WOMEN
WHO
influence

WOMEN WHO
influence

A COLLECTION OF INFLUENTIAL
STORIES THAT WILL INSPIRE
YOUR SOUL'S JOURNEY

kate butler
BOOKS

First Edition

© 2018 Kate Butler Books

www.katebutlercoaching.com

ISBN: 9781948927253

Library of Congress Control Number: 2018902735

This book is dedicated to you. We see you, we feel you, we relate to you and we connect with you, because ... we are you. At the core we are all the same. We are beings of light and love who deeply desire to make a positive influence on the world with our unique type of brilliance. The pages of this book promise to fill you with the wisdom, insights, and inspiration that will align you further on your soul's path. Our hope is that the vulnerability and authenticity of these stories will remind you deeply of who you are and inspire you to share your influence with the world. It is your time. It is our time. It is time.

enjoy the unfolding ...

FOREWORD

Welcome to *Women Who Influence!*
I am honored and humbled to have the privilege of introducing this book to you.

You are reading a collection of personal stories from an array of amazing female influencers. If you open your heart, mind, and soul to its contents, these stories will resonate with you and change your life.

Women Who Influence is the sequel to *Women Who Ignite* and *Women Who Inspire*—both published by Kate Butler, a role model and dear friend who has a truly remarkable ability to bring exceptional women together for connection and inspiration. Kate has touched the lives of so many women through her books, workshops, events, and personal-coaching business, relying on her guiding principle that "not only is anything possible, but everything is possible."

In every sense of the word, Kate is a true influencer. I am personally excited about this topic because I believe there is an influencer in all of us—someone who inspires or impacts ordinary people to do extraordinary things.

Kate and I met in 2012 at a women's retreat led by our mentor, Patty Aubery. All three of us were embarking on our own unique paths to embrace our "inner influence" to share with the world.

Kate was a young mom with a successful career, finding her voice and realizing her true purpose. Patty was coming into her own as a female thought leader, committed to empowering women. And I felt called to "inspire and reach the masses."

Three women, intersecting, just as the lives in these chapters are intersecting with you.

At the age of thirty-three, I was in the middle of a seemingly great life. I was surrounded by incredible friends; I had a consistent career and the ability to travel. Yet something was always pulling at me, always missing—my true path. One night, I stood alone, feeling frustrated and unsure of my existence, and asked aloud, "What do you want from me?" I asked because I wanted to know, because I needed to know, but most importantly, I asked because I knew there was a greater purpose for me. In that moment, the answer became clear—to inspire and reach the masses.

As a goal enthusiast, I knew I could accomplish almost any task that lay before me. I had just asked for the ultimate task, how to fulfill my purpose, and my answer came immediately. Now I had a quantum goal to achieve. My fears and insecurities had to take a back seat. I had work to do.

And that is the story of how GoalFriends® was born.

That conversation happened almost twenty-five years ago. At the time, those words terrified me. I'd never thought of myself as a leader. I was too shy. I wasn't qualified. I didn't know how to inspire the masses! And yet I knew I was purposeful.

Today, those words, "inspire and reach the masses," are etched into my soul and form the foundation for everything I do. Since that night, they have been the fuel that drives me. They keep me humbled and determined. They are my reason for being.

Through the journey of embracing my purpose, I've learned this: Within each of us is an influencer. That includes you. I discovered that there is no magic formula of traits or experiences you need in order to impact the people around you. An influencer may have been a leader her whole life, all the way back to kindergarten when she organized games on the playground, or she may be an activist who promotes social change. But an influencer might just as easily be a quiet person who rarely speaks up, a shy person with bold ideas, or someone with whom you have a chance encounter. Mine was my mother.

My mom worked her entire career as a waitress. She influenced me by being a great role model and fostering my ideals. While working relentlessly to help provide for her family, she impacted everyone she served. Her work ethic influenced me to begin babysitting at age ten, to get a worker's permit at thirteen, and, through the years, to go on to start my own business. This eventually led me to launch a global platform for women just like you.

Today I sure do miss my mom's presence. Her absence makes me cherish, all the more dearly, the legacy she imparted. You see, my mother's legacy, the inheritance she left me, has funded part of my own efforts to influence.

I created GoalFriends, a global platform designed to connect and uplift the influencer in each of us. GoalFriends brings women together in intimate groups to encourage and help one another, just like the women in this book. When we women enlighten one another with our hard-won knowledge and experiences, when we support one another to realize our dreams and goals, and when we share and bond with love and laughter, we can accomplish anything together.

The GoalFriends movement has grown exponentially, spreading organically across the globe, inspiring women of many nations and cultures to connect, to celebrate, and to grow. Each woman has her own unique path and is becoming even more extraordinary every day. Each is learning to listen to her own voice, be true to her own purpose, and live the life she always wanted. And each is learning to embrace her influence, because the best influencers step fully into their roles.

In this book, you'll read stories from women who do exactly that. Each author shares her journey in the spirit of leading *you* to fulfill *your* destiny as a woman of influence. These women have turned challenges into opportunities. They've conquered their fears and taken the road less traveled. They've discovered the joy of pursuing their highest callings. Their stories will rivet you, embolden you, and transform you.

It is my honor and privilege to present this book to you. My hope is that you will connect with these stories and discover the influencer in you.

May faith and love guide your unique journey,
Darlene Whitehurst
Founder, GoalFriends, LLC
President, Adsource Media Inc.

table of contents

INTRODUCTION

A note from the creator of *Women Who Ignite*,
Women Who Inspire, and
Women Who Influence, Kate Butler.

Thihis book series was created to provide a united platform where women could share their powerful stories with the intention of uplifting others.

This series began with our first book, *Women Who Ignite*, when a group of women came together to share intimate stories about the moment they truly decided to ignite their life. Through the success of this book, more women stepped forward to share how they were actually living out their purpose in the second book, *Women Who Inspire*. We are so honored to now introduce the third book in our series, *Women Who Influence*. In these pages you will connect with women who have ignited their life, are living their soul's purpose, and are using their influence to better the world. We have poured our hearts into every page of this book and our collective intention is that our heart connects with yours to create a movement of positive change in our beautiful world. We are all in this together.

the women who influence

shall we begin?

It was the morning of Mother's Day. The cinnamon rolls were baking in the oven, filling the air with their heavenly scent. This was a very special day. We all woke up early and snuggled in front of the TV.

We began to hear the familiar theme song of Sesame Street, "Sunny days, sweepin' the clouds away...". But as my daughters and I watched our faces come across the television screen, this was something that was not so familiar. This was far from familiar, this was ... extraordinary. We squealed and jumped around and did our happy dance. It was a surreal moment.

A few months earlier a colleague had reached out and shared that she was invited to write the music for HBO's new series of Sesame Street. She also played a hand in the casting, so she invited me and my daughters to New York to film for the new series.

As much as that moment felt surreal, I had to admit those moments were happening more and more.

In a short period, this was the third time I had been on TV. I was invited to speak alongside some mega thought leaders like Marianne Williamson, Jack Canfield, Peggy McColl, and Patty Aubery. I was featured at the Open Center in New York City. I had the privilege of speaking to thousands of children at schools across the country. I had published six best selling books. I had facilitated the publishing of ninety-one best selling authors ... and counting. Five of my books were accepted into The Library of Congress. And to seal the deal, the Huffington Post published an article saying, "Kate Butler is the real deal."

So as surreal as that moment was, it was also all starting to get more and more real.

But to understand the magnitude of these accomplishments, you must first understand where I started.

*** *

The night my fifth book was accepted into The Library of Congress.

I wept. I screamed. I stared at the screen in disbelief.

How could this be me? My books? My publishing copy?

I was the girl who failed English in the ninth grade. I had gotten a legitimate F in the class.

When the story is told now, my mom always says, "Are you sure you got an F? I think it may have been a D." She is always so sweet for trying to make it better.

But the fact is that I failed. I was a FAILURE.

I could not pass ninth grade English.

For a girl who loved to write, this was devastating. Math wasn't my strength. Science wasn't my strength. But I thought English was my strength. This is where I was supposed to shine. But instead of shining, I was met with a big, fat F on my final report card and I was heartbroken.

This failure hurt. But I wouldn't let me stop me. Not then. Not now. Not ever.

I had a deep sense, even as a young girl, that I was meant to do something big in this world. I know you have also had this feeling inside of you, because you chose to read this book.

This feeling deep in my soul pulled me out of my pain and allowed me to connect with my core brilliance. I knew then that I may not fit the exact mold people were looking for, that I may take a different approach than most people, and I may not subscribe to the "norm", but this was not failing ... this actually was *part of* my core brilliance. And so I made a decision to embrace it.

My brilliance was stronger than my failures. My brilliance was there to make a positive influence in the world. I knew my heart would guide me on my path.

***

After having children, this pull became even stronger, and I knew I needed to connect deeper with others who shared my desire to have a positive influence in the world. This led me to seek a mentor in the personal development industry and eventually led me to attend his workshops. There was so much value in the information and being around like-minded people that I returned to that same seminar the following year.

I remember the second time I attended the exact same training. Many of the attendees came back from the year before as well. All of those who recognized each other gathered the night before the conference and started to share updates of all that had transpired in the past year. Only something unique was happening in our circle. I wasn't sharing my updates, but everyone was commenting and asking me about everything I had done over the past year. They knew. They knew everything. They knew things I had forgotten about. They knew things I thought no one even noticed. And the same question began to repeat itself, "How did you achieve all of that in just one year?"

Back in my room that evening, I reflected deeply on what had occurred and began to record some of my thoughts:

1. **Keep your eyes on the road.**

I had no idea what everyone else was up to or what he or she had accomplished. Sure, I would see an occasional update through email or as I scrolled. But I did not make it a habit of following others' success. It distracted me from my focus. When I did allow myself to see what others were doing in the world, I found it created a comparison mindset, which is deadly for growth. It also kept me small. I would find myself thinking it was ok if I hadn't accomplished all I set out to do, because others were not doing those things. I found comfort in playing it safe. I would think, "Well, others haven't done this yet, so who am I to go out and do this?" But in those moments when I got silent and connected to my truth, I knew the answer. Even though it had not been done before, there was no reason I could not do it. I was here to make a difference and make an impact on the world. I knew this in my soul. So I had made a conscious choice to stay in my own lane and focus intently on the vision and goals I had set.

2. **What are you willing to do today? Not tomorrow, not next week, not next year ...** *today.*

Since the question of "how" was presented to me so many times, I had to take a closer look. How had I accomplished so much in such a short period of time? And why was this different than the others? When I looked back on what I had done, one word came to mind. Commitment. It was one thing to understand the information that was being taught to us at this conference. The second layer was to apply the information to our lives. But the last layer was the commitment to that action. For me it was a daily choice. Each and every day I had to consciously make the decision of what I was willing to do that day to meet my goals. I had to decide how much I desired it, what it would mean to me to achieve it and what it would mean for my family. Each day I chose this commitment.

3. **Master Your Craft**

The third thought that occurred to me really summed it all up. I did everything our mentor taught us to do. Everything. Not some of the things. Not all of the things some of the time. I did everything and all of the time. Not only did I do it, but I mastered it. I did not return to the conference the second year to learn something I had missed. I came because I mastered it all and I wanted to learn how to leverage this mastery. Mastering a craft does not mean being perfect, but it does mean that you are dedicated to the necessary progress each day to continue to expand your core brilliance. I continued going to this same conference five more times. When most people would learn that, it surprised them. I would often hear, "Oh, I would have moved on a long time ago." I get that. But I also see that often times we move on so fast from one thing to another thatthere is not enough time for lasting change to occur. I realized in this moment that what set me apart was willingness to take the necessary action to master my craft.

So how does someone who didn't pass a ninth grade English course go on to start a publishing company, publish ninety-one best-selling authors and have five of her own titles accepted into The Library of Congress to be available for generations upon generations to come?

Simple.

I allowed my core brilliance to shine through. I stepped up to the influence I was meant to make on this world. I followed that knowing deep in my heart. And you can too ...

People ask, "What does it take to be an *Influencer*?"

This is the wrong question to ask.

You are already an influencer. You were born an influencer. We are all meant to leave our unique influence on this world.

So the question becomes ...

Are you stepping up?

Are you honoring your core brilliance?

How are you using your unique influence to impact the world?

Whatever your failure is or was, it's part of you. It's part of brilliant you. And that is beautiful.

I had to reconcile that I may never ace ninth grade English.

But I also became very clear that **no one cares about a typo when you are changing their life.**

So now it's your choice which side you focus on. Every day you get to choose again. Do you focus on the typo? Or do you focus on your brilliance? The choice is yours. The choice has always been yours.

Welcome to The Women Who Influence

from inspiration to influence

Adrienne Dorison

I woke up in the middle of the night to the sound of crashing; someone was in my bedroom right there with me.

The person was standing at my tall five-drawer dresser, pulling out each drawer with anger and dumping the contents onto the floor. The person repeated this over and over until all the drawers were empty and then started on the closet. The clothes, the shoes, and the toys all mounted into one huge pile in the middle of my bedroom while I cowered in fear in the bed, just watching.

"Clean it up by tomorrow morning," she said as she walked out of the room.

I was eight years old, the intruder was my mom, and that was the norm in our house. Not the emptying of drawers specifically, but the midnight wake-up calls to the unknown. These late-night events had occurred almost every night since my dad had left three years earlier.

Vodka was her drink of choice. Some nights she wanted me to dance with her or asked me to twirl in the living room to John Anderson's "Straight Tequila Night." Other nights she'd do things like pour out the contents of my room or interrogate me for hours about my father, asking questions I didn't know the answers to.

Most nights I'd end up a punching bag of sorts and then head back to bed once she was done with me. I'd crawl back into bed and pray that it was over for the night. I'd pretend I was asleep if she came back in, hoping she'd leave me alone for just a few more hours and then I could go to school.

I loved school. It was an escape from the sleepless nights.

This was my normal for the better part of my childhood. Maybe that's why I'm highly functional on very little sleep, now that I think about it.

But here's where the real story begins—my biological mom had received multiple DUIs, and because she had full custody of us, the state let her serve some of her jail time on the weekends. This meant I needed someone to watch me while she was gone. My brother was old enough to just stay at a friend's house all weekend, but I ended up staying with one of my mom's closest friends instead.

It was a weekend leading up to the Thanksgiving holiday, and I had no idea what was about to unfold. My mom's friend always had dogs and even bred Weimaraner puppies, so needless to say, I was excited. But little did I know we weren't going to be playing with new puppies this weekend; we were going to be volunteering.

We pulled into the parking lot of a local high school that morning, and I noticed there were people walking with a real purpose through the doors to the gymnasium. They looked excited and cheerful and they laughed with one another, but I still had no idea what we were actually doing there.

As we walked in, I saw brown paper bags, the kind you can ask for at the grocery store when you check out and don't want to use plastic or don't have your own. They were being filled with canned foods like green beans and cranberry sauce, fresh sweet potatoes, and other Thanksgiving trimmings.

There was a picture of a really large man all over the event signs. He was tall and handsome, with strong features, and had a generous presence like none I had never known until that day. I found out his name was Tony.

I found a book at the event with Tony's photo on the front cover too. I figured out through some deductive reasoning that Tony was the man in charge around here, and he had a career in which he wrote books and motivated people through speaking. I wouldn't really understand the real depths of this or our greater connection until much later in life.

The man was Tony Robbins, and the event was one of Tony's early Thanksgiving Basket Brigades.

The Basket Brigade is built on a simple notion: one small act of generosity on the part of one caring person can transform the lives of hundreds. Now every year Tony's program feeds and serves more than two million people all over the world.

We packed bags full of Thanksgiving goods that day, loaded them into cars, strapped on our seat belts, and drove into neighborhoods that I'd never been to before. We bear-hugged each bag and carried turkeys up to the doors of strangers that day.

Strangers who hugged me. Strangers who cried when they saw the food we were delivering to them. Strangers who fell to their knees in prayer because they hadn't thought they'd be able to give their families a Thanksgiving meal, and now they could share thanks with the ones they loved over a home-cooked meal.

I felt good that day. Really good. And for the first time in a long time, I wasn't thinking about what I didn't have at home; I was thinking about how much I had to give.

Even when I wasn't receiving love, I could give it.

Even when I wasn't feeling safe, I could provide safety.

Even when I wasn't grounded, I could share stability.

I was able to pour into others even when I thought I was empty.

My love affair with giving was born that day.

That day at Tony Robbins's Thanksgiving Basket Brigade created an awareness in me, even at a very young age, of what it meant to feel ignited by something bigger than me.

Giving made me feel loved and lovable, safe and grounded, valued and valuable, joyful...all the things I never felt at home. There was a clear energetic exchange happening in those moments of handing over the Thanksgiving meals to people in our community who needed them.

I handed over food, but I gave them the same feelings that they were giving me.

They felt loved, safe, cared for, valuable, grounded, and joyful, just as did I.

In that moment, something in me changed forever, and while I didn't fully understand it at the time, I knew that even when we have nothing, we have more to give, and that the giving is what fills us back up.

That day and that feeling have been with me ever since, but I'd be lying if I said I was always the most generous human being after that moment. Life happened, stress got in the way, and I found myself still giving, but only when it was convenient for me.

And often it was not convenient.

I always spent that extra cash at Target or splurged on the almond butter...

Or made beach plans for the day instead of making the time to volunteer...

Or my debt repayment seemed to max me out each month before there was any money left over...

It all came bubbling over for me when my now husband graciously offered to use his own savings to pay off all my debt once we got married...and I cringed. He wanted to clean my slate, start our financial future together with zero debt, and I wanted to crawl into a hole and die at the thought of it.

I had more than $50,000 in student loan debt when I left my graduate school program. I had jobs throughout my college years, I received scholarships, grants, and an assistantship, and I still managed to take out enough loans to last me twenty-eight years of repayment.

For years, I had judged myself based on my financial status. I felt less than and unworthy of love because of my less-than-stellar credit score. Yes, I know it sounds silly, but we emotionalize our money, and at the time debt and poor credit made me feel unlovable all over again. I felt angry at myself for taking on so much debt and treated it as my own scarlet letter.

A big *D* might as well have been stamped across my forehead. *This woman has debt and poor credit: don't love or marry her.*

So when my boyfriend at the time offered to use his hard-earned cash to pay it all off someday when we wed, I didn't want that gift. But what he had given me instead was a wake-up call. It was a reminder that money didn't define who I was, yet I had allowed it to have a stranglehold over me all those years. I had let it run me, I had let it change my values, and I had let it get in the way of what was most important.

I felt the heaviness within me again, the same heaviness I'd felt as a little girl. And at the same time, I felt the lightness because I knew clearly at that moment what the answer was…give.

It was overwhelming to say the least, and giving money away when I had that much debt seemed unrealistic and irrational.

How could I possibly give to other people when I had nothing to give? I literally had negative money…

When you feel empty and as if you have nothing to give, you give to fill yourself up.

I got focused on chipping away at my student loan debt, and for the first time in over ten years, consistently, every single month during that debt-repayment period, I was giving away money to people in our community who needed it more than I did.

But I wasn't just giving through monetary gifts—I was spending my time serving the community and sharing my expertise in ways that supported others. There's more than just one way to give, especially when you feel your finances are tight or your time is limited.

There is no one-size-fits-all method for giving. There are tons of different ways for you to bake this into your life, but it's important to figure out which one is going to be the right fit for you so that you can comfortably commit to it.

There are three different ways you can start to give:

- Time—this means being hands-on with your giving and volunteering your time to causes that need it.
- Skills—this means pro bono work and giving with your expertise and skills.
- Money—this means giving with your cash.

Here's what that looked like for me:

Time: I was taking my dog, Church, to local schools to meet with students every week, where he was serving as a therapy and literacy dog. (Literacy dogs are used with students in remedial reading programs to help them feel more comfortable and safe to practice their reading skills out loud by reading to the dog each week.)

Skills: I was teaching financial-literacy classes in our local community alongside my now husband to individuals experiencing financial hardship and an overwhelming amount of debt. Every Sunday we went through the curriculum to help strengthen and improve their relationship with money.

Money: I was giving financially to local nonprofits that supported things I personally felt aligned with, such as animal shelters and programs for children facing domestic abuse.

Even when I was trying to pay back my debt as quickly as possible, I was still focused on giving away 10 percent of my income. I found that if I took it out first, I never even missed it, and it connected me with what I really cared about and valued enough to spend my money on even more.

Six months later, I was completely debt free.

Giving is part of who I am and who I've always wanted to be; I just needed to get realigned with the belief that it was possible for me to give at any given moment in my life, no matter my circumstances.

And when I really reconnect to the idea that I can give even when I have nothing to give, I know that it's the truth because of that day I spent over twenty years ago giving away turkeys and Thanksgiving meals to people who needed them more than I did.

As I started my own business, I knew that giving needed to be baked into everything that I did. This idea had served me so well in my personal life, and because I wanted to build a business based on my core values, giving was a nonnegotiable.

Starting my own business showed me that I can create limitless income. No longer are we capped by a low salary or limited by a 3 percent annual salary increase. We control what we earn in our businesses. And as more and more of the global economy turns to entrepreneurship, we can make massive changes in the world.

I believe that as entrepreneurs we're in a powerful position to eradicate world problems very quickly if we're all willing to bake giving and generosity into everything we do. Because when we begin to earn more money, we can give more back to those who need it.

To make this a reality, you have to do a few things:

1. Get comfortable with the idea of earning lots of money (as much as you want, the more the better).
2. Pay attention to your finances and honor your values through them.
3. Commit to consistently giving back through your time, skills, and money to causes that you feel aligned with.

You should start small, as you're likely building a new habit. Donate one dollar for every sale you make. Spend one hour a week serving at a local homeless shelter. Tutor a student once a week whose family can't afford it.

Our world needs your big heart more than ever right now, so don't put this off until you feel that you're ready. It's time to *get* ready and get started.

And because I believe in the energetic exchange, I'd like to ask for something in return. If any of this has resonated with you, connects with your heart, or has influenced you to give in any way, the best thing you can do is share this chapter with someone else. Just as I felt the exchange of reciprocal feelings when I gave those first Thanksgiving meals away to families in need, you can create that ripple effect as well.

I gave love and felt it in return. I made someone feel safe, and I felt grounded. I showed people they were valued, and I also felt valuable. I saw joy radiated, and I felt joyful. The ripple effect of giving is real, so pass this on and become a woman of influence along with me.

ABOUT ADRIENNE DORISON

Adrienne Dorison is the CEO of Lean Growth Group, a business-operations consultancy that helps companies double their results with half the effort. Adrienne is a certified LEAN Six Sigma consultant and SCRUM expert trainer from the world of corporate manufacturing who has created her own proprietary systems and tools specific to small-business owners.

Adrienne has helped hundreds of businesses (from Fortune 500 companies to fast-growth start-ups) meaningfully expand profit margins and cut costs in ninety days or less. She understands how to simplify complex business problems and help teams restructure so they can scale to the next level.

Adrienne has been featured in a number of publications, including *Entrepreneur, Business Insider,* and *TIME,* and she is leading a movement called Good Businesses Do Good™ that focuses on helping entrepreneurs earn more to give more. Her company has personally given away over $120,000 to meaningful causes in less than two years and has empowered and equipped her clients to do the same. Adrienne lives in St. Petersburg, Florida, with her husband, Tyler; her Bernese Mountain Dog, Church; and their rescue terrier, Airy.

Connect with Adrienne at www.adriennedorison.com.

WHO DO YOU *THINK* YOU ARE?

Tammy Anczok

A m I what I have? Am I what I do? Am I who people think I am? Am I living a life of purpose and meaning? I thought I knew the answers to these questions...

Our twin daughters were the last of our four children to leave for college. They chose schools in different states and would pursue their dreams independent of the lives they had had in each other's shadows. As we shifted the bins from the back of the SUV into their dorm rooms, my identity began to shift as well. My identity was caught up somewhere in the bottoms of those well-appointed, organized clear containers.

For the first time in three decades, I didn't have any children living at home. I enjoyed the easy mornings of sleeping in, lounging over coffee, going for a run, taking a long shower, catching up on reading, online shopping, binge-watching Netflix, and so on. I went out for lots of lunches and dinners with friends and family, complete with champagne, cocktails, and wine! This kind of self-indulgence was like being on vacation. But I wasn't on vacation. It was my life and it was becoming my new normal. I was filling my proverbial tank with busyness and beverages.

Our empty nest was peaceful, quiet, and *clean!* Once the house was clean, it stayed that way! This gave me the freedom to dig deeper. I cleaned out closets, drawers, and cabinets—purging the accumulated clutter of more than twenty-plus years of family life. I cleaned and perfected everything, making many trips to the donation center. It was invigorating!

But…there were days when I wandered through the empty bedrooms of our home missing the kids. Missing our *family*. As I closed each door to those empty rooms, I felt as if I were closing the door to my identity. It was painful to consider the space within myself that was empty like those empty rooms. My life *looked* perfect, but something was missing. *I* was missing. My emotional tank was draining.

It's amazing what you hear when things get quiet. I heard a deafening silence within myself. As the days and weeks passed, the quiet got louder, nagging for my attention.

I had reached an unspoken yet admirable goal of raising four amazing kids. I should have been celebrating, but instead, I was taken aback. I had fulfilled a lifelong goal, and it left me feeling unfulfilled! For as long as I could remember, I had been a mother. That had been my identity for most of my life. Now what?

The void within me asked a simple question: "Who am I?" Every answer I came up with described who my family was, what I did, what I had, or where I lived. But those things did not describe me. *Who am I?*

By definition, an identity crisis is a feeling of unhappiness and confusion caused by not being sure about what type of person you really are or what the true purpose of your life is. My loss of identity and purpose was my private, personal tragedy.

I began to suffer from insomnia. I awoke almost every night around 3:00 a.m. My mind couldn't rest. In the quiet of the night, as I wandered out into the kitchen, I prayed, watched TV, ate an array of snacks, brewed sleepy-time tea—anything to settle down! I was exhausted, and I was unsettled. So I picked up my journal and wrote this letter to God on September 16, 2012...

Dear God:

Please show me who I am. Please show me what it is that I am supposed to do. Show me my strengths and my weaknesses, my talents and my gifts. Help me to share them. Help me to let people in. Help me to put myself out there for the greater good. Help me to find my voice and listen to it. I want to contribute. I want to be successful. I want to do something remarkable and be financially rewarded. I want to be recognized and well known. Please help me to manage these answers even though it may be difficult. Please show me how I can be a positive influence on others. Please help me to forgive people I have not properly forgiven. Please help me to get unstuck.

Love, Tammy

Who did I *think* I was?

Frankly, looking back, I am a little embarrassed by parts of that prayer. Recognized? Well known? I wanted to be known, and I didn't even know myself!

Slowly, over the course of the last five years and counting, God has answered and refined my thoughts and desires. It has not been a quick process, but gradually answers began to show up in unexpected ways.

During one of my cleaning frenzies, I was rummaging through the shelves of bins in the basement when I came across a bin containing bits and pieces of my past. I believe God led me to a bin that contained a glimpse of who I had been. It was a step in the direction of who I am. I slowly leafed through this container of nostalgia from my high school days, revisiting yearbooks, photo albums, prom pictures, and finally an old journal from 1981.

I sat on the basement floor reading this secret journal from my youth. I barely recognized the main character as myself. The pages described what my older, wiser self now recognized as a very abusive, controlling, manipulative high school relationship that continued beyond graduation and resulted in my teen pregnancy. It became clear to me that I hadn't known myself very well back then either, judging by my passive behavior.

I did what most girls did back then. I turned to my friends before I turned to my parents. With their youthful yet experienced advice, I scheduled an abortion for the following week. I was easily influenced because I didn't know *myself*. My best friend drove me to the appointment and assured me that everything would be OK and my troubles would soon be over. I hoped she was right.

In my own teenage-girl handwriting, I read my description of the experience at the clinic. "Lying on the table, black plastic trash bag beneath me, and the sound of the suction machine running, I pulled myself up and stopped the procedure." I vividly remember that moment of clarity. With the help of two nurses, I got off the table and left the cold, sterile white room. As I got dressed, I wondered how I would face my friend in the waiting room and tell her that I could not do what she had done. To avoid the inevitable, I concocted a story that I was too far along for the procedure that day. It was the beginning of the end of our teenage friendship.

That pivotal moment changed the trajectory of my life and solidified my purpose for many years to come. Reading my long-forgotten journal reminded me of how long ago my purpose of motherhood began. Tears rolled down my cheeks as I turned the pages and was reminded of the details of that uncertain time, of an uncertain future placed on hold for the life of an unborn child. It was my life, my body, and my decision to embrace motherhood.

Pamela, my sweet baby girl, was born just before I turned nineteen. My dad was my labor coach. My mom waited anxiously in the waiting room. My young experience of motherhood was successful thanks to the love and support of my parents. Their influence became my strength.

I grew up fast being a young, single mom. Motherhood became my new identity and purpose. As my baby girl grew, I grew as a parent. In many ways, we grew up together.

I enrolled in college, got my degree, and was working full time as a sales secretary at the Hilton Hotel when I met my husband,

Mike. Pamela was an active kindergartener. Mike was an entrepreneur and had started his own business distributing oil, employing about twenty-five people. As Mike focused on his growing business, I focused on my growing girl and my new career. Together we focused on our relationship and took it to the next level.

After we were married, Mike adopted Pamela, and I went to work at his company as quality manager. I saw more of my husband, and the hours enabled me to be home when Pam was home from school. We became a *family*.

The following year, on New Year's Eve, our son, Michael Jr., was born. It was a totally different experience having a newborn with my husband at my side instead of my dad! Less than two years later, we were surprised and blessed with twin daughters, Elisabeth and Alexis. Suddenly, we became a *big family!* My purpose of motherhood was in full swing, and my role as quality manager had ended. Sometimes I longed for a day at the office!

The years clicked by as they do for all of us raising kids. At first, it feels as if every day is Groundhog Day. But soon my days were varied and busy.

I volunteered a ton, ran the children's school library, went on field trips, and attended sporting events, dance recitals, piano lessons, concerts, and plays. In my spare time, I worked in and out of the office. I attended business dinners and business meetings and accompanied Mike on business-award trips all over the world. My parents continued to help and support our family, caring for the children during our travel schedule.

While I was at home with four growing children, Mike was hard at work growing his businesses into four separate companies that employed more than two hundred team members.

I was the best supporting actress in the feature movie of my husband and family. I was the girl behind the scenes running the show as director, costume coordinator, caterer, producer, Uber driver, designer, decorator, and personal assistant to my team of five.

I put *their* needs ahead of *my* needs. Motherhood and marriage were my focus and, ultimately, my purpose. My identity was wrapped up in everything I was doing. And now I felt I was *worth* less because I was *doing* less. What had *I* achieved? What had *I* accomplished?

A few years ago, we bought a second home in Florida and became residents of the Sunshine State. We were living in a new neighborhood and a new community. I didn't really know myself at that point, and no one else knew me either.

Mike stayed busy and fulfilled running his businesses via phone and computer from our Florida home office. I, on the other hand, was *not* fulfilled. I was bored. I was lonely. Mike was there working but not there for me. It started to have a negative effect on our marriage. Not only did I miss my friends and family, but I also missed my *home* in New York. I began to resent him for everything he was doing and not doing. I blamed him for my unhappiness. Although I never could imagine myself divorced, I was beginning to think that the only way back to myself was to leave my marriage. My life looked perfect, and I felt guilty for being unhappy and unfulfilled.

Once again I was awake at 3:00 a.m. In the darkness of the family room, I was channel surfing. I landed on OWN, the Oprah Winfrey Network.

Imagine this. You are depressed, exhausted, having an identity crisis, feeling no clear purpose, contemplating leaving your marriage, and Oprah is saying these words in a calm, whispery voice...

> What do you really want in your life? Do you think everybody has a calling? We are all looking for the same things. What inspires you? Can we heal from everything? How can we live an awakened life?

This stopped me dead in my tracks. On this episode, Oprah was interviewing Jack Canfield, the cocreator of the Chicken Soup for the Soul series. Jack was talking about his book *The Success Principles: How to Get from Where You Are to Where You Want to Be.* About halfway through the interview, I hit the pause button and rifled around for something to write on. I restarted the interview and began feverishly taking notes. I definitely wanted to get from where I was, but I had no idea where I wanted to be.

Oprah and Jack were talking about passion, purpose, and being in flow. Passion? Purpose? Flow? I had no idea. I also had no idea that this was the beginning of my transformation.

We all headed back to New York for the summer. I was reading *The Success Principles,* the kids were home from college and working, Mike was working, and I enjoyed a full house again. I was so inspired by the book that in August, Mike and I attended Jack's five-day seminar, Breakthrough to Success (BTS).

The strengthening I was experiencing within myself was flowing into our marriage. The identity crisis belonged to me, and it was my responsibility to address it. Principle number one: take responsibility. During one of our lunches, I met Kate Butler, the creator of this book series. Some would call it a wink from the universe; I call it a wink from God!

I began shifting my focus from my family to MY personal development. I was looking for a new purpose. I created a vision board of new experiences I wanted to welcome into my life. While combing through magazines for pictures and inspiring words for my vision board, I came across an article about abortion. I put the article aside in a file to review later. I felt that the discovery of the article was God speaking to me. I felt a tug on my heart to share my experience and insight to help others. That summer, I became a certified crisis pregnancy coach. The closed door within me started to open to new possibilities.

Mike and I took our experience with the success principles a step further and attended a luxury retreat in Maui with several others. The retreat gave us the opportunity to work one on one with Jack Canfield, Patty Aubery, and their amazing team. It was during that trip that I was able to identify my passions. I spent a great deal of time and energy really focusing on what brought me joy. Joy comes from living passionately. My joy tank was at an all-time low. Living with passion and doing what we love leads to a life of purpose. And then it hit me. I am most passionate when I am connected. My greatest passion is connection! No wonder I was in such a deep struggle. I was experiencing disconnect on all levels. The reconnection began in five areas of my life.

My life is ideal when I am doing these things:

connecting to self and soul
connecting to family and friends

connecting to God and spirituality
connecting to leaders/top performers/authors/mentors
connecting to the world through travel

I moved myself to the top of the list. I had to make myself a priority because of the focused work I was doing. I was worried that God came in third! I know God was waiting to hear from me. And I in turn had been waiting and listening for him. I needed guidance. My personal GPS had become unplugged. God reminded me of my struggles and reminded me of his presence during those times of struggle. God was speaking to me all along, guiding me, helping me recalculate my course.

There is a space inside all of us where God belongs. If God is missing, there is a chance something may be missing for you too. Get quiet and hear the voice within you. Connect to your creator, your source, and your soul! Connect through stillness, meditation, and prayer. I know that I am the best version of myself when I make God my number one connection. My identity is based not on who *I* am but on who *He* is.

Everything you need is within you because you were created and wired for something divine! Discover what purpose God has in store for you. I imagine it's much bigger than you may think!

We strive to know more, do more, be more, and have more, perhaps at times losing sight of who we *really* are. I believe with every twist and turn of life's challenges, our purpose is continually changing and shifting, like the contents in those bins.

Who Am I?

I am a child of God created in his image.
I am forgiven and granted eternal life
I am shining God's love and light.
I am evolving.
I am connected.

Who do you think *you* are?

ABOUT TAMMY ANCZOK

Tammy Anczok is an author, speaker, trainer, and transitional life coach. In her upcoming book, *Can You Fill My Tank? If My Life Is So Full, Why Do I Feel Empty?*, she dives deeper into identity and connection. Making good use of her business degree and life experience as a wife and mother, Tammy hosts Fill Your Tank retreats in both New York and Florida to inspire women to discover their true identities and their passions.

A perpetual student of life, Tammy always seeks to learn, to constantly evolve into a more powerful version of herself, and to help others to do the same. She holds an associate's degree in business management and is a graduate of Tony Robbins's Mastery University and Dale Carnegie's management training; she is also is a Canfield-certified trainer, and a Crisis Pregnancy Coach.

Tammy has been married to successful entrepreneur Mike Anczok for twenty-seven years, and they have four children. Tammy and Mike reside on the west coast of Florida in Port Charlotte and spend the summer months in their hometown of Niagara Falls, New York.

When she isn't speaking to groups of eager listeners or writing inspirational words in her latest book, Tammy enjoys Pilates, yoga, running, biking, swimming, skiing, playing the drums, singing in church, boating, and connecting with others. Having an eye for detail, she delights in the art of interior design and personal style.

Connect with Tammy Anczok at www.tammyanczok.com.

PERFECTLY IMPERFECT

Susan Faith

I awaken to a new day. Not just on the calendar, but within me. Like yours, my journey has been filled with bumps in the road. Now I breathe in life. My awareness flows from sixty years of challenges, lessons, and embracing faith and trust. Always knowing that I am meant for greatness, I listen to and follow my intuition. I accept the flow of life and connect to my divine authenticity through love, compassion, kindness, and respect, first for myself and then for all others.

I am grateful for those experiences that created physical and emotional pain, fear, hurt, anger, sadness, grief, shame, guilt, self-judgment, negative self-talk, insecurity, and sometimes self-hatred. These didn't magically heal with a wave of my magic wand. I had to learn to walk my talk. I had to deeply *feel* and go through, not around, each challenging experience. It took years for me to realize that I was shutting out love. I didn't think I deserved to be loved. I demanded perfection from myself. Now I know that I am perfect just the way I am.

Some of the greatest spiritual and inspirational teachers with whom I have been blessed to work with in person or online include Jack Canfield, Deepak Chopra, Oprah, Nick Ortner, Gabby Bernstein, Louise Hay, and Dr. Wayne Dyer. And some of my greatest teachers are my friends, my family, the people who cross my path, and the everyday challenges we each face.

It's a *new day*.

I'm alive.

I take a deep breath.

I look in the mirror and say,

"Susan, I love you.

I love you, Susan.

Susan, I really love you."

I take another deep breath and say,

"I am grateful for…"

I list at least ten things, such as…

"I am grateful for breath.

"I am grateful for the sunshine."

The list changes daily.

I continue my routine of self-care and recite, "Life loves me." (I repeat it ten times.) I state it playfully, sometimes dancing as I go. I continue with, "One way life is loving me today is…" (It varies daily.)

My birth name, Susan Faith, is no accident. My parents knew I was a blessing. I am the youngest of three, born considerably after my siblings, when my mom was thirty-five. I was frequently teased and bullied by my siblings. I doubt they know how deeply isolated, hurt, excluded, and different they made me feel.

I was a natural leader in school and many extracurricular activities. I was "perfect." While in high school, I was chosen to attend an academic program in Israel. My parents were unable to pay, and gratefully I received outside financial support.

The high school campus was located on the grounds of a training facility for Israeli soldiers. Overtired from the long flight from Miami, I went to the student dorm and chose to climb into my bottom bunk to go to sleep while the others chose to go swimming. I felt different from my classmates. We were from various high schools.

The dorm was quiet without anyone else present. I felt safe. Then, the door opened and a boy came into my room. He didn't go to my school. The next thing I heard was the lock turning on the door. My heart began to race.

Mostly asleep and not fully present, I felt nauseated as the boy climbed into my bed and began to kiss me. I remember he told me that he thought we should date. Date? Other than seeing him on the plane, I didn't know him. Why was he in my bed kissing me? The kissing continued, my heart raced faster, and I was engulfed in a wave of dizziness. I was five feet one and about one hundred pounds, so he easily and forcefully held me down until the penetration was over. I was sixteen. He unlocked the door and left.

I felt liquid running between my legs. I thought I had peed. I saw blood. Confused, I walked down the hall to the bathroom. Several students in the hall were laughing and asked if I had had a good time. Naïve, I didn't realize the blood was from losing my virginity.

Burying the deep feelings of shame, disgust, fear, guilt, anger, and distrust, I believed that this was my fault. I felt unsafe. I should have gone swimming and not to bed. Why me?

I had several other unwanted sexual encounters during high school. Through it all, I maintained the highest grades, received numerous awards, and graduated at the top of my class. However, the seeds were planted deep within me from years of abuse and many years later blossomed as disease. I felt "perfectly imperfect."

From the time I was in elementary school, my father's dream was for me to become a lawyer. His younger sister had been murdered, and he knew I was a born voice of justice. I was the "perfect" candidate for a prestigious university as part of my transition to an exceptional law school.

During college, my life remained full of challenge. In my junior year, someone stalked me and left threatening notes on my car. But I met a senior with whom I had much in common. His compassion and kindness provided me with physical safety as he met me nightly at my car and slept on my dorm floor. I accelerated and graduated in three years, and we got married the summer of our graduation.

My high school best friend, Tami, attended our small wedding and wept uncontrollably as she left for the airport. She had given me roses throughout high school, and some people commented that that was not what girlfriends did for each other. Others judged our friendship as "perfectly imperfect."

When our son turned five and was enjoying kindergarten, I entered law school. I chose a school that honored my priority to be a full-time mother and supportive wife. We had a beautiful home, many friends, and a loving family. Law school required an immense amount of commitment and time, and I continued my perfection syndrome to be the best. I received awards and strong recommendations for future employment after my first year.

In 1990, during my second year, one student offered his belief that date rape wasn't rape because the girl could say no and leave. I became dizzy and nauseated and passed out as I slid from my front-row chair onto the floor.

I was rushed to my doctor's office and left carrying a large red container marked "biohazard materials." As I walked through the waiting room, I felt an inner shame, as if I were wearing a scarlet letter *A*. My mind was creating its own story. Shortly thereafter, I was hospitalized. The top-notch Boston hospital doctors concluded that the brain scans were showing something within my head that was inoperable. I would not survive.

I became increasingly weaker and was barely able to carry any weight. I could walk only very short distances, and I was frequently transported in a wheelchair. I needed help for everyday chores. I was told that it was time to prepare my son and say good-bye. This felt eons from "perfection."

On a leave of absence from law school, every day I would watch as children in the neighborhood went off to school, carefree. In contrast, my intuitive, caring, loving, kind, and compassionate son had a very sick mother. I felt incredibly guilty that I missed many of his activities and felt sad that I was missing part of his life. I hated depending on everyone. I began to have episodes of terror. In absolute horrific fear, I would cry uncontrollably. Men in particular heightened this fear. Terror. I had a total and unequivocal feeling of being unsafe. I would see visions of people or a person totally clad in black, and they overcame me. Where was the "perfection" in my life?

Fully engulfed by post-traumatic stress, I climbed into the closet and sat crying hysterically. My son joined me. His presence magically transported me into the present and a safe space.

While visiting my parents in Miami, I was evaluated by my father's lifelong friend, a prominent neurosurgeon. After he examined my brain scans, he concurred with the other doctors: "Susan will not survive." The tears rolled freely down my father's face. My father wept as I had never seen him cry. In that moment, I felt that I took a piece of his heart. All his dreams for me disappeared. His love and admiration wept out of every pore. Although the doctor's office was moments from my parents' home, it was the longest car ride of my life. Now, I felt "perfectly imperfect."

I will always remember the horror on my mother's face. Suddenly, I felt a miraculous inner strength. I turned to my parents and said, "I will not die. I am meant for something much larger than me. G-d has a plan." In that moment, I had no recollection of those seeds that had been planted years before. I knew I would overcome my challenges.

Upon returning to Boston, I joined an advanced meditation group. Although I had never meditated, the transition into the group was seamless. Finally, I felt a sense of belonging and immense support from other women. I was comfortable sharing my clairvoyance and new ability to do energy work while studying various alternative healing modalities. Within weeks, clarity, bright white healing light, and the immense love, faith, and trust that I knew were within emerged. I spent my days in meditation, receiving messages for healing, and frequently I saw the color purple. I received a strong message to go to yoga. The synchronicity in my life began to flow, magically and miraculously.

I drove to the yoga class where the handicap space was always available. At first, I was unable to get down on the floor. A clergyman who was a yoga participant would silently extend his arm to gently guide me. Within weeks, I was able to get to and from the floor on my own. Within a month, I could fully engage in the yoga postures. I felt embraced by G-d.

As I meditated, listened to music, and did yoga consistently, I heard the message to play the African *djembe* drum, and doing so came naturally. The color purple I saw represents royalty, spirituality, and healing. I embraced it and the connection with my divine authenticity for complete healing. When I wear purple, I am happy. I spread my love. I spread my light. I always carry the light within me, and therefore the sun always shines within my heart. As my awareness and connection to my inner strength increased, visions of previous sexual assaults and unwanted interactions heightened. My gratitude for the challenges grew as I embraced them as opportunities for deeper healing. I forgave the assailants and myself. I surrounded myself with love, compassion, kindness, and respect. Part of the elevation to my being came from my willingness to let go of people in my life who didn't thrive in a positive environment. I accepted myself as I am: "perfectly imperfect."

In the fall of 1998, my son located my high school best friend, Tami, in Atlanta. There was an instant connection when we first spoke after thirteen years. Like me, Tami had overcome major challenges and sought to learn from the opportunity. Tami is a gay woman fully connected with her authenticity. Over time, we came to understand her deep sadness and tears at my wedding. Without many role models, Tami hadn't understood the strange feelings she had for me in high school. All these years later, our love for each other was undeniable. I was overtaken by my intense inner sense that I am a gay woman. Until Tami came back into my life, I supported gay rights, but I didn't connect as being gay. Gratefully, I had tremendous love, compassion, kindness, and respect from almost everyone in my life to help me transition into my sexual authenticity. I knew I was born this way, and I lovingly embraced my sexuality and Tami. I remember telling my son that I wanted to be true to myself. He fully and completely accepted me just the way I am.

The years that followed were filled with many blessings. Tami and I deepened our inspirational and spiritual knowledge and practice. We got legally married when the US federal law for same-sex marriage passed.

In December 2013, Tami and I traveled to Hawaii with our special friends, Karen and Gina, to celebrate our mutual birthdays. While there, things didn't seem right. I felt fear that I had never felt in my many visits to Hawaii, where I've found incredible spiritual connection.

When I meditated, I kept getting messages around health and safety concerns. I wanted to ground myself and spend time writing and meditating. I felt surrounded by fear in a way that I hadn't felt in many years. On almost our last day there, I suggested that Tami and our friends go snorkeling without me so I could watch from the lanai. I had an overwhelming sense to be ready in case of an emergency.

It was a beautiful sunny day with the ocean as clear as a sheet of glass. Tami and Karen swam out as I stood on the lanai, wondering what would happen if I dialed 911. Would it reach local help? Why was I having these thoughts? What was my intuition trying to tell me? When they safely returned to shore, I took a long, deep breath. But I quickly learned that Tami was incredibly winded, wheezing, exhausted, and barely able to walk up the path to the condo.

After our flight home, one of our friends commented that it looked as if Tami might be in congestive heart failure as she was incredibly swollen and retaining a lot of fluid. I was appalled at the suggestion. Where did that come from? Tami had no history of heart issues. Her blood pressure, cholesterol, and everything else were all fabulous. Congestive heart failure? Nope, that didn't exist in my world of healing.

Several nights later, I lay listening to Tami wheeze. A few minutes later, she went to the bathroom, returned, and sat on the edge of the bed. I didn't like what I heard. I turned on the light, and Tami was blue, shaking uncontrollably, wheezing, and having trouble catching her breath. For many years, I had no interaction with the Western medical world. I had left that behind when I began to meditate, do yoga, play native drums, embrace positive thinking, do daily healing affirmations, and embrace other holistic methods.

At 2:30 a.m., as I saw my wife struggling to breathe, every ounce of my belief system was shaken to the core. She looked at me and said, "I can meditate through this." I heard myself say, "Tami, I can't get you through this. You are not able to meditate through it. I must call 911." My thoughts floated back to my feelings while on the lanai, knowing something wasn't right. I recalled my meditations before we left Hawaii in which I kept getting messages about Tami's chest. I had expressed to her earlier that day that I thought we needed to pursue a mammogram.

Within minutes, I saw the flashing lights of an ambulance and fire engine in the freezing air outside our home. Eight men entered carrying equipment and wheeling a stretcher. I thought, "She'll be fine. They'll check her and away they'll go." But my intuition told me otherwise. I could feel every ounce of my being sending me a red alert. I felt as if I were outside, watching someone else's trauma.

Soon the monitor was displaying medical information. "We must transport her now. No, she is not having a heart attack. She is not getting enough oxygen, and her heart is racing uncontrollably. We have very little time. I need your permission to transport her *now*. If we leave and you call us back, we may not get here in time." They had started her on oxygen and were trying to start an IV but couldn't. I trusted this kind man who was gently stroking our two pups. "Susan, we need to take her now."

I looked at Tami. She was weeping and didn't want to go. In that moment, I had to go against everything I knew to have been my world of healing for over twenty years and agree to let them take my wife, barely clad, into the freezing night on icy roads in an ambulance with its emergency lights on.

I took a deep breath and relied on my inner strength to get my mind to function. I called our dear friend Sandy to come be with our cats and two service dogs. Although she lived ten minutes away, Sandy came so quickly that she was almost to our home as I passed her while following the ambulance up our street. Was this a nightmare? Was this really happening? I had seen this exact scene in my meditations. Crying and trying to stay coherent to do what needed to be done, I made the phone call that I had heard in my meditations for many months. "This is Susan. I'm following an ambulance with your daughter in it. She's barely breathing."

As the ambulance made it up the city's longest hill on an icy road, it pulled over to the side and stopped, and the interior light went on. My heart raced faster. *Why did they stop? What are they doing?* Someone was leaning over my wife. Oh my G-d, was Tami alive? Would my car make it up that hill? The ambulance went through red lights. I followed.

We arrived at the closest hospital. Tami was on the gurney, shaking uncontrollably, covered with a thin blanket and almost purple. The hospital personnel calmly told the ambulance driver that they couldn't accept Tami because she was too critical. He responded, "On the way, we pulled over but couldn't get an IV line in. She won't make it the twenty minutes to the nearest trauma center." *What? Did I just hear that? Won't make it? Is this happening? She just turned fifty-four.*

Tami's emergency-department room filled with medical personnel moving quickly. At 4:45 a.m., I called a friend who is a cardiothoracic surgeon. My friend knew my beliefs. Recently, I had energetically intervened with a relative who had a lump near her lung that he planned to remove. When he examined her after the energy work, it was gone.

Now, he cautioned that if we went home and didn't transfer Tami to the trauma center, she might not survive. I called another friend, an interventional cardiologist, who met us at the trauma center. I felt respected by both medical professionals for my belief system.

I took a deep breath and received guidance to embrace the Western medical world. My spiritual awareness and gratefulness heightened as I accepted the positive opportunities available by combining the Eastern and Western methods of healing.

The next days seemed like months. When we originally arrived on Saturday, the news was not good, and it revealed life-threatening heart challenges. On Monday morning, it was confirmed that Tami needed open-heart surgery.

I don't know how I had the courage to leave Tami when I was told there was no room for me in the Guardian Air helicopter. The flight nurse, ironically also named Tammy, took my hand, looked into my eyes, and promised that she would take great care of Tami. I felt comforted as Tammy told me that the hospital was already informed that Tami's wife would arrive by car once the helicopter landed. As I raced home to pick up a few things, I was praying gratefully that we had all the paperwork so I would be respectfully included and treated as Tami's legal spouse.

As it had never before done and never would again, the Guardian Air helicopter flew over our home. As I stood there with Sandy, we both looked upward and knew Tami was being flown on angel wings. In moments like this, I am completely connected to my divine intuition and know all is well.

However, the next weeks were a blur. I slept by Tami's side, never leaving the hospital. Her recovery from open-heart surgery was filled with many complications and took much longer than anticipated. By the time we arrived home, weeks had passed.

Little sleep. Constant stress. We arrived home totally depleted physically and emotionally and somewhat spiritually.

I maintained my practice of meditation but also spent a lot of time in a zombie-like state. I struggled to process the magnitude of this change in our lives.

I didn't have energy to answer the onslaught of questions. No one understood. How could they? One day I was speaking to thousands while traveling with our documentary film, *Bullied to Silence*, and only weeks later I was watching my wife fight for her life.

Everyone meant well, but the endless comparisons of Tami's challenges to other people's experiences created tremendous frustration, anxiety, and my need to learn everything possible about Tami's unique situation. I tried to be the perfect spouse and perfect patient advocate. With such a new, complicated, and sudden onslaught of health challenges, I welcomed being "perfectly imperfect."

As Tami's health challenges continued, it was time to make a choice. I could be a victim of my circumstances, or I could elevate to my magnificence. One thing I knew for sure was that I could embrace the positive in every challenge and accept it as opportunity. I meditated. I wrote group updates to keep people informed. I prayed. I visualized Tami healthy and active.

Once I began to express gratitude, acknowledge the challenges, work through them, and connect with my inner intuitive strength, I saw the positive energetic results. I felt a huge shift in how I perceived my reality. Gratefully, I had love, support, compassion, and kindness aplenty from friends and family near and far. Sometimes it took my only remaining energy to warm the delicious meals and soups that our earth angels delivered. Embracing the gift of those in our lives, I recall the beautiful warm smiles, the joyous laughter, the private music concerts that uplifted our souls, and the heartfelt messages, pictures, and blessings. Our rabbi Alicia's visits and prayers and the support of our congregation rooted my faith and trust in G-d. I always felt held in the light. After a year, special friends made it possible for me to spend a few days at a nearby hotel, journaling and nurturing my soul. Acknowledging the necessity for self-care was one of my greatest lessons.

All our friends and family fueled the magnificence within me to appreciate the love, compassion, kindness, and respect so readily available when I allow it in. Whenever challenges present themselves, and life is full of them, I seek to breathe in my faith and trust, express my gratitude, and look for the opportunity created by the experience.

In June 2015, our house was for sale. I was busy doing, doing, doing and losing track of being, being, being. Sometimes I would meditate. Sometimes the ever-present to-do list won the attention for my time. Time. I didn't seem to get the living-in-the-*now* concept then.

We left the house early on June 25, as the house was being shown to prospective buyers. We had no time to meditate, no morning affirmations, no mirror exercises. We were feeling incredibly stressed to make the house immaculate, get our cats inside the laundry room, clean up the dog poop in the yard, and get out the door. Minutes later, the agent called to say we could return. All that energy and the people were there for ten minutes. However, all the doors were left wide open. The neighborhood chipmunks appreciated the open invitation and happily scurried inside. The agent had left a note telling me that she had marked a tree with pink tape. "You need to top the tree to open up the view." Oh my G-d! Our homeowners' association did not allow tree topping.

OK, note to self...get the chipmunks out of the house (I was the only one hearing them, so I was questioning my sanity), find the flag on the tree before a nosy neighbor does, call the vet, and read the real estate agent's text. As I walked across the hard stone floor, speakerphone in hand while conversing with the vet's office, looking out the window for the pink flag, and searching for the text message, I slammed into the concrete Mediterranean post. Instinctively, I extended my left arm toward the dining room chair to keep from falling,

It was too late. I heard a huge cracking sound and looked down to see my arm completely turned sideways. I dropped the phone and wailed, "I broke my arm!" Pain. I immediately began to breathe deeply. Slowly, I scooted along the cold, incredibly hard floor toward a chair to brace against it. Pain. Pain. Pain.

I remember closing my eyes, envisioning a beautiful beach, and removing my mind from the presence of my body. I held my arm tightly and closely against my body. I began the mantra that lasted for over a year: "There is no pain. There is no pain. There is no pain." The ambulance and EMTs arrived quickly. What would I like for pain? "I'm allergic to all pain meds. I can't take anything." Silently, "There is no pain. There is no pain. There is no pain."

I remember thinking that I'd request a purple cast and be home soon. The ambulance ride—pain. The emergency department—pain. During the x-ray—pain. When my bladder and bowels let loose, I was scoffed at. Humiliation. Repeatedly, I heard, "We must start an IV drip with pain meds."

"I'm allergic to all pain medications."

"We need to transport you by ambulance for immediate surgery."

"I'm allergic to all anesthesia."

"Your blood pressure is high."

"I don't have high blood pressure; I'm in pain."

"You must take this pill to lower your blood pressure."

"I'm allergic."

"We can't send you home unless you take it."

I complied and got all the allergic reactions, and I was in pain! I repeated my new mantra, "There is no pain. There is no pain. There is no pain." Only there was A LOT of pain! The x-rays revealed that the break in my humerus bone resembled the capital letter *T*.

Now I knew I was "perfectly imperfect."

We arrived home, and Tami quickly assembled a brilliant team of homeopathic and energy healers. I entered into a meditative state and continued my mantra, "There is no pain."

Fitted with a full upper-body immobilizing brace, I could not move either of my arms, shoulders, or hands. Weeks turned into four months wearing that poorly fitted contraption. I could not sleep comfortably, getting rest only as I became exhausted and overwrought by pain. I remained meditating around the clock. I removed myself from my body and its pain. I needed help to get out of bed, go to the bathroom, brush my teeth, wash my hair, have a sponge bath, and yes, adjust that barbaric brace.

At least twice daily, the brace needed to be adjusted. It was an extremely stress-inducing time for everyone because it could not be done without exacerbating my pain tenfold. The cornstarch we were instructed to use to lessen the skin chafing grew mold! The brace cut deeply into my flesh, creating a deep open sore. And I wasn't on pain meds! I would envision myself snorkeling. I'd put myself on an island. I'd send myself energetically anywhere away from the pain. "There is no pain!"

Severe lymphedema developed. I was grateful that some incredible earth angels were present with me during this ordeal. Amazing physical therapists; occupational therapists; energy healers doing Reiki, Jin Shin Jyutsu, and deep energy-flow work; craniosacral massage therapists; friends singing; and huge amounts of unconditional love surrounded me.

I focused on the vision of a healed bone. Faith and trust. What opportunity arose from this challenge? My meditations were revealing. Over the past years of being a caregiver first, I had lost myself. My mind had written stories that didn't resonate with my authenticity. My wife's continued health deterioration created a deep-seated fear that she could die any day, and it immobilized me. I needed to release that fear. It was deep and hard work and continues to this day as I embrace my new mantra from Gabby Bernstein, "I proactively heal my body."

I have learned to adapt to my new norm as opportunities arise daily. When I go to the grocery store, I bring multiple bags so that each of them is extremely light. Sometimes the person in line behind me just wants to get home to enjoy some ice cream. I am aware that the person has defrosting items. I offer my freezer bag! I interact with the cashier and am certain to ask how his or her day is and am truly interested in the answer. I let everyone know that I appreciate him or her. My happiness and gratitude just to be able to go to the grocery store, to be able to wheel a shopping cart, to have the abundance to purchase what we need and some extra for those who have less, and to be present in the moment and fully aware of my magnificent life is abundantly apparent. I share my smile.

Yes, like you, I have had challenges throughout my life. Yes, as in your life, sometimes tears, frustration, anger, sadness, fear, negative self-talk, or any of many other overwhelming and anxiety-producing events transpire. Yes, there is physical pain. Yes, there is real disease.

Pain is the body's way of getting our attention. When we have a trauma or an event, we encourage the creation of an imprint within our cells. It may lie dormant for years. For me, the law school discussion of rape parted the soil away from the seeds that had been buried years before. Likewise, the trauma of Tami's ongoing life-threatening illness planted new seeds. In each case, a full-grown blossoming imprint upon my cells was manifested as a physical disease. My journey has led me to become aware of my triggers.

My awareness focuses on the opportunity the experience creates. This isn't easily said or done. It's the hard, challenging work of going through the pain, the experience, and letting it go. I know I can't go around it. I must go through it, fully feel it, and diminish the power of its energy. I find that after its release, my growth includes gratitude for the experience. I embrace it as an opportunity for more magnificence, more awareness, more authenticity, and complete connection to my soul's purpose, the reason I am on this planet, here and now.

I've developed an acronym for how I choose to show up and connect to the world with a voice that is the positive change. The acronym is LCKR (pronounced "looker"). LCKR stands for "love, compassion, kindness, and respect." As LCKRs, we can engage with others from a positive space. First, we embody this openheartedness within ourselves. Then, we can share our love, compassion, kindness, and respect with everyone we meet, whether it is for a minute while passing on a street or in a longtime relationship. Wherever we go, we can share a smile. Compliment someone. Hold a door open. A simple "I appreciate you" makes someone feel special, happy, loved, visible.

Some of my greatest teachers are the ones who cut me off in traffic or illegally park in the handicap space. These opportunities allow me to take a deep breath in and breathe out my positive attitude while being a LCKR. Also crucial are the lessons I learn as I share my love with those who might otherwise be unnoticed. My heart soars when the trash collector turns and smiles after I've been telling him weekly that I appreciate him; when the person making my sushi lights up when I exclaim in delight that she created a beautiful masterpiece; when a young adult, previously mercilessly bullied, writes me a loving note of gratitude for the positive impact I've had on his life, and it's addressed, "Dear Momma Susan." My tears of happiness effortlessly flow.

You create your positive reality with your positive thoughts. Your openheartedness is contagious and should be spread. Wherever you travel, always carry your most prized possession—your smile.

Today is a new day.

I AM. Magnificent.

I AM. Strong.

I AM. Perfect. Just the way I am.

And so are you.

I love you just the way you are.

Please join me in being a LCKR by spreading your light, your love, your compassion, your kindness, and your respect—first for yourself and then with everyone you meet.

Together, our love will be the change for a world full of peace.

ABOUT SUSAN FAITH

Susan Faith (Broude) is the proud mother of an adult son and joyously married to her wife for sixteen years. Trained as an attorney and with thirty-five-plus years of business experience, Susan is an acclaimed author, filmmaker, and international inspirational speaker.

Susan Faith founded Purple People Inc. twenty years ago after experiencing life-threatening challenges. As she was told to say good-bye to her young child, Susan experienced a lightning bolt of divine clarity. Her message is to live in purpose by igniting others to honor our differences, celebrate diversity and to shine her light for others to know they are innately able to heal.

Susan's vision to impact a broader audience beyond books expands into documentary films that make a difference with the creation of Dog Eats Hat Productions. She is the executive producer and writer of several films, including *Let It Begin! A Filmmaker's Journey*, nominated for the 2011 Student Academy Award in Short Documentary.

Recognizing the global impact of bullying, Susan produced and wrote the award-winning feature film, *Bullied to Silence,* which focuses on verbal and cyber-bullying. Susan brings awareness to diversity as *Bullied to Silence* shares stories of dozens of youth and adults from all walks of life, ethnicities, physical challenges, sexual orientations, and international communities.

Susan champions the Movement to Be the Positive Change of Verbal and Cyber-bullying. She contributes to publications and speaks at conventions, symposiums, on radio, and television.

Susan Faith's films and award-winning books including *Purple Love* and *Purple Puppy* enable her to meet children and adults worldwide who embrace her presence and message that, "You are perfect just the way you are."

Susan's passion is to inspire others to connect to their soul's purpose and live a life full of love, compassion, kindness and respect. As a spiritual intuitive and visionary, she empowers us to overcome challenge and create opportunities. Susan accomplishes this through her books, films, and live events.

Susan nourishes her soul by spending quiet time with Tami, taking walks in nature, frolicking at the ocean, going to movies, laughing with friends, playing with dogs, and singing off-key!!

Founder/CEO: Purple People Inc.

Founder/Executive Producer/Writer: Dog Eats Hat Productions

Education: JD, New England School of Law; BA, Brandeis University; Elementary Education Certification, Brandeis University Certificate, Jack Canfield, "Breakthrough to Success."

Purple People Inc. promotes love, respect, equality, peace, compassion and kindness through openhearted service.

Email: info@PurplePeople.com

Websites: www.PurplePeople.com www.BulliedtoSilence.com

Facebook: www.facebook.com/SusanFaith

LinkedIn: www.linkedin.com/in/susanfaithbroude

Twitter: @RealSusanFaith

SLIGHTLY GREENER

Tonya Harris

My childhood started out normal enough. I lived in a small town where everyone knew everyone, and I lived with my parents and my younger sister. I remember it as being a very happy childhood; we lived in the woods, and I remember climbing trees, going for hikes, and running back and forth to my grandparents' house next door. It was a pretty fun, normal childhood!

In first grade things changed. I remember complaining of back pain, and soon I also couldn't raise my right arm past shoulder level. I remember saying, "Look! I can't raise my arm past this," raising my arm just about halfway up, and then feeling as if it wouldn't go up any higher. A little strange for a first grader to be complaining of these things, so maybe it was just a fluke. Plus, I really didn't know how to describe my pain. A couple of days later, though, I collapsed when I tried to pick up my cat. That's when my parents knew it was time to call the doctor.

We went to my regular pediatrician's office right away, and they did some tests. I remember being shuffled off to the nurse's office to color, and I thought that was so cool! Luckily the nurse that day was a family friend. I went into her office happily, thinking it was special getting a chance to go in and color with her, not knowing that just a few rooms away, my parents were getting some pretty scary news.

The doctors weren't sure what I had, but they knew it was serious. We were sent to the hospital across the street for more tests. I still didn't know for sure why I was in the hospital, and I overheard the doctors telling my parents that if my tests came back clear, I could go home. So while I was enjoying the visitors, flowers, and gifts (I got a teddy bear taller than I was—what almost-seven-year-old wouldn't love that), I also remember that I was telling everyone that if my tests came back clear, I'd be going home soon. I was super excited to get back to normal!

But the tests didn't come back clear, and I didn't get to go home. Ironically, it was my dad's childhood pediatrician who told my parents, with tears in his eyes, that it was a worst-case scenario. They were pretty sure it was some sort of cancer; they just didn't know what kind. He sent us straight to a hospital in Chicago and said there was no time to pack, that we had to leave right away. My dad recently told me that they didn't know if I'd make it through the weekend. It was in that hospital in January 1982, two weeks before my seventh birthday, that I was diagnosed with acute lymphocytic leukemia.

I don't remember a whole lot about that hospital stay. I do remember it being nighttime and hearing the hushed voices of my parents talking to my hospital roommate's parents. I remember thinking, "Wow, that doesn't sound great," but I still didn't know what was going on. And I also remember my doctor coming in and introducing herself to me that first night, but I remember thinking, "OK, cool, but why do I need a doctor?" She also didn't look like a doctor to me, so I was doubly confused! Then again, I didn't really have an idea of what a doctor would look like. But I can still recall the shirt she was wearing—it was like a velour material with thin, colorful stripes that reminded me of *Sesame Street* colors—red, orange, yellow, green, and maybe some blue. And somehow it comforted me.

My doctor had told my parents that the survival rate, which back then was approximately 20 percent, depended on several factors. One of the biggest factors I had in my favor was that I was female. Some of the other factors were the type of leukemia that I had, how quickly I went into remission, and my age. All those were working in my favor.

One of the things I find fascinating is how my treatment plan came about. Early on, my parents had to decide whether I would get two years of chemotherapy followed by one year of radiation therapy to my brain or three years of chemo with no radiation. Or they could go with the option of putting me in a study, where my medical information would be input into a computer, and the computer would decide how to treat me. Since the survival rate was low and they didn't like the sound of the side effects from the radiation, they decided to go with the study. The computer chose three years of chemotherapy with no radiation.

One of the other things the doctor told my parents was that I had to be careful not to get the chicken pox. If I did, it could be fatal. Soon enough the chicken pox was going around school, and my doctor said I needed to stay home from school until I got a chicken pox vaccine, which was almost unheard of back then. I was terrified of the shot because back then it was a shot in the behind, and I definitely did *not* want that. But the next day I didn't need the shot, because guess what I woke up with? Yep. Chicken pox. So I was back in Chicago and in the hospital. To make matters worse, I also got pneumonia at the same time. That was when I started on an experimental drug treatment. The drug was acyclovir, and today it is commonly used to treat chicken pox, among other things.

I also missed a lot of school, at least the first couple of months after the diagnosis, but I was lucky enough to have a teacher who came to my house to tutor me so I didn't get held back. And from that point on, everything changed. Painful tests—spinal taps and bone marrow aspirations and biopsies—were frequent, and it took several nurses to hold me down in the beginning. I like to think, "Ha! Several nurses, not just one."

The next few years were filled with those tests, along with having to stay in at recess and missing birthday parties, slumber parties, and school. I missed being able to go outside at recess, but I must admit it was pretty cool to have kids fight over who got to stay in with me.

And the chemotherapy, as the doctors told my parents, would have its own side effects. One was soft teeth that would be very prone to cavities, and I had to see a special dentist while I was going through chemo. Learning issues, especially with math, were also a possibility (they nailed that one), and I was always in the lowest math class. Another side effect from the chemo was the possibility that I would not be able to have children.

Then of course there was the hair loss. Having a wig in second grade comes with its own set of issues. It was hot and scratchy, but if I didn't have it on, my head would freeze. And being called a boy—not my favorite.

Despite all this disruption, I still feel that I had a pretty normal childhood. I knew I was considered different because of the strange stares I got and some of the things that were said, but I was lucky to have a strong support system both at home and at school. I am very blessed to have strong parents who kept me very normal and grounded through my three years of chemo and beyond.

We would celebrate a lot, so that also made things easier. For every trip into Chicago for a doctor appointment, we would plan something fun to do afterward. We took a lot of family vacations. And when I was finished with chemo in fourth grade, I had a big party with friends and family that we all still talk about. My parents also let me choose a trip to anywhere in the United States to celebrate the end of chemo. I remember how excited I was to choose where to go (I chose California), and this helped me get through some of those tougher times.

I have been asked many times how or when I knew I was cured or healed, and the answer is… I don't know. I was considered cured after ten years, but I'm sure I felt well way before that. I can't say when because I always felt as if I was just myself.

By the time I was in junior high, I was in a sport for every season. I really feel that this was when I was coming back to myself, and I felt healthy—normal. By this time the painful spinal taps and bone marrow aspirations were pretty much finished, and the trips to the hospital for checkups were growing fewer and further between, so they weren't something I thought about as often. High school was the same. I was busy with sports and friends, and by that time I was getting just an annual checkup. For me, things felt pretty normal.

As I became an adult, those bad teeth I was supposed to develop didn't happen; in fact, I didn't even get a cavity until age thirty. The fear of infertility disappeared my senior year of college, and I am now blessed with three amazing children. And the part about being bad at math? Well, that one still rings true to this day!

But those lingering thoughts stuck with me. I think on some subconscious level, I didn't buy into the story about what I was told could (or might not) happen, and this also contributed to my sense of normalcy. Little did I know that soon I was going to be told a similar story about two of my children, and I would have to decide whether to buy into those stories.

When my son was in second grade in 2006, I got called in for a meeting with his teacher to talk about testing him for ADHD because he was showing signs of attention issues. I was not ready for that yet, although I had definitely seen the symptoms at home.

For some reason I can't explain, I just wanted a little more time to investigate; I had a feeling that something wasn't quite right and maybe there was something in our home, food-wise, that could be aggravating symptoms. So I asked for a little time before testing and poured my energy into researching natural alternatives. We made small changes to our diet, including the removal of preservatives (such as sodium benzoate) and artificial colors, and when I went back to the school just a few weeks later, I was ecstatic when the teacher told me she no longer saw a need to test him! I am definitely not saying he was cured or that we don't see the symptoms crop up again from time to time, but there was a noticeable difference, and the symptoms had lessened to a point where they were interfering less with his school performance.

A couple years later, we got another phone call from the school, this time from my daughter's teacher. This time, though, I was ready for it. I had seen the signs since preschool, when she wasn't able to write her name. I would try to teach her, and she would say, "No, this is my name..." and proceed to write in letters that looked like hieroglyphics. My original college degree was in elementary education, and I had some teaching experience, so I knew this wasn't quite right. But I was hoping as she went through school that she would catch up.

The night before we were supposed to go in and talk to the teachers to find out the results and to see if she qualified for special education or an IEP (a legal document that spells out your child's unique learning needs and the services the school will provide), the school psychologist called to tell me the results before I had to find out in front of the team. I'm so glad she did. The exact words she used were "severely learning disabled." When we hung up, I went to ugly-cry in the garage, where no one could hear or see me break down. I could hardly even get any words out when my husband came out to see if I was OK.

But talk about motivation. We knew we had a long road ahead of us, and this was an entirely new challenge. Learning disabilities, such as dyslexia, are not something that can be helped with medicine. But again, I wondered if what worked for attention issues would now at least help with her learning disabilities. What we began to see as we continued to make dietary changes was a little more focus and a longer attention span. And while she didn't show any signs of hyperactivity at school, we noticed them decreasing more and more at home.

Those changes were mostly made through eliminating foods or certain ingredients, but as I continued my research, I realized that what we put on our bodies through our personal-care products such as shampoo, shaving cream, and toothpaste can also affect health and behavior. I also discovered that the word "natural" on the label doesn't really mean anything, and toxins can hide in products in other ways.

Some, which I call hidden toxins, can contaminate a product but don't need to be listed on the label because they are considered by-products. For example, a product may not have formaldehyde listed on the label, but it can be slowly released into the product if that product contains a formaldehyde releaser, such as DMDM hydantoin or diazolidinyl urea. A formaldehyde releaser is an ingredient used as a preservative that releases formaldehyde (a known cancer-causer) into a product in small amounts, meaning you are still getting exposure to it through these ingredients that release it. The scariest part is that we get multiple exposures to it every day through all the products we use on ourselves and our children, and some products even contain multiple hidden toxins, so it's important to know what to look for on ingredient lists.

Frustrated by the amount of money I was spending on these "natural" products only to find out they were anything but, I talked to my husband and said I needed to open an online store that sold only truly safe products that I had used and for which I had carefully vetted the ingredients. So in 2008 I got a business and a retail license and opened Naturally, a business through which I shipped products out of my home. I wanted a place for parents of children with health and behavior challenges to go and know that the products they were buying were truly safe.

One of the biggest misconceptions about my online store was that I was creating it to promote particular brands of essential oils or skin-care products and things of that nature, when in fact the reason I created that store was that I couldn't stand behind, affiliate with, or endorse any product, regardless of brand, that didn't meet certain criteria. I had also decided not to affiliate with or receive any monetary reimbursement from any companies I recommended, a decision I still stand by today. What I did was research products and thoroughly read their labels to make sure there were no hidden toxins or ingredients on my "avoid" list, and I would approve them only if they met my strict criteria.

But soon I realized that this was not enough. Parents were coming to me with questions about their home environments, how to clean out their pantries, and which toxins could be contributing to their children's health issues. Even though my business was thriving and I loved blogging and answering questions, I knew there was more I could do. My true desire was (and is) to reach and support as many parents as possible with what I had learned and give them a safe place to go for answers.

So I closed Naturally in 2011 to go back to school to get my master's degree in holistic nutrition. I graduated in 2014 and then went on to become board certified in holistic nutrition so that I could help families and give them the best information possible.

And I came back to environmental toxins, not only in our food but also in our everyday personal-care products and cleaning products. I have gone on to receive several certificates in wellness and environmental health, and I've started a business through which I show parents simple ways to create a safer home environment through simple substitutions and learning how to read product labels for toxic ingredients. I show them that even small steps can have a big impact on their family's overall health—without turning their family's lifestyle completely upside down.

So many of the chemicals we're exposed to every day are affecting us, whether we know it or not, but they are affecting our children even more, which is why it's so important to me to talk about it. Children don't have detoxification systems developed enough to flush toxins out of their bodies quickly; plus they are exposed at a young age, meaning they have more years of life ahead of them for potential health issues from these toxins to occur. We don't even know what many of these health effects will be yet because so many of these toxins are new and a majority have never been tested. And children are more closely tied to their environments. They put fingers in their mouths, crawl on the floor, and chew on toys, which gives them multiple routes of exposure.

Experiencing my own wellness journey at such a young age and then becoming a parent and guiding my own children though their wellness journeys has all led me to my passion for protecting our children. I want parents to know that creating a less toxic household doesn't have to be as overwhelming as it seems. In fact, once a few systems are put into place, it becomes very easy—almost automatic—to have a less toxic household. Plus, it can actually be fun, believe it or not! And the peace of mind you get knowing that you have made some simple changes that can have a huge impact on your family's health is priceless. It's not about perfection—it's OK to be just slightly greener.

ABOUT TONYA HARRIS

Tonya Harris is an Environmental Toxin Specialist and the founder and CEO of Slightly Greener, the place to be for moms who want to reduce toxins without having to toss their mascara, lay off their favorite ice cream, or DIY their kids' shampoo.

She's an advocate for keeping detoxifying life simple, doable, and mom friendly—because if you're like other moms, you're horrified to discover modern family life is riddled with toxins.

Believing mom guilt is as toxic as the three-thousand-plus additives we're being fed through our favorite foods, Tonya is an advocate for putting a stop to scaring moms into change and is loved for her approachable style of showing the way.

Tonya is also board certified in holistic nutrition, a mom of three, and a childhood-cancer survivor. When she's not busting toxic products or explaining why you can keep your favorite mascara, you'll find her raising money for her organization Clubs to Cure Kids, which has donated over $160,000 to childhood-cancer research and family-support programs.

Hop over to www.slightlygreener.com/saferbrands to grab her *Safer Brands to Buy* guide, which contains over 150 safer product brands and explains how to buy them on a budget.

LOVABLE. VALUABLE. CAPABLE.

Lindsay Smith

For as long as I can remember, I have wanted people to feel included. In seventh grade, I befriended a new student who lived near me. I wanted her to feel welcomed, to know she had a friend, and to feel as if she belonged. I did the same with another new student the following year, and in high school, I joined the new-student committee, striving to make each person coming into our environment feel cared for and important. It wasn't until recently that I realized why I was so invested in making people feel included.

In a therapy session, I recalled an incident from the fall of sixth grade. I had two best friends, and the three of us spent every moment outside of class together. We would walk the halls together, eat lunch together, and hang out together after school and on the weekends. We were inseparable. I felt so full of love and life when I was with them. One day during break in between second and third period, I went to the lawn to hang out with them, as I did every day. Only that day, they told me that they didn't want me to be in their group anymore. I was crushed. It felt as if my world was crumbling. I had belonged. I had been part of something. I had felt loved and included and worthy. All of that came crashing down in an instant. I was sobbing and absolutely overwhelmed with feelings I didn't understand. I couldn't imagine facing those girls again that day, so I went home. I couldn't pull myself together. I had never felt so unloved and so unworthy.

I never wanted to feel that way again, and I never wanted others to feel that way. So from that point forward, although I was not conscious of the reasons at the time, I worked hard to make sure others always felt included.

But how could I ensure that I wouldn't feel like that again? I could do everything within my power to help others feel included, but to guard against feeling unloved and unimportant, I needed to build up my inner reserves. I needed to know, without any doubt, within myself, that I was truly lovable, valuable, and capable. I spent many years seeking to feel those feelings deep within myself. What I came to understand was that I could not be shaken in that same way again if I internalized and embodied those traits so that they, along with God's love for me, were my core foundation. Would people still do and say mean things sometimes? Yup. Might someone important to me leave? Maybe. Could I weather the storm? Absolutely.

It seems crazy to me that one moment in sixth grade affected me so deeply, especially since I was thirty-five before I realized the true impact of this incident. I had carried those feelings of being unlovable and unworthy into every friendship, every relationship, every action, and every choice from that day forward—I just didn't know it. Those feelings were locked so deep within me that I was unconsciously living from a place of unworthiness. Once I really came to understand this, I was able to focus on learning how to love myself, to know my value, and to know that I am capable.

I am lovable. You are lovable. When you know that you are inherently lovable, you know that you are worthy of giving and receiving love. It starts with loving yourself. You must truly love yourself before you can know the fullness of the love you are capable of giving to and receiving from others.

Loving yourself is a choice—but it is not a surface-level choice. It is a deep-down-in-the-soul-of-your-being choice. For years, I was doing all different kinds of therapy, self-help, and transformational-growth work trying to get there—so wanting that feeling of really loving myself. No matter what I did, I never felt it. I felt as if it was easy for me to love others, but loving myself was a different story. Then one day, just a few months before my thirty-seventh birthday, I was at a healing and wellness retreat, still searching for that elusive self-love, and it finally dawned on me that it was a choice. Loving myself was a choice I could make then, so I did. I decided to choose to love myself right then and there and forevermore. I looked at myself in the mirror, and I chose to really, truly, from the depths of my soul love myself. I said "I love you" to myself many times that night and in the coming weeks. I allowed love to fill every inch of my body—every cell from head to toe. From that point forward, every time I have had a negative thought about myself or my body, I have stopped and said to myself, "I don't think like that anymore. I love myself," and I have allowed myself to feel that love. I have begun to radiate with love in a way I never knew was possible.

Once I understood that self-love is a choice and began truly loving myself, I realized I was also able to love others more than I could before, and I was able to receive love from others more deeply than I ever had because I knew I was lovable and worthy of that love.

You, too, are lovable. It is my hope for you that you will choose to love yourself. When you do, people who say or do mean or hurtful things cannot tear you down. When you know, deep in your soul, that you are lovable, you can weather the storm and allow comments that don't lift you up to float by like the clouds in the sky. That doesn't mean they won't hurt—it means just that you know you are lovable and another's words or actions cannot change that. It is a choice, and I hope you choose it. No matter what has happened to you in the past or what you have done or not done in the past, you are worthy of your own love today and forevermore.

I am valuable. You are valuable. How do I know? I know because you were born. Whether or not your birth was planned by your parents, it was planned God. Every single one of us has inherent worth and value. God made you in his image. You are precious. You are worthy of love. You are worthy of respect. You are worthy of time. You are worthy of your dreams. You are worthy of kindness. You are worthy of whatever it is you want.

My sister and I are two and a half years apart and have been best friends since she went to college. We went to college in different states and then went to different graduate schools. After we completed school, we moved back to the area where we grew up and ended up purchasing homes just a five-minute walk from each other. My sister is my rock. She is always there for me. We have the same group of friends and would spend a lot of time together. A few years ago, she got married, and now she has a precious baby boy. After she got married, we didn't get to spend as much time together. Much of the time she used to spend with me she now spent with her husband. And unfortunately for me, somewhere along the way, it was ingrained in me that when people spend time with me, that means I am valuable to them; therefore, when people choose to spend their time in other ways, that means I do not matter to them, and I feel unworthy and unimportant. Of course, from an outside perspective, it is easy to see that just because she is choosing to spend time with her husband does not mean that she does not value me or our friendship. I know she loves and values me, just as I do her. And I get to make a conscious choice to remember my own value. That my sister, or anyone, for that matter, has another priority in that moment does not diminish my value or our friendship. But when these situations come up, I often have to remind myself of this.

You determine what you will allow to affect your value and your worth. Most of the time, people are not trying to diminish your value; they just have different priorities or beliefs or a different focus in that moment. It is my hope that you will know you are valuable and choose not to allow others' priorities, words, or actions to affect your value.

I am capable. You are capable. You are capable of doing anything you want. You are capable of being who you want to be.

You are capable of loving yourself. You are capable of achieving whatever dreams you have.

When I was working as a psychotherapist at juvenile hall, it was my dream to start my own therapy practice working solely with teens. People told me it would be too hard. They told me I wouldn't be able to fill my practice with just teens. They encouraged me to keep the job I had with good benefits and a great retirement package. Nonetheless, I knew I was capable of making my dream a reality, and I knew that was what I needed to do. I started my practice, filled my practice solely with teens, and became so busy that I began bringing on additional clinicians a little over a year after starting my practice. Eight years later, we have many clinicians dedicated to serving teens and their families, and we have the honor of helping hundreds of teens and families each year. Additionally, six years after starting Teen Therapy Center, I started a second center, where we now get to serve adults, couples, families, and children.

When I started my practice, I wanted to touch lives on an individual basis. I wanted to make a difference one by one. I wanted to bring light into the darkness. One client I worked with when I first started my practice was a fifteen-year-old girl we will call Josie. Her mom brought her in to see me because her grades had dropped, she was using drugs and alcohol, she was lying, and the family was constantly fighting. As Josie and I worked together, we discovered that many of these behaviors stemmed from the way she felt about herself due to her parents' separation many years earlier. As we worked through these feelings, Josie began feeling more lovable, valuable, and capable, and her behaviors improved. She became more connected to her mom and her siblings, her grades improved, and she eventually got a scholarship for college. I loved getting to be a part of her journey.

While I have loved being able to make a difference in the lives of teens on an individual basis, I am now shifting my focus to making a difference on a larger scale. With the time I spend in my centers now, I am focused on creating a warm, inclusive, and supportive culture in which therapists want to work and can achieve their dreams, and in which we are able to touch the lives of our clients every day. In addition, I have time to work on other projects that allow me to make an even bigger difference in the lives of teens and families. I have created a card-and-dice game called Talk About It! to enhance communication between teens and adults. This game is changing the way teens and families interact and is bringing them closer. I continue to dream, to grow, and to live into my dreams.

It is easy to believe others when they tell us we can't do something, when they say that something is too hard or just won't happen. But this is not true. You can make it happen if you want it badly enough. Do you want to graduate from college? You can do it. Do you want a certain job? You can have it. Will the path always look the way you think it will? No, but this does not mean it can't be done. It might take longer than you want, and the path might look different than you expect, but you can get there. You can do it.

If what you are doing isn't working, do it differently. Visualize the result—what it will look like, how you will feel, what you will be doing, saying, and thinking once you achieve it—in as much detail as possible. Do this visualization every morning and every evening and really allow yourself to feel the associated feelings.

This will help you to stay connected to your goals and dreams and to live into them. Commit to your vision, and you can make it happen.

Sometimes parents, teachers, or others, without intending to, lead us to believe that we cannot do something. Please do not allow yourself to internalize these beliefs. If you have internalized these beliefs in the past, it is not too late—you can change them now. You can be, do, and have whatever you want. You are your only limitation—so don't stand in your own way. Believe that you are capable.

When you live from a place of knowing you are lovable, valuable, and capable, everything is possible. You are in a world without limits, and this is the world I want for us and for our youth.

It is my mission to empower all people, especially our youth, to know without doubt that they are lovable, valuable, and capable and to treat themselves and others as lovable, valuable, and capable. Can you imagine a world where this is true? When we know we are lovable, we give and receive love fully. There is no hate. We when know we are valuable, we know our worth, and we value the worth of others. We build one another up and support one another. We don't cut one another down. When we know we are capable, we follow our passions and achieve our dreams. No one says to another, "You can't do that."

When children are born, they don't know hate. They don't know unworthiness. They believe all things are possible. They have love in their hearts. Through living in this world, children come to learn about hate and unworthiness. And so it begins with us. We get to choose to know that we are lovable, valuable, and capable so that we can model these qualities for our youth. If we try to teach these values to our youth but do not truly believe them ourselves, then our efforts will fall short. It starts with me. I have made my choice. It starts with you. Will you choose to love yourself? To know your value? To know that you are capable?

ABOUT LINDSAY SMITH

Lindsay Smith is a licensed clinical social worker and the founder of Teen Therapy Center of Silicon Valley and Family Therapy Center of Silicon Valley. If you are interested in receiving services through these centers in Silicon Valley, visit www.teentherapycentersv.com (for teens and their families) or www.family-therapycentersv.com (for families, couples, adults, and kids) for more information.

Lindsay created a game called Talk About It! to enhance communication between teens and adults through fun and familiar card and dice games with a twist. To learn more about how this game can support you and your teens or how to get this game, visit www.talkaboutitgames.com.

Lindsay is the founder of I Am LVC. The mission of I Am LVC is to empower people to know they are lovable, valuable, and capable and to treat themselves and others as lovable, valuable, and capable. If you would like support in knowing that you are lovable, valuable, and capable or if you are interested in supporting this mission, visit www.iamlvc.org. Lindsay can also be reached at Lindsay@iamlvc.org.

VISION BREAKTHROUGH

Violeta Potter

I was nervous and shaky. In front of me was a sea of eyes. Waiting.

It was the moment I'd been anticipating for months, and now that it was here, I stood there frozen.

Twenty-five of them. One of me. And somehow, in this dynamic, *I* was supposed to be the leader in this room full of twelve to fourteen-year-olds who were sizing me up and expecting to hate me.

What they didn't know was that it was my first day of teaching and that I had no clue what I was doing—or that I had only had six weeks of *partial* teaching experience just a few weeks prior.

They didn't know that Teach for America had placed me in that school in Gary, Indiana because it's considered an impoverished, underserved, and high-needs community. They didn't know that my whole life I felt I was born for greatness, and that I repeatedly failed to make my dreams come true. They definitely didn't know that I had always considered being an English teacher as the opposite of greatness, and that it was the last job in the world I had ever wanted. Or that I had only taken the job because I felt that I was running out of options.

With their eyes on me and all of those circumstances in mind, I felt like the sham of the century. I mean, I couldn't get *my* own life together. How was *I* supposed to lead these kids?

But I had landed the job, and these very real kids were depending on me to help them progress.

I started class, not knowing that the year ahead would be the hardest of my life yet.

They were tough kids. But I soon realized that their toughness was a big front, a mechanism of their system of self-preservation. Many of them had difficult and traumatic lives and were accustomed to losing important people in their life without notice.

The fact that their school was a revolving door of teachers made it worse. Many teachers came in, but few of them stayed. The kids learned not to let teachers in, and almost prided themselves on driving teachers to quit. It was a taxing environment for sure.

It took a while, but I earned their trust and respect. In a school with all Black students, it helped that I was Mexican and understood many of the struggles of being a minority in America.

Plus, I wasn't like many of the teachers they'd had in the past. I actually held them to high expectations instead of letting them goof around. They knew that I cared about them and their success.

I vowed to push them to grow and make a *positive* impact in their lives. I didn't care if they thought I was mean or if they didn't like me. I was there to break the culture of low expectations and wanted them to see that they could achieve great things if they worked hard.

So, I went all in for my students. I spent evenings and weekends creating the curriculum, planning lessons, grading work, and tutoring myself in the concepts I had to teach the next day or following week.

Of course, all this work cost me my health. I hardly slept and often was so busy that I would forget to eat. It also took a toll on my personal life and heavily contributed to the downfall of my first marriage.

But for the first time in my life, I was 100 percent focused on caring for people other than myself. I felt responsible for my students and grew to love them. Teaching them gave me a sense of purpose that I had never felt before. I finally felt like a leader and that I was doing something that mattered.

***

Because I was lost in this cause, time flew by. And by the end of my second year, I was one of the best teachers in the building. My students saw so much growth that I received quarterly bonuses and was able to negotiate a raise 4 percent higher than the standard.

But devoting myself wholeheartedly in such an environment was wearing my spirit down. Save for a new relationship with a fellow teacher, I had very little life of my own.

The fact that my school was in a constant state of turnover made me feel like a hamster struggling to keep up on a wheel. New principal. New requirements. New staff. New curriculum. New lesson plans. New surprise electives to teach. Every year started from scratch.

All of this paired with the reality of working in a place like Gary, with its consistent cycle of poverty, violence, and dysfunction, weighed on me. It didn't seem like I was truly making an impact.

My old feeling that I was meant for something greater started creeping up and gnawing at me from within. I felt like I would be the one to pull my family from the cycle of struggle we had been in since my parents sacrificed everything to bring us to this country.

I felt torn. I knew I was doing important work, but it was becoming clear that it wasn't what I was called to do. But what could be more impactful than working in an area that so many ignored and thought a lost cause?

Besides, getting good teachers in Gary, teachers who not only loved these kids but also held them to a high standard, was difficult. And even though I had been there longer than most, I would be another entry on the long list of past advocates who had abandoned the area by leaving.

The guilt settled in, and I felt stuck.

I tried to go about business as usual. But my unhappiness and inner calling to create something of my own would frequently sneak up on me at the worst possible times. Like the time I showed my students Steve Jobs' commencement speech to the Stanford graduating class of 2005. In it he talks about how for the last thirty-three years he's asked himself the same question every morning: "If today were the last day of my life, would I want to do what I am about to do today?"

It hit me hard. I knew in my gut that for me the answer every morning was a resounding *NO!* I cried from the back of the room as we watched the remainder of the speech.

More than anything, I felt like a giant hypocrite. Here I was, showing my students a speech I hoped would inspire them to chase after their dreams, but here *I* was, not doing that very same thing.

Something had to give. And little did I know that something was about to.

***

On the eve that my boyfriend went to buy an engagement ring in secret, I found out that I was pregnant.

The pregnancy was the surprise gift of a faulty IUD. It was a shock. But once we knew the baby was thriving and that we'd become parents in nine months, I knew this would be my last year of teaching.

The timing meant that I'd have to take my maternity leave in the middle of year four of teaching. But I didn't dare leave the job in the middle of the year because I knew that would mean leaving all my students to an inadequate substitute teacher who wouldn't teach them anything. I was determined to finish the year.

When the time came, I promised to return for the second semester. Keeping that promise, of course, proved more difficult than I imagined.

The heavy schedule my fiancé and I kept as teachers meant we would hardly ever see our baby. Plus going back to work meant that I had to find daycare for a newborn in the very expensive city of Chicago. I would be working just to cover the cost of having someone else raise my child. And the stress of being a new mom would likely affect how I did my job as a teacher.

It felt like a bad move all around. I wouldn't be able to be a good teacher or be a good mom.

I tried to make some kind of compromise with the administration. I thought I could come up with an arrangement that served both my students and my child. I would still plan all the lessons and do all the grading. I would come in to teach major lessons, and I would record minor ones from home.

Of course, they didn't go for it. It was a bittersweet moment because I was about to leave a job that forever changed how I looked at life. A job that had given me a taste for serving minority people who are forgotten and underserved. But at the same time, having my beautiful baby gave me the out I couldn't give myself.

I was finally free to take a chance on myself and search for what the purpose that I called for. And after years, of feeling miserable giving all my time and energy to something I wasn't called to do, living that way for another minute wasn't an option.

I was determined to find what I was here to do. And though, I didn't know what it was, I knew I was meant to help people and that I wanted to build something completely of my own. And as a new mom, I spent every spare moment, however few and far between, searching for what it could be.

My searching led me to the online-business world, where I found many women sharing and making money from their knowledge. I knew I had bumped into something interesting, but I didn't quite know what. I dove in deeper. One blogger lead to another until I came across a woman of color who blogged at www.mayaelious.com.

My heart jumped! It was so rare to see a non-celebrity woman of color doing something outside the norm, and here was a strong black woman being a leader and unapologetically doing her thing. I quickly devoured everything she had written.

I learned so much from Maya's content, but I kept finding grammatical and writing-style messes that made it difficult to understand her point in some of her blogs. After teaching it, I knew written English well, so I decided to reach out to her:

Maya,

I love your blog! I admire the polished brand you've created. So, it's a bit troubling to me to find grammar and syntactical errors in all of your posts. They are minor, but they smudge your polished look.

I find that correct grammar is doubly important for minority women. Without it, people don't take us as seriously. People care how we look on paper. We simply have to prove ourselves a little more. I wanted to reach out because, in a sense, I feel invested in your success as a fellow woman of color.

I hope you get someone to look into this or reach out to me for a fresh set of eyes.

All the best,
Violeta
PS: I was a high school English teacher for nearly four years.

I didn't really expect it to go anywhere, but she replied! She asked me if I knew anyone who could help her.

In not so few words, my response was, "Yes, me."

And she hired me.

I found out after she hired me that she had built a name for herself and was an influencer in her field. And now, *I* was her editor. Somehow, I had gotten myself into a world that had been a complete mystery only a few months prior.

I didn't realize it at the moment, but seeing Maya create her own truth showed me that I, a Mexican woman, could also do the same.

***

Working with Maya was a blessing. She trusted me and let me poke around her site and make suggestions. I came in as her editor, but before I knew it, I had rewritten all the copy on her website as well as for her products.

Now came the biggest test. Could my copy sell? She asked me to write copy for her sales page. With no hesitation, I delved in.

One hundred sales in three days! I was officially a copywriter!

I went all in on this business. It was perfect. I fell in love with the idea that I could help people who, like me, had big aspirations, wanted to change their narrative of struggle, and leave a legacy for their children. But most importantly, I fell head over heels with the ideas that I could make money while helping people and having more free time to spend with my son.

I thought I had found my calling. And I pushed myself to grow fast.

I was eager to change my narrative and build my legacy. But somewhere along the way, I started believing that doing all those things meant that I had to get money, lots of it. I had these nebulous goals of getting rich and being successful. I let other people's ideas that the people I wanted to help couldn't afford me sway my decisions.

Making an impact quickly turned into chasing clients. Big-fish clients who had money. And having fun, turned into working more while my son grew up in the other room.

I had lost sight of my vision.

No matter what I did, no matter how many hours I poured into my business, nothing felt right. None of the pieces fell into place the way I had thought they would. All those hours didn't lead to more money. I was still in the same place. The only thing I had succeeded at was building a business I didn't want to be in.

Then I came across my business doppelganger. She was a fellow copywriter and also a woman of color. We had both been tagged in a post in response to someone looking for a copywriter. Unable to resist the urge, I clicked on her website.

I was awestruck. I noticed that we had a similar writing style and that her entry into copywriting had been similar to mine. And then I saw that she had been featured in a popular magazine's article highlighting people's income in unique careers ... *Wait, she makes how much?*

I was dismayed. We had a similar writing style and a similar amount of experience. But why in the hell wasn't I making as much as she was? I knew that something wasn't right.

There was no reason for me to be struggling the way I was. I was an avid learner with an incredible work ethic. If I failed, I picked myself back up. If something went wrong, I immediately sought to fix it. If one thing didn't work, I tried something else. I never let anything keep me down, and I never let myself dwell on my disappointments.

I had been working under the impression that what I achieve was a direct result of the amount of work I put in. Yet here I was, doing so much work to level up, and nothing was changing.

It was becoming clear the problem wasn't tied to something I could work on outwardly, which meant that the real issue was somewhere within me.

The idea made me squirm because it meant that I had to look at all the baggage I never let myself dwell on. But I knew instinctually that if I really wanted to find what I was seeking that it was time to face the ideas and feelings I had tried to bury for so long.

So, for the first time ever, I stopped hounding myself to work and achieve, and without judgment I let myself explore what I was holding internally.

What I found was astounding. I realized that deep down I was committed to a story that was limiting the growth and advancement I wanted to see. It went something like this:

You're just a scrappy Mexican girl who is lucky to have made it this far. With all your failures, it's evident that you're not a person who produces results. You're meant to fail, and you're greedy for wanting more.

And why do you want to be rich? Money is for greedy white people who care only about themselves. Money is for people who care only about excess in spite of the suffering and poverty happening in the world.

And besides, if you get money, you'll betray your roots. You'll betray your community and leave behind your familial and cultural identity. You'll abandon your shared experience of struggle and lose your culture, your people, and the only ones who like you to begin with. It's better for you to stay where you are.

I was shocked. The only thing holding me back was my beliefs and ideas!

I quickly realized that the things I believed were all lies, messages I had picked up from the world. Instinctively I wrote what I really believed—what I wanted to be my truth.

This exercise proved to be therapeutic. I understood that the only limits that exist in life are the ones we place on ourselves and that we all have the power to create our own narrative.

It became clear that to go where I wanted and become who I'd always dreamed of, I had to shed the idea of who I had been.

I had to let go of my story.

There was no room for the *permanently-poor-scrappy-Mexican-girl* narrative where I wanted to go. That scrappy Mexican girl was scared and trying to keep me in the same place. So, I thanked her for getting me to where I was. Then I told her it was time to say goodbye, because I needed the room to elevate myself to the power woman I knew I was born to be.

The next step was to reconnect with my vision for impact. I knew that I already had an idea of the change I wanted to see in the world, and that it was a matter of piecing together everything I had picked up along my journey. The answer was clear: I was uniquely called to serve women of color.

It made so much sense. The things in life that most bothered me, and made me most angry were the injustices of racial inequity and the lack of advancement for people of color. And I felt that helping women of color would help me tackle those problems and create more equality.

But instead of feeling relief, finding my calling only brought up resistance. How could I make a business talking about a touchy topic like race?

I kept wondering things like: *What impact can I really have? How can I address something so big? What will people think of me if I do this? Will people think that I'm being exclusive? Will I offend people?*

I had no idea how to progress, and was worried about how all of this would affect *me*.

Then a blessing came at a retreat. A mentor guided me to visualize the fullness of the impact I was called to make. The experience changed my life.

In my visualization, I met and spoke to thousands of women I had helped. They shared all the ways I had moved them and the impact I had had on their lives. One woman told me that my work helped her up-level not just her life, but her family's life. Another told me that because of me she was on the path to creating a legacy for her son.

I was deep in the visualization, but tears started running down my cheeks.

When I opened my eyes, all my resistance and fears had vanished. This wasn't about me, and there's no way I could ignore this calling.

My purpose was completely crystalized. I was called to lead and guide women of color to positions of power, circles of influence, and economic stability.

And for the first time in this long and winding journey, everything felt aligned.

The universe seemed to agree. All the business and leadership opportunities I had been so desperately clamoring for began to fall into my lap. I landed bigger clients, received tons of requests for features and interviews, and even gained a team of supporters who rallied around me because of this message.

It's as if all the growth that hadn't happened while I was stunted was making up for lost time. But none of it could have happened without three crucial steps:

1. Releasing the limiting ideas that kept me playing small.
2. Accepting my highest mission for impact in the world
3. Elevating my mindset to match my vision for impact

I've been uniquely called as an example for women of color of the power that comes when we allow ourselves to show up as our highest selves.

I'm here to create a legacy of change and equality, and I know in my bones that *all* women have the power to do the same.

ABOUT VIOLETA POTTER

Violeta Potter is a vision & conversion strategist. Her vision of having more women of color in the highest levels of leadership and influence will lead to racial and gender equality is at the core of everything she does.

Violeta serves her vision by providing high-level mindset and business consulting and conversion strategy services to women of color and the allies who support this cause. Her goals are to help women reclaim their power and rise to their highest vision for their life and legacy. Learn more at http://www.violetapotter. com/vision-breakthrough/

Her rich history as an immigrant child who wanted to break the cycle of poverty and honor her parents' sacrifices is rooted in her a deep passion for teaching women of color that they have the power to change the narrative of their lives and histories and shatter the limiting expectations placed on them. She believes that self-development paired with business and entrepreneurship is the key to doing that. Learn more at www.violetapotter.com/ vision-breakthrough/

I AM TOTALLY W.O.R.T.H.Y.

Brenda Walton

I think it's rare to find a woman who is completely confident in herself or her choices. That's because we have been taught in so many spoken and unspoken ways that we just don't measure up. But the truth is that this is one of the greatest lies that we have ever been told.

We can all recall experiences of feeling rejected, diminished and ridiculed. Eventually, we learned to fear these feelings. We learned how to change our behaviors, thinking and feelings to avoid feeling shame. In the process, we changed who we were and, in many instances, who we are now.
—Brené Brown

I started my first business in 1999 and have since gone on to build it into a multiple-six-figure company. I have designed and delivered strategic public and indigenous-engagement programs for corporate clients, regulatory agencies, and three levels of government. I have been successful in my profession, but there were also times when I didn't always feel I was living an authentic life.

One of those times came not long after I was offered a full-time job, which I accepted because my consulting work had slowed substantially and I was worried about finances. I was initially excited to work for the company. I reported to two vice presidents who fully supported me and the work I was doing, and as a result I was very successful at achieving my goals. After my first six months with the company, I received the equivalent of an annual performance bonus and maintained that level of reward for the next two years. Eventually, though, I began reporting to someone new—someone I didn't connect with well at all. Things became much more challenging for me at work. Eventually my partner and I began having conversations about my quitting. After careful consideration, we agreed that the salary and bonuses were just too good to walk away from.

A few months later, on a typical Monday, I was in my office making plans for the rest of my week. There was a knock on my door, and as I turned, I saw my supervisor and our HR representative. I wasn't expecting either. They closed the door and informed me that my job was redundant; my anxiety and fear had already kicked in, and I heard the words "you're fired." I wasn't allowed to pack up my office or gather any of my belongings other than my purse, my briefcase, and my coat. Instead they informed me that my personal items would be packed up and sent to me. Then security escorted me from the building.

I was in shock, devastated that my professional and personal credibility would be lost. It was humiliating being walked past my coworkers, who appeared equally shocked. I remember thinking, "But why are they firing me? I'm good at what I do!" Shock turned to anger. But as my partner drove me home, my anger turned into relief, and as coworkers started to call me, I began to experience compassion.

As I look back now, getting fired was the best thing that could have happened to me—honestly! I had known for months that it wasn't the right work environment for me. I was stressed, and at night I would grind my teeth so much that I eventually ended up breaking one of them. And yet I consciously chose to stay—fearful that I wouldn't find other work that paid as well. I know now that I had settled for less than I deserved, a pattern I can see clearly as I look back at several challenging moments in my life.

Being fired was just the motivation I needed to *wake up* and honestly face what was and wasn't working in my life. For the first time ever, I hired a personal coach—I have since worked with several and find them invaluable. Ironically, though, my initial motivation for working with a coach was so that I could figure out how to fix all the negative people and events in my life. Instead, she wisely introduced a book written by Louise Hay called *You Can Heal Your Life*. As I listened to that book on my iPod, I felt as if I were hit with a lightning bolt of insight—I was the one who needed to change! Those negative people and events were part of my life because I had set such a low standard for myself. If I wanted that to change, then I needed to raise my standards.

And that began a journey that I could never have imagined. I summoned the courage to be brutally honest for the first time in my life about my finances, my business and career, my relationships, and even what my legacy could be. I realized that at the root of everything that wasn't working in my life was a belief that I wasn't good enough...that I felt *unworthy*. Inside I didn't feel that I was good enough, despite what the world was reflecting to me.

I was caught in a cycle of self-criticism. For example, even though my marks in school validated that I was smart, I downplayed that fact. At my ninth-grade graduation, when I was asked to be the valedictorian, I turned the opportunity down. I didn't feel worthy of such an honor and suggested one of my other classmates have that distinction instead. And I never saw myself as others did, despite being told repeatedly that I had the most expressive and incredible eyes. I compared myself to other women in my life—the most popular girls almost always seemed to be tall, thin, and blonde, and I was none of those things. And the saddest part of all was when I realized that I had become so consumed with external validation that I couldn't see that I was perfect just the way I was.

I never talked to anyone about my self-doubt because I was convinced that I was the only one who felt that way. Ironically, people often commented on how confident and self-assured I seemed to them. I even had one woman say that whenever she had to make a big decision in her life, she would always ask herself, "What would Brenda do?" Instead of taking in that compliment, that evidence that I was an inspiration to others, I remember thinking, "Wow, if you only knew how often I feel insecure in everything I think, say, or do."

I started to explore what needed to happen for my life to be different, to begin living the life of my dreams. That's when I noticed on the Internet that Jack Canfield, coauthor of the Chicken Soup for the Soul book series, was looking for people to attend his Train the Trainer program and learn how to deliver his transformational work based on his book *The Success Principles*. I immediately downloaded the application form. But as I began to fill it out, self-doubt set in once again. I remember thinking, "Who do I think I am?...He's not looking for someone like me...He's been on *Oprah*...He was in the movie *The Secret*." And then I then set the form aside for two days.

Finally, I realized that everything in life is a choice, and there is so much power in choice. I realized that it was just like dreams of winning the lottery—it wouldn't happen if I didn't buy a ticket. Accepting that I had nothing to lose, I eventually submitted my application and waited for confirmation that they had received my form. After a couple of day of not hearing anything, I contacted them. Assuming they had received thousands of applications, I just wanted to know where I was in the queue. That's when I found out that they hadn't received my application. I quickly resubmitted the paperwork. Then the next day I was being interviewed, and a few days after that I received notice that I had been accepted into the program. Can you imagine? What if I hadn't made that one simple phone call? Had I not taken action, I wouldn't have been accepted into the program, and my self-doubt would have received confirmation that I wasn't good enough, that I wasn't worthy, when in fact they had never even heard of me.

Have you ever let self-doubt take over and prevent you from achieving something that you really wanted?

It was during a meditation while in the Train the Trainer program that I first received a message that has led to the development of the W.O.R.T.H.Y. program. I want to create space where women can learn from my journey through self-doubt and discover their innate courage and sense of self-worth. I'm on a mission to support women in discovering who they are, what they stand for, what they believe in, and the unshakeable knowledge that nothing can stop them from achieving their dreams.

Each of us—every single woman—has other females following in her footsteps. As we begin to step into our greatness, to *own our power*, we shine our light so that others can follow our lead and step into their own greatness. I believe that the greatest way to influence others is to own your power.

Many of us have limiting beliefs that were often formed when we were children. Maybe it's a belief that life is hard, or that there is never enough money, or that people always let us down. I use a body-centered transformational technique called RIM ("regenerating images in memory"; the initials also refer to the book *Releasing Your Inner Magician*) that frees women of negative thoughts, feelings, and memories so that they are empowered to live their best lives. This technique was pivotal in helping me break free from my limiting beliefs. I was able to reframe my beliefs in a way that empowered me rather than holding me back. That's when I noticed how often events started happening in my favor.

For example, I was having a conversation with my mentor about an event I was scheduled to volunteer/assist at, and as I was explaining to her that I was no longer available (due to a paid corporate-client project), she asked me, "What do you really want to have happen?" I wanted the project to be delayed by a few weeks so that I could attend her event and still be able to work on the project. And that's exactly what happened. A few days later, I received word that the project was going to be delayed, which then afforded me the time to be able to assist at the event. Ask and the universe provides.

Another important step for me has been to *relate with love*, which I believe involves two aspects. First is an unconditional love for self, and from that comes greater unconditional love for others.

Rest and self-care are so important. When you take time to replenish your spirit, it allows you to serve others from the overflow. You cannot serve from an empty vessel.
—Eleanor Brownn

It has been interesting to develop compassion for myself. I've had to learn how to turn my inner critic into an inner coach. My self-talk now sounds more like what I would say when comforting a friend. I no longer beat myself up about what went wrong. Instead I get curious. I learn the lesson. I recognize and appreciate myself for refraining from picking up that proverbial stick and beating myself with it. Self-compassion is not vain. It's not self-indulgent. It's critical.

I believe that unconditional love for others must come from a place of forgiveness and nonjudgment. Yes, I've had some moments in my life that were very hurtful. Do I believe that people meant to hurt me? No. I believe that what they did or said was triggered by their own fears or feelings of inadequacy. When I can see their actions from that perspective, I have empathy. After all, I can relate. When I was living less than authentically, I'm sure there were moments when I too said hurtful things, which I regret.

As my compassion for myself and others increased, I began to explore intuition—*trusting myself and my source.* I believe we all have an inner knowingness that can guide us, advise us, and teach us. But most people have no idea that tapping into that energy is even possible. I certainly didn't. But now it's something that I do daily. I find it grounds me. It keeps me more present and aware in my life.

There was a time when I had traveled to a major city for meetings in the downtown area. Since I know that I am directionally challenged and was unfamiliar with my surroundings, I took note of where I had parked my car—I noticed a building with a large mural of a violin on it. "Perfect, I should be able to find my way back to that," I thought.

As I left my meetings and exited the building, I paused to get my bearings. I took a few steps to the right and then paused, certain my vehicle wasn't in that direction. I turned and walked in the other direction for about forty-five minutes, pausing every so often to see if anyone knew of the violin mural I was seeking. A kind woman eventually came to my aid. As we reached our destination—outside the very doors I had exited after my meeting—she pointed and said, "It's just over there." Sure enough, I found my vehicle less than half a block away—to the right of those doors in exactly the direction I had first headed. Had I listened to my intuition, I could have saved myself forty-five minutes of stress.

Sometimes our greatest teachers in life really have no idea that they had any impact on us at all. We all have people who have contributed significantly to our betterment, while at the same time there have been others who have treated us terribly. By *honoring your past*, you can find closure to those things that are keeping you stuck and truly embrace the future.

I worked with a client who had suffered from multiple traumatic childhood events. Through my use of the RIM method, she found a box of those childhood events locked away in a closet. She remembered putting them there so they couldn't hurt her anymore. But when she opened the box and remembered each event, it didn't seem so painful anymore. And she was able to see the lesson in each event. She even felt gratitude for the people who had treated her badly because of the life lessons in those experiences.

Why would anyone do all this work? So you can truly and finally say a heartfelt *yes to life*!

Our deepest fear is not that we are inadequate. Our deepest fear is that we are powerful beyond measure. It is our light, not our darkness, that most frightens us. We ask ourselves, who am I to be brilliant, gorgeous, talented, fabulous? Actually, who are you not to be?
—*Marianne Williamson*

Through my own journey, I have reframed limiting beliefs that had held me back for years, and my inner coach now encourages me. I know with certainty who I am and how I want to show up. I have clarity about my life purpose. I have clearly defined goals and action plans that keep me on track. I feel optimistic about my future. But most importantly, I feel empowered and alive.

ABOUT BRENDA WALTON

With an excellent track record in business and interpersonal communications, Brenda Walton was chosen by Jack Canfield to be one of the first one hundred people to attend his Train the Trainer program. She has studied his methodology and can tailor keynote addresses and workshops for audiences around the world.

She is the founder of Brenda Walton Inspires and creator of the W.O.R.T.H.Y. program. She is an international best-selling coauthor of the book *Success University for Women in Business*, and she empowers women worldwide through her one-on-one coaching, online programs, and luxury women's retreats.

Brenda has achieved accreditations in the following roles:

- cultural transformation tools (CTT) certified consultant
- certified professional RIM facilitator
- certified transformational coach
- master practitioner of neurolinguistics programming (NLP)

Brenda has a professional background that is complementary to her work as a women's empowerment coach. She is the founder of Kairos Creative Solutions, a consulting firm that designs and delivers strategic public consultation and community-relations programs for corporate clients, regulatory agencies, and three levels of government. She has worked closely with business leaders in the oil and gas industry as well as Aboriginal communities to successfully balance business plans with community needs.

You can find Brenda at http://www.brendawaltoninspires.com and www.worthywomen.com.

DISRUPTOR

Desiree Peterkin Bell

WHERE ARE WE?

P urpose, not position. I have written about this concept before, and it is a powerful belief that you not only live a purpose-driven life but also operate to make an impact in the world around you, no matter your title, role, or position. I have dedicated my career to operating through purpose and not position. I have had conversations with women all around the world about impact and making change. How do you make an impact? How do you move the needle forward? How do you wake up every day living a life driven by purpose, not position, despite the obstacles and the severe insecurities of others? Given the impact of the presidential election, the outcome, regardless of what side of the aisle you've chosen, has created a time, space, and environment where many feel lost, afraid, uncomfortable, apprehensive, mistrusting, and even disrespected and discounted. Don't worry—I have felt this way too; I have often cried about the world I see blasted on the media channels and the disgruntled nature and hate that exist in this country. I have cried many a night.

Many people used their energy to plan and march in the largest single-day protest in US history, the Women's March, while some have participated in marches with tiki torches and chants that have instilled fear, marches reminiscent of Klan marches at the turn of the century. Marching has become a way to express what you believe in to the world. Even at the same events, the same marches, we have found that many people participate for different reasons. During the Women's March, there were many black women and white women who were marching for different things. How do we create a real alliance? How can that alliance create policy change and make a lasting impact? These are some of the questions that I have asked at breakfast, lunch, and dinner tables for the last year. How? It starts with you. It starts with each of us. How are you making your voice heard? How are you challenging yourself? How are you using your voice? Where do you start? One day at a time. One conversation at a time.

LET'S START HERE

I have been involved in politics, government, and policy for over twenty years. In that time, I've learned a lot about myself and even more about how some people in this field are driven by the wrong thing. They are driven by ego and forget the people they serve and the purpose for which they committed to be public servants. There are many who seem to struggle to stand for something and therefore are led to fall for anything. I have learned through my family, my lineage, and my experience to define my own path forward. I drink deeply from wells I did not dig, and I seek to make a difference in this world every single day, but especially for my daughter.

When I became a mother, I began to look at the world in a completely different way. The idea that you exist to participate in something so much bigger than yourself is a beautiful thing, and motherhood is its epitome. It is my hope that my life experiences and hurdles serve as my daughter's greatest lessons. It is also my hope that this world we live in recognizes her differences and celebrates those differences in a way that doesn't seek to perpetuate intolerance and ignorance. I pray every night that this is the case.

WE MUST ACKNOWLEDGE OUR DIFFERENCES AND RESPECT THEM

Diversity is important. Real diversity. Diversity of gender, thought, age, political ideology, socioeconomic circumstance, culture, religion, ethnicity, and race. For everyone who seeks to truly believe in diversity, ask yourself this question: Have you ever invited anyone over to your house to eat who didn't look like you? There are many people who say, "I know plenty of black, Asian, Hispanic, and gay people," and in the same breath they can't name one of those people they have taken time to get to know.

I want my daughter to know she comes from a long line of powerful black women who are *fierce*. These women have been firsts, warriors, disruptors, and trailblazers; they are battle-tested. Unfortunately, some people will judge my daughter because of how she looks and what she has, and they will make assumptions based on this. That is the world of small people, small thinkers, and small impact makers. Small. These few may try to deter my daughter from her dreams. Which is why it is important that I teach my ten-year-old daughter about who she is and the power and fire she has inside her. I also have taught my daughter to know that all our experiences are different. We welcome the truly diverse backgrounds of her friends. My husband and I have her friends over, we enjoy the company of their parents, and we learn from one another. This is intentional. We are intentional about creating a space where our daughter both knows who she is and also understands that differences exist in the world that we can acknowledge and celebrate. My daughter knows she is a young black woman, but she also knows that unfortunately there are some who are not ready for her truth, for her existence, and these are the reasons I do what I do every day.

Feminism is about intersectionality and is not monolithic. The ideas of feminism are often debated, but what cannot be debated is that the concept of feminism and the fight for the right to vote did not include black women. Black women were not seen as equals to white women. This history, this context, is very important.

Let's do an exercise. Close your eyes for a moment. Picture that you are in a room waiting for the CEO of a business to meet with you. Two women walk in—one is black and one is white. Which one do you think is the CEO? Why?

You are walking down a relatively safe and well-known street, and you see a group of young men of color coming toward you. Do you clutch your purse or smile and make eye contact?

Responses matter. How you respond matters. But the truth about how you feel and how you carry on in your everyday life matters even more.

Whenever my husband, who is African American, travels to work via the turnpike, I have a lump in my throat. I make him call me when he arrives at work, and if he is ten minutes late, I am already fearing the worst. This is my reality every morning during the week.

When I book my first-class flight for work travel, arrive at the airport, and am asked to stand aside to let the first-class passengers on, there are days when I am fed up and I don't smile at the ignorance.

I don't teach my daughter that the world is color-blind. Why would I? She isn't colorless, and neither are we. My husband and I are black. My heritage is partly Latina and Caribbean, but I am black. I remember when people would tell me that they didn't see color; I would always feel confused because I knew then that they didn't really see me as a black woman. My experiences as a black woman are very different. Acknowledging the difference, respecting it, and celebrating it while not letting it serve as an impediment to progress and an excuse for discrimination, ignorant behavior, and racism is key.

While this may seem simple, it takes work for some.

You have to be the change you seek. Nothing in life is given, and effort has to be made to make an impact, to influence, and in certain cases, to understand difference. Listen, we all have our prejudices, our likes and dislikes, but to live in this world—a melting pot of experiences, rich culture, and diversity—means we have to acknowledge that we aren't all the same.

The key here is to allow yourself to be uncomfortable enough to make an impact. It's tricky, I know. And be honest with yourself. So if you are committed to making change, being an ally, using your voice, and being impactful, but your circle looks just like you, then you are not making change that will lead to real impact. If you witness something that is unjust and you don't say a word, then you are complicit. You are not challenging your circle. For the last few years, I have been committed to challenging my circle and creating a larger one. The election, the context in which we now exist, has only heightened my desire to expand this idea even more.

I have chosen to make my impact in the industry of politics, policy, and government. Politics is hard. Being a woman in politics is especially hard; just ask Michelle Obama, Condoleezza Rice, Meg Whitman, Jill Stein, Carly Fiorina, Shirley Chisholm, Kamala Harris, or Hillary Clinton. But if you're a black female in politics, that can be game-changing.

Lately, we have seen that black women are often tested in ways that seek to devalue their roles and their existence and in some cases even try to silence their voices and experiences. We often must "reclaim our time," just as Congresswoman (Auntie) Maxine Waters proclaimed. Black women are reclaiming our voices, dignity, and purpose. We are also reclaiming our place in history and in the world to make an impact for a better future.

Former first lady Michelle Obama recently revealed her treatment as the first African American first lady of the United States and the harsh criticism and venom she faced. She said, "[I know] that after eight years of working really hard for this country, there are still people who won't see me for what I am because of my skin color."

Hearing Michelle Obama share her experiences both saddened me and gave me hope. It saddened me because as my mother used to share with me, there will always be people who, because of their position, will seek to try to make you feel less than or test your resolve. I felt hope because, despite the ignorance she endured, she still prevailed with grace and eloquence. She persisted, and more importantly, she represented.

Maya Angelou once said this about black women: "There is a kind of strength that is almost frightening in black women. It's as if a steel rod runs right through the head down to the feet." But still, for many the experience of being in politics and being a black female can sting like a thousand paper cuts. The intersectionality of the hierarchies of race and gender speaks to the challenges that black women face both as women and as black people. So the idea that we are all color-blind erases the fact that not only are our experiences different, but so is our history. But how do we move forward and use this to make an impact and not further divide? Speak truth to power and acknowledge where we are and our history. It is difficult to be an ally to someone if you don't know his or her history or story and you don't recognize your own bias.

In my conversations around the world with women from India to the Caribbean, from urban communities to rural ones,

I have challenged the notion that we can make an impact if we don't allow ourselves to become uncomfortable first. I began to have conversations about difference, experiences, lifestyles, and beliefs with women at breakfast, lunch, and dinner tables. I call these talks "Chat and Chew with Someone Who Doesn't Look Like You." I have also gathered leaders from around the world for dinners with a theme of purpose, not position. Creating an open environment with different kinds of people in a space that is safe has allowed varying levels of conversation to take place, voices to be heard, and opinions to be explained. In the end every single person leaves the table having learned something new, with a renewed sense of purpose and perspective and more heart.

Listen, we are living in a world where we can choose to allow our differences and in some cases ignorance of the unknown to further divide us, or we can make the choice to leave this world a better place for our daughters and sons, to give them a fighting chance to live with and understand the differences within us all. That is the impact we can make. If you speak to someone kindly who doesn't look like you and invite him or her over to eat at your table, in your house, you may see that despite the differences between you, you have more in common than you think. We cannot be complicit with bias; instead we must rise against it, be disruptors, and make an impact for purpose regardless of our positions in this world.

ABOUT DESIREE PETERKIN BELL

Desiree Peterkin Bell is an award-winning political and communications strategist whom world leaders, visionaries, and change agents turn to when they desire to build not only a rock-solid brand but also an enduring legacy with global impact. As president and CEO of the public affairs firm DPBell & Associates, she serves her clients by leveraging her hard-won expertise in problem-solving, crisis communications, strategic counsel, thought leadership, and brand development.

Desiree's impressive career is one that is defined as being driven by purpose, not position. From an early age, she was raised to be a self-reliant and critical thinker who always persists through adversity. These skills, along with a potent mix of diligence and discretion, would become the reason she has served as a trusted advisor to a dynamic group of American cities and leaders for over twenty years.

As the director of communications and strategy for the city of Philadelphia and former mayor Michael Nutter; director of communications for Newark, New Jersey, mayor Cory Booker; and vice president of government affairs for New York City mayor Michael Bloomberg's administration, Desiree has had an undeniable track record of producing results. In these roles, she led initiatives and campaigns that elevated the profile, awareness, and digital presence of each locale and its respective leader.

In 2012, Desiree oversaw an extensive communications strategy that positively impacted the reelection campaign efforts for former president Barack Obama in the battleground state of Pennsylvania. Additionally, she served as the lead in drafting and negotiating the successful bid for Philadelphia to host the Democratic National Convention that took place in July 2016. During the convention, Desiree served as a senior adviser to the CEO of the Democratic National Convention Committee and her team.

Desiree recognizes her success as the result of drinking from wells she did not dig. To honor those who have pioneered paths before her, she endeavors to dig wells for those who come behind her through mentorship of young women of color. She regularly delivers talks to audiences around the world on her life theme of purpose, not position, and lectures in urban communication at the University of Pennsylvania's Annenberg School for Communication. Described by those who know her best as passionate, ambitious, and a fearless disruptor of the status quo, Desiree is also a loving wife and mom.

Learn more at www.desireepeterkinbell.com.

FROM CAUSE TO CURE

Deanne Deaville

I am a nutritionist. I walk the talk. I eat right. I exercise. I am my ideal weight. I don't take my health for granted. I consider myself to be proactive. Sure, I have a family history, but I know the statistics about genetics—that isn't what causes cancer. Why me? How could I be diagnosed with breast cancer?

That question didn't take long to answer. I know why it was me, and it wasn't something that happened overnight. Cancer never is. It was a long time coming. Many cancers, including breast cancer, take years to develop and form into a tumor that can be seen on imaging. They can take even as much as ten years, although some are more aggressive and faster growing.

Looking back to ten years earlier, I can see that's when a lot of the problems began. That's when I started to ignore what I saw and felt. I had my head in the sand. The view was nicer somehow.

In the early days, it was like a fairy tale—I got married, and after an eighteen-month sailing sabbatical, we returned to California to start a business and a family. A year later we bought our first home and moved in with our first baby. The business was growing. We adopted a black Lab from a local rescue. It was really the American dream. The years passed, bringing another baby and a lot more animals. We were creating the life we had envisioned. Life was good.

There were tough times, of course, as there always are, but we had made a pact to stand by our values and what we believed in. Some of the times were tougher than others. We thought our business in the semiconductor industry in Silicon Valley would be solid, would weather any storm. There are always dips, but ultimately this information age would be digitally based, so we would be OK. There would always be demand; therefore there would always be business. But with economic dips and the Internet opening global trade and huge competition, it became harder to earn a living. We stopped paying ourselves to keep the staff and manufacturing going as long as possible and lived off savings while borrowing against the house to invest more into the business. My husband was the risk taker, and I was the conservative one, but in order to win big, we needed to take these risks, or so we were told. People were still selling these small businesses for $10 to $15 million, and we were on track. I heard little alarm bells ringing, but I reluctantly went along, still believing in the distant picture but terrified of the one immediately in front of us. The economy improved, we got new contracts, and things were good again. I had worried for nothing.

In early 2008, the entire world changed. Within what seemed like weeks, the value of our home dropped by a quarter. We had current orders, but nothing new was coming in. Just one month later, our home had dropped to half its value, which was what we owed on it. Things had been scary before, but this felt far more serious than what we had seen in the past few economic drops. The alarm bells weren't so little now—they were blaring.

One of the rules we had in our marriage was that we would not both break down at the same time. What good could we be for each other in a time of need if we couldn't even hold it together ourselves? I was scared. I didn't know what to do, but I knew staying on this path was wrong. But my husband came to me in this time of need, and I couldn't voice my fear at the same time. So I kept it together, held my feelings in, and was supportive of him. I ignored the warning signals. I was good at repressing, not allowing myself to feel. By now I'd had a few years' practice, and it seemed to work, as things had been OK in the past. Things will be tough, I thought, but we'll get through just as we have before.

What I wanted to say was that we should bail. We should look at a plan B, something totally different from what we had done before.

By that summer, forecasting the potential future based on how far we had dropped in that economic depression, my husband had started to drink a lot more. He was always a drinker; he would have a few beers after work, or we'd share a bottle of wine over dinner. But now after dinner it was another beer and then another. It was just stress, of course, and a way to escape. I knew it was driven by fear. But every morning we kept to our routine. He went to work around 3:00 a.m. while I got the kids off to school, and he picked them up in the afternoon while I continued my workday. By the time I got home for dinner, he had already had a few drinks. I would then be engaged with the girls, helping them with homework and the bath/bedtime ritual. By then my husband was asleep, only to get up at 3:00 a.m. again. I thought, naively, that if he was able to keep that schedule, I really had nothing to worry about. But the little voice asked… did he fall asleep from exhaustion, or did he pass out? It wasn't a question, really, but I kept it ambiguous to avoid the truth, which meant something harder. Those bells were clanging.

The value of the house continued to drop. No new business was coming in. And then my daughter wound up in the hospital after a horseback riding accident. Things really spiraled then. It seemed my days became focused on keeping everything together. Get my husband off to the office for another day to work on something, to try for business somewhere. Get the kids to school. Keep the finances organized enough to keep things afloat, paying minimums. I had a lot of balls to keep in the air, and he was going out to the garage to take hits from his bottle of vodka. I preferred ignoring him over facing a fight.

I was terrified of everything falling apart, yet there I was in the middle of it, scrambling to make it look as if everything were fine. And to the outside world, it was. No one had any idea about the truth of our reality. My husband had become a different person. He blamed me for his drinking. So as the responsible one, I responded the only way I knew how—by trying to be more of what he needed and to keep the peace. He was so unpredictable.

And I had no clue what I could do. I was in so deep over my head. I finally told a few people around me—my sister, my dad—that things were really a problem. I knew I had to leave. But I was making hardly any money, not enough to move out and leave him. I didn't see any options. I was terrified.

Until one day I knew it was beyond any point of return, and I had to leave. I had no clue how to do it, how to actually execute my intentions. I had to make a plan completely on my own. The kids were fourteen and sixteen then—old enough to see and understand that things were really bad but too young to be able to work through things logically. Heck, at forty-seven, I didn't feel capable anymore. For the past twenty years, my husband had made all the decisions. He had made all the plans, and I had helped only in the details and supported the execution. In other words, I had followed directions. Now I didn't know what the right direction was. I was so focused on a specific outcome that I failed to truly acknowledge the multiple warnings along the journey. I repressed them.

But we did leave. With financial help from my dad, we got a place of our own. Friends and neighbors loaned pots and dishes and table lamps.

Life became a blur in this next phase of my life, with new legal tasks arising from the choice I had made. I had to justify how I could take the kids from my husband without being charged with abduction. I needed to file for divorce. This was devastating to him, and he played my emotions. And at first I fell for it. We had agreed never to get divorced. We were not going to be just another broken family, another statistic. We were going to push through and make it work. These were our agreements from years earlier. This was crushing to my values. Yet I knew, for the first time in years, I was making a decision that was right. As hard as it was, and as much as it went against what I wanted and believed in, it was right in this situation. It was right for me and for the girls, but it came with conflict.

Money became an even bigger issue with these added expenses. I was constantly looking for jobs that would pay more. Fortunately, a former coworker was now a department head and offered me a job. Reluctantly, I accepted. I was reluctant because the job was not in an industry that I enjoyed or even wanted to work in. But I did need money and a foundation of stability. I needed something I could really count on. Plus, it had the added bonus of being a demanding and stressful job, so unless there was an issue with the kids, work would need to come first. No excuses, no exceptions. This diversion gave me an excuse to escape my life and my emotions, which were bigger than I could handle. I could continue ignoring my feelings and keeping my head in the sand. Then the phone call came with the news that my now ex-husband had stepped in front of a train. I thought life had already been derailed. That day and the ones that followed brought new meaning to the word. I had never believed something like that would happen.

I was angry while feeling guilty about being angry over such a tragedy. I felt that my husband had taken the easy way out, as if he couldn't hack this life, the recovery, the challenge of living life when things weren't easy, without a drink to escape. So good-bye, world. Good-bye, kids. Good-bye, everything we had ever believed in and set out to do in this life. I felt betrayed, sad, and so incredibly hurt. But continuing the trend, I denied my anger, my loss, and my feelings in general. I went numb. All the while, below the surface, the anger festered along with the grief.

And I was left picking up the pieces. I had to be there for our two daughters, seventeen and nineteen at the time. I didn't feel I could be there for myself at the same time—there just wasn't enough of me. I remained emotionally disengaged and filled my days with the items on the task list and the thought that someday it would be better or different. Someday, after some lucky break.

Then summer came, and I found a lump. I was never great at doing self-checks; I certainly didn't do them monthly. And it had been a few years since my last mammogram. I'm not a huge believer in mammograms anyway, since they bring on penetrated radiation to an area that is highly sensitive and reactionary to radiation, basically promoting the very thing they are designed to detect. Plus, as I mentioned before, I was doing all the right things. I ate right. I exercised. I was my ideal weight. I didn't take my health for granted.

Yet I found a lump. I knew innately something was seriously wrong. It was why I was doing the self-check to begin with. I had already been contemplating a comprehensive blood workup, deciding on which tests I wanted for myself. I was exhausted, and not just from the stress of life and lack of sleep—this was much deeper. The cumulative stress had been going on for ten years, but up until then, I had been able to recover after a month of decent and focused rest. Not this time.

I kept checking it in disbelief. It wasn't really there, right? It was just a weird anomaly. But sure enough, it was most definitely a lump. I didn't want to tell anyone. I couldn't tell anyone. I didn't want to feel the rush of emotion I had been damming back. I wanted to keep that structure in place for fear I wouldn't be able to handle the flood. I couldn't go there. How could I manage this one? I'd barely been handling all the other shots in the last few years. It was more about deflecting than handling. Here was another, a whopper, potentially very serious.

Then it occurred to me that maybe I was done with this life. Did I really want to live? Maybe I was just done. It had been a very long road, a very emotionally challenging one. It had been ten years spent on a road I had never intended to walk, one that was so painful, even though I refused to actually feel most of it. I couldn't bear to feel it; I had to skip through it to survive. But that energy was still present—whether I chose to feel or not, it was still part of me and chipping away at me, wearing me down. And now there was a lump. I wasn't sure I had the strength to take the next steps. It had been ten years of so much stress, so much anxiety, so much pain, and in the process I had lost the love of my life. It would have been so easy to say *I'm done* and not do anything. I didn't have to tell anyone about it. I could just ignore it. That was an option, a choice I could make. I would probably have a miserable life as the cancer overtook me, but I could do that, as a martyr, while receiving love, care and sympathy in the process.

While I was contemplating this option, my brain was working on the problem, looking for logical next steps. From my nutrition background, I knew it wasn't good enough to treat only the symptoms; you've got to get to the underlying cause. Why wouldn't the same apply to cancer? Cancer isn't something that randomly attacks us. And we don't just destroy the cancer and all is well. That is possible with some people, but in many cases, the cancer returns. It's not only about the mutating cancer cells—it's their environment too. Despite all my healthy habits, my internal environment had allowed cancer to grow. Something needed to change.

Support, for one thing. I had taken so much on myself, thinking my troubles were my burdens and problems and my responsibility to clean up. But I was again overtaken by fear of the possibilities, by the what-if-it-really-is-cancer thoughts. I needed support, so I asked my sister to go with me for the biopsy. The results confirmed I had invasive ductal carcinoma, triple negative. It was highly aggressive, replicating at an extremely fast rate. The oncologist was adamant that action be taken immediately; he had never seen such an aggressively growing cancer in his years of experience.

On the surface I put up a good front. I couldn't deal with other people's emotions or fear or even their questions. I was still trying to process things myself and keep my own fear under control. I felt ill-equipped to deal with this issue and was completely overwhelmed with information about what to expect regarding surgery, chemotherapy, and radiation. I was given information on various cancer support groups, but I didn't want to talk about my options or my emotions with anyone. I didn't want to go to a support group where this would be the new focus of my life. I had already allowed my life to be sidetracked; it was time I started living it. I felt a small spark that told me I wasn't done. There were things I still wanted to do. A different path became clear. My life was not going to be about cancer, nor was it about to become a battle against it. Cancer was not my enemy; my way of living was. Cancer was simply the symptom that showed up.

My battle was with old, habitual patterns that were disguised as protection. I knew in my heart that this would be not only a war on cancer but also a surrender to the current situation. I could feel that the way to healing was to become fully present to all that was, whether perceived as good or bad, and to create a new foundation to build upon. It would not be enough simply to focus on killing cancer cells alone. Although that would be the first priority, this was just one of many things that needed to change. These patterns had created the environment for my cancer to grow, and left unchanged they would likely allow it to return.

No, it was no surprise that I was diagnosed with cancer. But it was a shock that I could no longer defer to tomorrow. I had to deal with this now. Tomorrow was no longer an option. I pulled my head out of the sand, dove into the deep end, and immersed myself in various aspects of cancer and disease. Several surprising things emerged about the nature of cancer, leading to a few key areas I needed to change.

First, from a nutritional perspective, even though I had been eating what was considered a very healthy diet, it was also apparently good for supporting the proliferation of cancer cells. Cancer feeds on glucose and glutamine, so I needed to shut off that fuel supply with very specific dietary changes. I was already on a grain-free diet, but with all the veggies and fruit I was eating, I was still burning glucose as my main source of fuel. After doing a liver cleanse, I went on a restricted ketogenic diet. I incorporated specific herbs and enzymes and other nutrients based on lab tests and symptoms. I monitored my blood glucose and ketone levels daily. I added other adjunctive therapies as well, including hyperbaric oxygen therapy. Within a few weeks of this, my lump was noticeably smaller. I had more energy, and I knew this was a key part of my formula.

Secondly, emotionally I still had a lot of work to do. Holding on to grief and anger while reacting from fear is extremely detrimental to the body. We know that energy cannot be created or destroyed, only changed. We understand the laws of energy, but very few of us apply them to our lives and our bodies. But the truth is that energy is everything. And emotions are just energy in motion. The emotions I had repressed when I was too scared to voice my fears, stand in disagreement, or express disappointment had been ignored, but they hadn't disappeared. They had only changed. Over time, this energy had eroded parts of me. And since I wasn't honoring my feelings, I wasn't honoring myself. My confidence had eroded—I no longer felt competent to make decisions. I had abandoned myself in this process. I had discounted my intuition and no longer trusted my judgment. In order to become well again, I needed to make a massive shift in processing and honoring my emotions and releasing stored negative energy. There are many techniques that can be helpful in this. I used guided imagery, affirmations, journaling, and daily meditation, and I worked with a skilled psychotherapist. I also incorporated specific essential oils and Bach flower remedies to help encourage an energetic shift.

Lastly, and most importantly, I needed to engage with life energetically from a place of trust. I needed to start showing up fully in each moment. As humans we are hard-wired with a perfect guidance system—we feel in our hearts whether we are on the right path or if we are off course. I had ignored this. I had let my head take over and use only logic to make my decisions.

But logic doesn't bring satisfaction, happiness, peace, or security. Those things would come only from nurturing my beliefs, values, and dreams. They would come as a result of being true to my nature and expressing what mattered to me. This also meant being aware of how life and responsibility could hijack my time and attention. I needed to stop reacting with clever thinking to come up with the right answer and instead step in fully from my heart. I needed to trust that this was all meant to be.

I wouldn't say that I was happy to get a cancer diagnosis, but I can say I trust that it ultimately sparked the life back into me. It was the shock and wake-up call that I needed. And through it all, I have learned some valuable lessons, which I'll share here in the hope of helping others alter their course before a life-threatening diagnosis or tragic event occurs. We never know when that day might come, and we can't afford to wait until tomorrow.

From a nutritional perspective, we have been misinformed over the years about what is the right diet, what is good for us as humans to eat—not only to prevent disease but for optimal health in general. The biggest tragedy has been in the adoption of a low-fat diet. The truth is that we need fat not only to survive but to thrive. We have been led to believe that fat causes clogged arteries, weight gain, and many other health issues. But it's important to note that not all fats are created equal and should not be treated—or avoided —as such. There is a difference between healthy fats—saturated fats and medium-chain triglycerides—and damaging trans fats and processed oils. Yes, we have different necessities based on our current physiology, our ethnic backgrounds, our geographical locations, and our physical demands, but the fact is that humans are healthier burning fat, or ketones, as a primary fuel and not glucose. Eating high-quality fat and burning ketones has so many benefits. For one, it combats sugar cravings, eliminates the sleepiness we feel at 3:00 p.m., and helps us sleep through the night. There are other important nutritional game changers on the slope to chronic disease, but I feel this is the most significant. So eat more high-quality fat. Eat an avocado every day. Cook eggs in lots of organic butter. Use coconut and olive oil liberally. And cut back (or cut out) grains and processed food products.

From an energetic perspective, it's not always clear why some people get cancer and others do not. However, it is known that all cancer cells have damaged mitochondria, which continue to divide and multiply in this mutated form. Mitochondria become damaged for several different reasons—and I believe that in my case, the damage was caused by years of repressed negative emotions in combination with environmental factors. Emotions, literally energy in motion, come without effort or thought because of some trigger. We experience them constantly, some more powerful than others, and they continually affect our body chemistry, altering our physiology, which then effects our behavior and responses. As Theodore Roosevelt once said, "In any moment of decision, the best thing you can do is the right thing, the next best thing is the wrong thing, and the worst thing you can do is nothing." Repressing an emotion—stifling it—might seem like inaction, but this energy stays as energy in some form. It doesn't simply disappear. Pay attention to your feelings. By judging them as foolish or immature, we unconsciously hear the message that we are not good enough and must pretend to be something different from what we are, creating inner conflict. Take some time to tune in to yourself every day. Are you living in alignment with your beliefs and values? Are you honoring agreements with yourself, or are you putting off handling situations to avoid confrontation and keep the peace? Compromise is sometimes the right solution so long as we have agreed to it as opposed to resigning ourselves to it. Live true to your values, and honor your heart. Listen to and trust your inner wisdom without judgment or fear. Step boldly into your life.

ABOUT DEANNE DEAVILLE

A nutrition expert and wellness coach—one who has had a variety of experiences, from sailing across the Pacific Ocean to running her own business to working in Silicon Valley—Deanne Deaville has not only survived an alcoholic husband who chose to take his own life and leave her as a single mother in California but has also mastered her practice through treating her own cancer diagnosis with alternative methods through diet and stress management. Deanne has done more than read books and take classes; she has practiced her skills through extreme challenges and has not only survived but thrived.

Deanne's Healthy by Heart program is a lifestyle shift that helps overworked and overstressed people restore their health, their sanity, and their purpose. She understands the challenges people face from her firsthand experience in a high-stress Silicon Valley job and our twenty-four-seven culture that led to her own cancer diagnosis. With so much conflicting information in the world of health today, Deanne doesn't take a singular approach to health but instead creates the plan your body needs. Deanne uses her personal journey and over fifteen years of experience to create a unique path for you, starting from where you are today and guiding you to the health you desire.

Deanne is an engaging speaker, and she offers classes in areas such as stress management and cognitive health and performance, among other topics. She is a certified nutritional consultant through the AANC and a certified trainer of Jack Canfield's success principles. She also holds a BS degree (with honors) in health and wellness. Learn more by visiting HealthyByHeart.com.

COURAGE TO BE CURIOUS

Alyssa Gavinski

It was the summer before seventh grade. I pulled a hand-rolled cigarette from the top of the breadbox, lit it, and took one puff. Despite my parents' daily smoking habits, they smelled the smoke as soon as they got home. I crumbled in overwhelmingness and guilt. This wasn't the first time I went to my mother bawling my eyes out about something I felt guilty over, usually something insignificant or out of my control. I wanted to be perfect. I *needed* to do everything right.

Nightly confessions with my mom were filled with nerves over things I felt extremely guilty for, even though they really were not guilt worthy. I couldn't explain exactly *why* I needed to tell her; I just knew that I *needed* to. This lead to my first experience with therapy. To this day, I enter that building and still remember the shame I felt back then.

Fast-forward three years and I'm in high school.

In every way possible, I was an overachiever: honor roll, IB courses, and extracurriculars to the max. I took everything from physics, chemistry, and calculus to choir, technical theater, and art class. I not only *tried* my best in everything I did but also had to *be* the best.

Amid the busyness of high school, with 7:00 a.m. choir practice, after-school drama rehearsals, and taking courses to earn enough credits to graduate practically twice, I fell in love.

I met him in tenth grade, we had our first kiss in eleventh grade, and he broke my heart in twelfth grade. Our relationship was on again, off again for years after that. We were schoolmates, then best friends, and then long-distance partners—our relationship was anything but simple.

This boy introduced me to the Church of Jesus Christ of Latter-day Saints (or what is more commonly known as the Mormon Church).

I had been baptized Catholic as an infant, attended Catholic schools growing up, and gone to church as much as most Catholics: on Easter Sunday and at Christmastime.

The Mormon Church felt different, and in many ways, it *was* different. Mormons taught that God, Christ, and the Holy Ghost were three separate beings. They had a community unlike what I had felt in the Catholic Church. Instead of official clergymen, members of the congregation spoke to us each week about their experiences with and research about the gospel, and it felt more relatable, more...human, less intense.

I was only sixteen years old when I met with the missionaries (who preached the gospel to recruit for membership) for the first time in that boy's home, and I followed him to six-plus hours of church every Sunday for years. I was entranced, starry-eyed with the enchantment of it all. I was in love.

When I was eighteen years old and living away from home at university, I got baptized. Because my parents wouldn't give permission for me to be baptized before I was an adult, it wasn't possible until then. I had to do it in secret, on a Sunday, when they didn't know where I'd be.

In a way, I was rebelling against what my parents (and sister and other family) told me to do, heading straight into a religion that would strictly govern how I lived my life.

Almost immediately, I stopped going to church because it was too hard. When I moved back home for the summer, I felt shame and guilt for having joined the church, and I withdrew completely. Like my relationship with that boy, my relationship with the church was on again, off again for years.

That boy went on his mission for our church from 2005 to 2007. We reunited at the airport on a cold winter day in February. This was a day I had looked forward to for two years. We had spoken about getting married when he returned, growing old together. It was like a fairy tale; my high school sweetheart and I would finally be together again.

The day he ended our relationship, only six weeks after he got home, was the worst day of my life.

Scratch that. The day he got engaged to someone else, fourteen days after breaking up with me, was the worst day of my life.

I found out years later that the reason that boy broke up with me was that I wasn't myself. I didn't seem to have a personality, my own opinions, he said. That's true—whenever we were together, I didn't care what we did as long as we were together.

I didn't have an opinion because I didn't want to disrupt what I had waited so long for. And yet that was the exact reason it ended.

I rebounded hard. At least, as hard as a virgin Mormon girl knows how to rebound. In less than six months, I had not only had my first date with but also married my now husband.

My husband and I were married for two years before welcoming our first child, and during the following three years, we welcomed two more.

My life looked good. I had two daughters, one son, three angels in heaven looking out for me, and a husband who worked hard for our family while I stayed at home with our kids. It was correct in the most correct sense of a Mormon woman's life. It was the dream life for many perfect-to-the-standard Mormon wives, like the "perfect" I had aimed to be for as long as I could remember.

Except I was a prisoner. (Although back then, I didn't recognize that; I thought the guilt was normal.)

I was chained to the rules of the church. I hadn't had any alcohol, coffee, or tea since before I was baptized. I paid thousands of dollars in tithing, as tithing was my ticket to the temple (and, by extension, heaven). I didn't shop Sundays as Sunday was the Sabbath, not meant for anything outside attending three hours of church. I had arguments in my mind about whether it was right or wrong to allow my daughter to participate in her dance recital, which was on a Sunday. I refused to eat tiramisu or Coffee Crisp (a Canadian favorite) because of the coffee or eat steak cooked in a wine sauce. I had to wash my hands profusely when I touched coffee or alcohol by accident. Witnessing a mother giving her child an iced tea made me as uncomfortable as most people would feel seeing a child with a martini. I had to do everything right. Everything was black and white. The rules were clear, so I had to obey.

I was chained to the guilt. I did all those things because I was told I should, not because I wanted to. I didn't know what *I* wanted, only what the rules were. The only thing I knew was that I wanted to have children.

When I was thirty-four weeks pregnant with my fourth child (my seventh pregnancy), I knew something was wrong. When I told my doctor about it, he tried to send me away, saying everything was fine.

I couldn't leave. For the first time, I listened to myself even when everyone else was saying something different. Their words should have been comforting, but I could feel in my heart that what they had done wasn't enough. They performed one more test, and they found it.

My son had developed hydrops fetalis, a condition that normally develops around twenty weeks and can be fatal.

The moments that followed were terrifying. They told me to call my husband, and I was rushed to another hospital to have the baby that night. Listening to the doctors give us the talk on resuscitation and at what point they would have to call time of death felt surreal. How could this be what they were saying about me, about my son? Even though I had had three successful C-sections in the past, I shook uncontrollably on that table, not knowing if he would live or die that night.

He lived, and he is now the most beautiful, curious, charismatic four-year-old boy you would ever meet.

It was in the strength that I found to stand up for myself and for my son, to trust my instincts and speak my mind, that I was able to save my son.

The shake that the universe gave me that day has carried me through so many times in my life and was the turning point in how I looked at it. After almost losing him, and having had three miscarriages before that, I finally understood that I needed to stop being afraid of doing what I wanted to do. I needed to stop trying to do what other people told me I should be doing. I needed to stop feeling guilty. I began to be curious about things, I began to ask questions, and I began to search for more.

Shortly after my youngest was born, I began two businesses, and my world opened. My design business began to skyrocket, and I loved the creative expression I had, the ability to help others tell their stories and express themselves in a real and vulnerable way.

In pursuit of learning more and asking questions, I took a business course in 2016, and the instructor asked us to share our stories. I shared with them the same story that I've shared with you now, up to this point. As I stood there, the instructor asked if there was anything else that I needed to share, anything else that I had left out of my story. And in that moment, I knew there was a piece of myself that I had been hiding for years, a piece of my story that I hadn't spoken aloud, ever, until that moment. And in six words, my life truly changed.

Those six words were, "I think I might be gay."

The weight lifted off my shoulders as the tears fell from my face. I was bawling. Except this time, I wasn't crying because of guilt; instead, I had released the shame and the guilt around everything I believed about myself. I was so overcome with emotion. No truer words had I ever spoken than in that moment. The sense of catharsis I felt after getting that off my chest was indescribable. From the second I released those words, I felt more like myself than I had felt before. It was absolutely terrifying in that moment but oh-so-freeing in the next.

Like the shake the universe gave me when my son was born, this woke me up even more. The weight off my shoulders wasn't solely because of the release of that secret I had carried for seventeen years; it was because of the realization that I am enough. It is OK to be me: imperfectly perfect, as I am, me.

What started as a picture-perfect dream of how I thought my life would play out if I simply followed the rules and listened to the church turned into a series of wake-up calls and the metamorphosis of my ongoing self-discovery.

It's been more than a year since the day I said those six words aloud, and I'm still figuring out my life one day at a time; only now, it is guilt free and intentionally driven. I am making choices that I want, without pressure from anyone or anything. I'm learning to live life for the process, not for the end result. Without being overcome by the guilt of what I "should" do, I finally have the freedom and the courage to be curious.

In case you're wondering, my husband and I are separated, but we coparent our four kiddos. We maintain a great friendship and are dedicated to raising our children happily and cooperatively.

ABOUT ALYSSA GAVINSKI

Alyssa Gavinski is a mom of four (yes, F-O-U-R!) little ones under nine and the CEO and founder of Felicity + Design Inc., and she knows a thing or two about branding and creating websites that showcase your business and what you love.

When she started her business in 2014, she took on 105 client projects in three weeks. After quickly building a portfolio, expanding her services, and building a team, she now runs a successful design studio that contracts out to over fifteen designers, developers, strategists, and other contractors.

It was one event four years ago that kick-started the course of events that led her to begin to figure out what she really wanted in life. She started living on her own terms by seeking happiness based on her own approval and not on what other people thought she should do.

Learn more at www.felicityanddesign.com.

HIDE AND SEEK

Tamara Benson

Waking up to who you are requires letting go of who you imagine yourself to be.
—Alan Watts

Dear Diary,

This is a story that took my whole life to write. I have very little, if any, recollection of my childhood and often wondered how everyone else seemed to remember being three...five... eleven. The following forty years are a blur from self-medicating and self-sabotage to hide from the overwhelming feelings of being an outsider, a misfit, invisible, and disconnected from the world.

What was written on those pages? Did her reality match her dreams, or did her dreams create her reality?

Who she was and was becoming had been lost among the cracks of what her childhood had looked like. In the darkness she feared sleep; in the light she feared living.

I remember never being able to fall asleep, a feeling of being in a tunnel spiraling down. A whole lot of daydreaming and staring off into space happened. I think all I heard was like something out of a cartoon, muffled and garbled—*wha wha wha wha*.

What did those pages tell of her story? Were there any words written, or were they blank pages of a lost soul?

I remember having a diary, year after year, always with a beautiful cover, always with a little lock and key. What was in those pages, I haven't a clue. Why can't I remember?

Why are the only memories brought to me through pictures and bits and pieces filled in, here and there, from my broken family? As I sit here now and think back, the pictures bring a flood of unsettling emotions.

My parents divorced when I was three or four. Both parents remarried. At that time, I was the youngest. My older sister and brother were suddenly just gone. They moved with my dad. I never understood why.

My next recollection is of my neighborhood friend. I loved to go to her house after school and just about any time I wasn't in school, for that matter. Her parents were so funny and always there together. We would play for endless hours in their basement and go everywhere around our little neighborhood, which smelled like chocolate when it was going to rain or snow, and sometimes cows depending on which way the wind was blowing. We often stayed up all hours of the night in their shed, which her father had turned into a little cabin of sorts, sharing our dreams.

Mine was that I would marry young, have triplets, and we'd be super, young, hip, fun-loving parents who were always around for our children.

This friend had witnessed his anger from out of nowhere, the fierce slap across the eye, the broken blood vessels. Had she seen my fear, my embarrassment? Did I cry, or did I laugh it off? I got pretty good at covering up my fear with nervous laughter. I even laughed as I left my sobbing mom to move in with my dad, which has always bothered me. I recently apologized for my actions, although she hadn't remembered.

I wish I could say this move made everything all better. I spent numerous hours, days, months, even years plotting how I would depart from this world. A full bottle of aspirin stands out, but really, would that have even done the trick?

As soon as I graduated, just before my eighteenth birthday, I flew the coop. Initially, I did well in college. I received an A in speech class…me, the person who always felt invisible. I had really prepared myself and learned everything I could from every source I could find. I asked questions, and my life was excelling. Ideas for my own businesses and inventions to bring into the world were forming in my thoughts…*Dunh dunh dunh*, in steps alcohol and drugs.

Because there was so much imbalance in my foundation, it left space for that recreational drink to become a bigger part of my life. I dropped out of college three weeks before the end of my third semester. What would have been A's in all my classes turned into F's. I found myself wanting to escape my thoughts, my mind, and my body, and alcohol and drugs helped numb that pain. I ran away from long-term commitments and went from guy to guy, always looking for something. What I was looking for I wouldn't know until many years later.

I was put on medication for bipolar disorder in my mid-twenties, but it took the doctor a long time to figure out I also had a hyperactive thyroid. By the time I was diagnosed, it had turned into Graves' disease. I was dealing with panic attacks, anxiety, anger—the list goes on. I think the doctor treating me had multiple issues as well. That first day when I walked into his office, he was yelling belligerently at his receptionist and then went on to tell me he couldn't believe that anyone liked me or that I even had a job. Radioactive iodine was used to kill my thyroid. That doctor was a mess throughout this process. I was a mess. I couldn't function. Luckily, with Synthroid (a thyroid medicine that replaces a hormone normally produced by your thyroid gland to regulate the body's energy and metabolism), I started to feel normal. Right? Normal. Ha. I stopped taking my meds for the bipolar disorder.

At that point I vowed to fix myself. I dove into working out. I did back-to-back aerobic classes, step classes, yoga—minimum two hours at the gym every single day. Sometimes I would go back for seconds. I worked out in the day and partied into the night. I did that year after year after year. There were more failed attempts at relationships. I was a damn good server, aiming to please. I was excellent at giving all…or nothing.

Finally, in my late thirties, I found a guy I kinda liked, someone who was nothing like the guys I'd dated in the past. It was a love-hate relationship the first week of meeting him, but I moved across the country (Florida to Colorado) three weeks later to be with him, only to figure out rather quickly that I'd made one of the biggest mistakes of my life. This was just another way I was punishing myself—I stuck with my decision for sixteen years!

Something started to change within me in 2004 when I watched *The Secret.* Even though we both watched this movie, my takeaways started to resonate with me immediately. I began to see everything in a positive new light. Instead of walking around angry and muttering "I hate you", every time we were around each other, I was happy and positive. I started seeing signs in nature, in everyday activities. I was growing! He wasn't. I began to flourish, but the more I flourished, the worse he got. It took another ten years of his belittling and verbal abuse to get me to the lowest point of my life. With no self-confidence and thirty extra pounds, I didn't want to see or be seen. I was fifty, fat, and a big failure. I assumed that was what happens after fifty and was resigned to staying miserable the rest of my life.

But then the universe handed me a gift in the form of a breakup, and I was able to enter into a new life. God showed me a new path. Looking to get myself back in shape, I found a fitness and nutrition system that helped me not only lose the weight but also gain the strength and self-confidence to reclaim what I had lost. With a lot of hard work, consistency, persistence, and personal development, I've regained my freedom, and at fifty-five, I feel fit and fabulous.

I always knew I had something special to share with the world. Why else would I still be alive after everything I subjected myself to?

I had spent all my life trying to find things or people to complete me, when everything I was searching for was already inside me. I have ceased struggling to change what is outside me.

Because I have relinquished the battle, I have won the war within myself. I now spend every day living in the moment.

What if it doesn't matter at all what is on those pages?

I found freedom in the personal-development arena, and it has translated into many different things for me. I discovered meditation, and through my daily meditative practices, my faith in God has taken on new meaning. My spiritual flow has been awakened, and the pieces to my puzzle are finally fitting into place:

Movement
Nutrition
Mind-set
Emotion
Spirituality

The set points that we choose for ourselves affect so much. We must be willing and motivated to take care of our physical bodies through exercise and good nutrition, but we must care for our mental, emotional, and spiritual selves as well.

I feel that to do this, everyone would benefit from implementing meditation and good nutrition into his or her life today.

Feeding your body live food, which is raw, uncooked, and sprouted vegetarian foods, not heated above approximately 115 degrees Fahrenheit, cleanses your body of disease and provides clean fuel to help your body function at its highest level. Eating raw food has been shown to have healing effects on some chronic illnesses, such as autoimmune disease.

There are tons of different autoimmune diseases, such as lupus, multiple sclerosis, cancer, diabetes, Parkinson's disease, and celiac disease. Thyroid conditions and fibromyalgia, as well as skin conditions such as psoriasis, are autoimmune as well.

Each autoimmune condition has its own form of medical treatment. However, it is possible to keep an autoimmune condition under control, and in some cases at a level close to nonexistent, through diet. A day filled with fruits, vegetables, seeds, nuts, sprouts, and fresh herbs is highly beneficial to anyone, but especially to those suffering from autoimmune diseases.

For me, years of stress had wreaked havoc on my body and caused chronic arthritic inflammation. After only five days of eating a live diet, that pain was alleviated. I maintain this by continuing to eat mostly raw foods.

There's no need to get caught up in labeling yourself as a vegan, vegetarian, or raw foodie. It's not about that. It's about feeding and nourishing your body with the very best foods to reach and maintain the very best health. Just listen to your body and eat foods that you thrive on—don't worry about how your eating habits fit into a diet category.

Meditation by definition is simply creating awareness. Yogi experts agree that any focused activity free from distraction qualifies as meditation. However, too often we find meditation a daunting, complicated, spiritual routine, and we're discouraged before we even begin. Luckily, meditation doesn't have to be so hard! There are many brain-boosting benefits to meditation, including the development of focus, which leads to a more tranquil, happier existence.

If you're not already convinced, here are four easy tips to get you started with a meditation practice:

1. Sit or lie comfortably.
2. Close your eyes.
3. Make no effort to control the breath; simply breathe naturally.
4. Focus your attention on the breath and on how the body moves with each inhalation and exhalation. Notice the movement of your body as you breathe. Observe your chest, shoulders, rib cage, and belly. Simply focus your attention on your breath without controlling its pace or intensity. If your mind wanders, return your focus back to your breath.

Maintain this meditation practice for two to three minutes to start, and then try it for longer periods. I've found guided meditations to be the most beneficial for me.

Each morning when I awaken, my first thought is, "Thank you! Thank you, God!" and then I become recentered in present awareness, the here and now, with meditation. This practice allows me to be in a place where I wake up every day excited for all the miracles that God has in store for me. Self-love, self-discovery, and self-acceptance are words I use frequently to describe how I feel. I have the tools to get through anything that isn't serving me, and I can release negativity and move on. I love every minute of every day that I get to share what I learn with others.

I am passionate about feeling and being healthy and having a positive mind-set. I want to help others reach their full potential of living a meaningful, healthy life in this very moment, at any age. I've dedicated myself to helping others achieve this, and that is exactly what this chapter is about. It's about owning and loving all of who you are, teaching yourselves how to live from the heart, how to have a voice, how to get unstuck, and so much more.

The only reason ever to look back is to see how far you've come.

My hope for all of us is that our lives are filled with fire, fearlessness, and things that we love.

If that's not where you are right now, then I hope that changes, and fast.

Life is way too short to spend it doing things you don't enjoy. This is your adventure. You have only one life. But you also have only one soul. It deserves to be set on fire. It's your gift to the world.

Light it up, and let it blaze.

We are the eyes and the ears of God. Together we can elevate the vibration of the planet through the power of self-love! Together we rise!

ABOUT TAMARA BENSON

Tamara Benson genuinely wants to make the world a better place. She's passionate about sharing total wellness with everyone so that as a collective we can rise above adversity, be in the moment, and live fulfilling lives.

Tamara maintained her own mortgage company for numerous years, currently holds her real estate license, and enjoys fixing and flipping properties. While she always loved helping people get into their dream homes, her true passion is helping others focus on their inner homes.

She immersed herself in her own self-growth and self-love through meditation, spirituality, workshops, online courses, and high-vibe events and retreats, and she shares what she learns through her innovative, hands-on approach. Through her programs, she helps women realize that it is never too late to regain their lives. If they can first focus within, everything else falls into place beautifully.

Her mission is to motivate others to be at their best. Tamara believes the foundation of living a happy, confident life comes from being an empowered individual and keeping up with continually moving happiness targets. This empowerment helps people be present for their children, their spouses, their family, their friends, and, most importantly, themselves!

Meditation and yoga are part of her daily existence, and you'll often find her running on the beach or simply breathing in the beauty of the sunrises and gorgeous sunsets of her Florida backyard. She loves to combine motivational thoughts with her beach photography to create inspirational artwork.

Her future vision is to own her own wellness resort, something you won't want to miss.

Find all her upcoming courses, freebies, and events at www.tamarabenson.com.

E-mail: tamarabenson444@gmail.com

Facebook: tamara.benson.79

Instagram: @fitfansunite

CHOOSING TO INFLUENCE AFTER A TRAUMATIC EVENT CHANGES YOUR LIFE

Alexa Bigwarfe

I believe that all of us innately want to make a difference in the world. But we may not let our true light shine until we are faced with a triggering event to propel us into action. Our self-limiting beliefs often hold us back from becoming the influencers that we could be. We might feel too small, too un-educated, too unimportant to make a difference. Or perhaps imposter syndrome—that belief that we are not expert enough to take a stand and make a difference—holds us back. That is, until the moment that something happens to us and we have a choice to make. We can choose to try to make the world a better place despite our own pain and tragedy, or we can choose to let the opportunity pass us by.

Sometimes things in life happen *to* us, and from that point on, everything we do is a choice. Our response is our choice. What we do in response to those life events is our choice.

I didn't choose the circumstances that led me to become an influencer. I didn't choose to lose my infant daughter. Obviously, I would never make a choice like that, and if there were such a choice, I'd happily be holding her in my arms rather than forging a path of advocacy. I wouldn't be driven to raise awareness, to make a difference and influence change, if I hadn't experienced the trauma that pushed me to the place where I am. I'd rather *not* be the person in this position, but this is the path my life took. And because I'm here now and I can see what a difference I can make in my efforts to help others, to be a voice for those without, and to influence action and change, I know that I'll never stop.

It all started with heartbreak unlike any other. Trauma, pain, and loss—these are powerful tools that you can use to propel you forward even when it seems difficult. But my journey to advocacy began before I held my Kathryn as she breathed her last breaths. I lay in a hospital bed, pregnant with identical twins, for over four weeks. They had been diagnosed with a syndrome called twin-twin transfusion syndrome (TTTS)—a syndrome that affects the placenta with identical twins and is highly fatal. I prayed for a miracle, undergoing numerous procedures to try to stabilize and help the babies, but the miracle never came. My daughters were born ten weeks early and were whisked off to the NICU. Kathryn was swollen with excess fluid, her lungs unable to develop because of all the swelling and her heart functioning on only one side of her body. While the medical staff did their best, the damage caused to her by TTTS was too overwhelming, and they could not get her little body stabilized. She was with us for two days before her body gave up the fight.

As I lay in that hospital bed during that bed rest period, I distinctly remember feeling as if I could do absolutely nothing to make any kind of a difference for my babies. I couldn't even change position in the bed, because when I did they would lose the heartbeat of one baby, and then it could be hours before they could get her back on the monitors again. I was trapped, I was hurting, I was angry at everyone, and I had lots of time to think. It was during this time frame that I started to realize how important advocacy for ourselves and children, particularly within the health-care industry, is. Even though I didn't realize what the outcome for our babies would be at the time, as I think back on it, I am certain it was during this time period that I decided I would do something to influence change when we got home from the hospital.

After my baby girl died, I was riddled with guilt that I had not used my voice to advocate for her or myself during the last ten weeks of my pregnancy. I had assumed that the doctors knew best, that they were doing the best that they could, even though my gut told me differently. I will never forgive myself for not asking more questions and pushing back harder, for not seeking a second and third opinion. Could I have changed the outcome? Who knows? But at least I would have tried. Over the last few years, I have come to learn that there are still many doctors who do not recognize the severity of TTTS, do not take it as seriously as they should, and do not educate the mothers, as I saw through my own experience.

This guilt and disappointment that I felt at not doing more to save my baby led me to take the first steps of what would become a grand journey into advocacy. I started a blog. Yes. That was my big first step. This may not seem like a huge action, but everyone has to start somewhere.

Once I left the hospital, I was on a mission. A mission to raise awareness for TTTS in the hope that other mothers in the same situation would feel empowered to use their voices and force their doctors to provide more information or seek second opinions. I hoped that my message might reach medical professionals so that our story would not become someone else's story. Did I start my blog to be an influencer? Not consciously. In fact, I started my blog under a pseudonym, and only after I became comfortable sharing my mission did I out myself. However, what I did set out to do was bring more awareness to TTTS, prematurity, the challenges of prematurity, and eventually more maternal health topics. I realized that someone needed to make some noise, and if it wasn't me, then who would it be?

I felt that there was a large lack of information in the obstetrics community, which is exactly who pregnant mothers rely on as their source of information and the people who are going to be making the best decisions for them. I knew that somebody needed to start talking about it and raising awareness; otherwise more parents would face the same outcome that we did.

Once you allow yourself to start speaking out and making a difference, I find that things grow quickly and in unexpected ways. What started as an awareness blog led to other elements of advocacy. I began to write about prematurity and the need for more research and funding. I started to share my feelings about grief and loss. I noticed that many people were at a complete loss as to how they could help, so I began to write about the ways friends and loved ones could support parents who have lost a baby. I made it my goal to provide information that could be useful in helping people respond. After my friend delivered her baby stillborn at thirty-seven weeks, I realized I needed more than just a blog—grieving mothers needed a book. I wanted to create something that could be placed in the hands of all grieving mothers to encourage them, to bring them hope, to show them that one day they would emerge from this awful situation. So *Sunshine After the Storm: A Survival Guide for the Grieving Mother* was put into motion. It's interesting because while I started my blog and my advocacy to raise awareness for TTTS, I soon found it would be in the grieving mothers' community where I would do my greatest work and provide the most comfort.

When I decided to put together the book, I really had no idea of how much bigger this would all become. I had no idea that it would lead me down a path of publishing and sharing other people's stories of hope, transformation, inspiration, love, and self-help. If I hadn't started that blog with just the desire to raise awareness and use my voice, none of this would have come to be. I would have never impacted the people I have impacted or left the mark on the world that I am leaving.

The most powerful thing that has happened to me in this process is the realization that even as a "nobody," I still have a voice and can still make an impact. Through my blogging, through my publishing, and through my business, I have been able to continue to increase awareness for the things for which I am advocating while having a positive impact on my community and in the lives of others. I have also come to the realization that in making noise on the topic, I am creating opportunities to be placed in front of the right people, who have more resources and have the ability to make even greater change than I can.

I realize that in the global scale of things, I'm small potatoes. I don't have millions of followers, and I'm not able (yet) to donate millions of dollars to really see change take place, but I'm actively using my voice to support those who don't have a voice, I'm building a platform to raise awareness, and little by little, we'll see great rewards from our efforts.

You *can* make a difference in the world. You *can* effect change, even if you feel as if you are small and insignificant. If you take nothing else from this essay, I want you to feel empowered to use your voice. Everyone must start somewhere, and you can start with very small steps. For me, it was a blog. A place for me to express my grief and my anger and to spread awareness for a disease that I didn't believe was getting nearly enough attention.

Even if it's scary, even if you feel as if you are talking only to your mom and your two best friends when you start talking and doing something about it, you can make a difference and you can do something. Start small. Start someplace. Use your voice. I challenge you to go forth and make a difference in this world. You never know how many lives you can change or save.

I didn't ask for this. I certainly didn't *want* this. If given the choice, I would rather have my daughter with me than be a voice for awareness for this syndrome and for grieving parents. But I believe I was born with a life mission and purpose, and when the opportunity presented itself for me to take what had happened to me and make something happen from it, I made the choice that I would do that. I chose to take this experience and leave an impression on the world. I chose to make a difference. We are all faced with times in our lives when we can choose to move forward and do something about a situation that happened to us, stay stuck in the bad place created by that situation, or do nothing at all. We are given opportunities along the way during which we can choose. We can choose whether to make something part of our journey or whether to go a different route. We can choose how we let it impact us. And while I didn't choose this, I felt prepared for it.

As I look back on the major events in my life, I wonder if I was being trained along the way for this role of advocate, or "momvocate," the term I coined for myself. It started early in my childhood. If I hadn't lived in Europe as a child, I don't know that I would have developed such an interest in international relations, which led me to joining the US Air Force. If I hadn't gone through what seemed like the most painful and excruciating training to learn how to stand in front of a room full of people and give presentations as an intelligence briefer, I would have been too petrified to stand up in front of anyone and speak. Now I have the opportunity to do so on a regular basis, but back in the day, I nearly passed out even just giving a presentation in front of my fellow officer trainees! If I hadn't been stationed in Germany, I would have never met my friend Fadia, who delivered her baby girl stillborn at forty-one weeks and provided me my first window into what infant loss and true grief look like.

You might look at this cynically and think I'm making too much out of what is just, well, life. But I recognize that these stages of my life gave me the tools I needed when it came time to use my voice. It could be coincidence, or it could be something more. Either way, what I do recognize is that when the time came for me to start making some noise about TTTS, preterm birth, and supporting grieving parents, I felt prepared to do so. If I had not held my sweet, darling daughter in my arms as she took her final breaths, I would have never had the same compassion and empathy for other grieving parents. And had our surviving twin, a force to be reckoned with, even at one pound ten ounces, had not spent eighty-four long days in the NICU, I would not have the awareness at all about the need for research, funding, and advocacy for maternal health and premature babies.

But I still had a choice. I could either allow my circumstances to define me or choose to take those circumstances and make a change for the better. I believe that because of the experiences in my past, the extreme trauma of our situation, and my desire to make a difference, I was well primed to be the voice.

I believe anyone has the capability of making this same choice. I'm just one little mama who started a blog to make those two days of her daughter's life matter and to help others who were also facing this diagnosis or grieving the loss of an infant. Wanting to do more to help grieving mothers, I then wrote a book to provide encouragement and support to grieving mothers. I fell in love with the publishing process, and before long, I knew I had a new mission—to help other women share their stories of loss, love, and inspiration.

Some of the most influential and powerful changes have come about in our country because of grieving parents. Mothers Against Drunk Driving, Everytown, Moms Demand Action— these are all groups that have pushed for and successfully achieved major legislative changes to protect other children because of their pain over losing children. New medicines, research, and advances in treatment for many diseases are the direct results of actions parents have taken to help their children. I decided I wanted to be in this camp of action takers.

The people who have the most influence in the world may not necessarily have the largest audiences or the biggest amounts of money, but they have passion and drive, and they understand that if they are going to influence change in a specific area, then sometimes it must start with them. When I started the blog, it was largely because of my desire to use my voice and reach people who might not know anything about TTTS in the hope that I would one day impact change concerning how these types of pregnancies are handled. I wanted to create a repository of information so that mothers pregnant with identical twins or diagnosed with TTTS would have access to more information than what was being provided to them. I wanted them to realize that they needed to ask more questions and dig deeper in the hope that it might save their babies' lives.

It *is* possible to overcome something tragic and make something beautiful from it. I want to encourage you, if you feel the urge to become an advocate or influence change, to take steps toward this goal, even if it feels uncomfortable. Even if it places you in a zone you've never been in before. Even if you don't feel as if you have what it takes to be an influencer. I made a choice that my daughter's two days on earth were going to be meaningful. Because of her short life, my family and I have given back to our community in massive ways, we've reached out and helped more people than we even know we've helped, and we're doing our best to influence change.

ABOUT ALEXA BIGWARFE

Alexa Bigwarfe is a wife, mother to three wildlings, devoted advocate, blogger, author, and publisher. Her writing career began after her infant daughter passed away at two days old. She has written and/or edited and published eight books, including *Sunshine After the Storm: A Survival Guide for the Grieving Mother* and *Ditch the Fear and Just Write It!* She uses that hard-earned publishing knowledge to support other writers and entrepreneurs at writepublishsell.co. She also owns the small hybrid publishing company Kat Biggie Press (katbiggiepress.com), dedicated to sharing women's works of inspiration and self-help. Alexa is passionate about women's, infants', and children's health topics and has had more than fifty articles published in regional parenting magazines in the United States and Canada. She enjoys drinking wine, spending time with her husband and friends, traveling, and just because life isn't full enough, hosting the *Lose the Cape!* podcast featuring inspirational mothers and women making a difference in the world. You can find her on Facebook at WritepublishsellLLC and on Twitter at @katbiggie.

BE THE CHANGE

Shalini Saxena Breault

A s I sit down to write this chapter, I notice it is October 2. October 2 is a date that has stuck with me since I was a kid. October 2 is Mahatma Gandhi's birthday. I learned this on one of my travels to India many years ago. When I was growing up, my family traveled to India every summer to visit family. One year we visited Gandhi's sacred site, and I learned much about him. I was drawn to his story of nonviolence, love, and compassion for all. Little did I know that my life journey was to live out his words, "Be the change you wish to see in the world."

I deeply resonate with goddess energy. I work with goddess energy in everything I do. I am the embodiment of goddess-like energy. Goddess energy in all traditions represents aspects of what is already inside us. We all possess qualities like love, compassion, fierceness, courage, wisdom, beauty, passion, wildness, and creativity. Again, little did I know the goddesses had been working and are currently working through me to make me the change I wish to see in the world.

I have developed a very intimate relationship with the supreme-trinity Vedic goddesses over the last four years. These goddesses are Durga, Lakshmi, and Saraswati. As a teenager I had always been drawn to Saraswati. She is depicted in the color white—she wears white clothing, sits on a white lotus, and has a white swan as her spirit animal. I always loved the color white for its pure, light, serene, and cosmic essence. Years later, I found out that my name, Shalini, means "purity," which then drew me even closer to Saraswati.

What I am offering in this chapter is the story of how the three goddesses worked through me to get me where I am today. Whether you work with goddess energy or not, it doesn't matter. The invitation is to reflect on your own journey and surrender to the possibility that the universe is working through you for a higher purpose. The universe is here to support you and encourage you to be the change you wish to see in the world. There are goddesses in a lot of traditions. There are angels you can work with. Perhaps you resonate with nature and would like to work with the trees, moon, sun, stars, or planets. Maybe after reading this chapter, you will want to explore Durga, Lakshmi, and Saraswati. You choose.

My journey begins with the goddess Durga. Durga is the warrior goddess! I refer to her as the no-nonsense goddess. If you decide to work with her, then know she will get to the core of your heart and soul. Whatever needs to be done for you to step into what you're meant to step into, she will help you. She is the strong mother. She is loving but fierce. Life can look a bit tumul-tuous or chaotic when working with her, but it's always for your highest good and is done with tremendous love for you and to help you find your truth. Durga knows your truth. She knows your heart and soul. Durga is depicted with many arms holding weapons. The weapons help you cut the cords and attachments you carry that are preventing you from living your truth. She helps loosen your grip on old memories, fear, and the past.

The way Durga worked through me was by redefining cul-tural rules and expectations. I grew up in a very loving and strong family. I was the first generation being raised in the United States. I was the firstborn. My dad, who also was the eldest, is a doctor. The expectation was that I too would be a doctor one day. However, the universe had my brain tuned in to mathemat-ics, foreign languages, psychology, and foreign cultures. Of all the subjects in school, I just couldn't understand and grasp the concepts of science. Can you believe that? The one subject that challenged me was the very one I was expected to embrace.

When it came time to pick a college, what I wanted to be-come needed to be addressed. I couldn't hide anymore. Durga came forth. I have always wanted to help people heal, to empow-er them and stand up for them. I have always believed in oneness, so my love for foreign studies was not surprising. However, this was new territory for my parents. They had thought all along I was going to be a doctor. After talking it out with my dad, I decided to explore a business degree. The business degree was not my heart, but it was the next best thing because I was able to major in international business. I was able to go deep in cultural studies, so I was happy. I went on to get my MBA in finance. My education served me extremely well, but my path took another turn, and I left corporate America in 2006. I didn't know it at the time, but the goddesses had plans for me.

It was not an easy road for me to go from the daughter who was going to be a doctor to the daughter who was in the business industry. My parents were always supportive, but I felt as if I had disappointed them. My parents had a dream for me, but they love me no matter what I do. This is where Durga's energy lifted me—I had to stand firm in my heart, follow my strengths, and not fall into cultural expectations. Durga had to cut my attachment to childhood conditioning—not just for me but also for the generations to follow. I had to be the change I wished to see in the world. I thought it was unfair for the culture to expect children to become doctors, especially living in the United States. The United States offers freedom to express your uniqueness. The United States offers unlimited possibilities. You can be anyone you want to be. I was raised in this culture, and I believed in the depths of my heart that we have an opportunity living in the United States to be who we are meant to be. We are all unique—no one is like you in this world. The gift and blessing the United States brings to everyone who lives here is that it allows us to be the change we wish to see in the world. Durga is the stirring of this fiery, passionate energy we all have inside of us. We need to have courage and release the conditioning and fear of the unknown to be that change. We need to trust our hearts. We need to release the ego. This is Durga—this is our warrior selves.

My journey continues with the goddess Lakshmi. Lakshmi is the goddess of beauty, love, fertility, and abundance. My Lakshmi blessing came forth in motherhood. I am blessed with a daughter who is now nineteen. She is a combination of Durga, Lakshmi, and Saraswati. She is my greatest teacher in this lifetime. She can be fiery, compassionate, and wise. I never know what I am going to get on any given day. But what I have come to see is that she presents to me what I need to experience to turn the wisdom and teachings I am learning at that moment into practice. She has taught me moon medicine. Her name, Chandini, means moon-light. It was a name I was so deeply connected to as a teenager that I knew I was going to name my daughter Moonlight if I were to have one. I've had a connection to the moon for as long as I can remember. During my daughter's teenage years, I was struggling with how to serve her well. She was the typical teen-ager, but I knew in my heart there was something I was missing. Raising teenagers is not fun, but this was a call from the god-desses to dive deeper into the mysteries of the moon. I heard in my meditation one day, "Chandini is the moon. Learn about the moon, and you will know how to serve her." And that is exactly what I did. The sacred teachings of the moon allowed me to un-derstand my daughter at a soul level as she was moving through life in sync with the phases of the moon. She was young. She couldn't understand her feelings or emotions. I was able to help her understand herself. I quickly learned that she was my direct link to my love for the moon. The sacred teachings of the moon in turn have become an integral part of my work today.

Lakshmi, for me, has redefined motherhood. When my daughter was born, I remember holding her in my arms and knowing she was given to me to serve her true essence. She was God's child first and then mine. I was responsible for her thriving in this world. And that meant serving her needs, not what society and culture thought her needs were. Nothing about raising my daughter has been what you would call traditional. I grew up not feeling encouraged to express myself. Every time I tried, I was not taken seriously. After all, what does a child know? Well, I believe children know a lot about their true essence. They are pure innocence until they go out and live more of the world. They just have a hard time processing and expressing their knowledge because they are not familiar with what they are feeling. This is where I feel that mothers come in. For me, I have always encouraged my daughter to express herself. When my daughter is expressing herself, I go beyond her words. I go to her heart. I am hearing it from her heart to mine. I take myself out of the mind—I remove myself from what I believe needs to happen for her and focus on how can I serve her needs. She is not me. What worked for me won't necessarily work for her.

Lakshmi has infused motherhood into my heart from a place of service. I am the warrior mother who will trailblaze the path for my daughter not to live by the world's rules and expectations but to live by her own.

This is no easy task. Parenting this way has shown me that the world is not ready for this. The world still has so many rules our children need to live by. This breaks my heart. The children are our future. To create passion and fierce compassion in our children to be the change they wish to see in the world, we must serve our children to their divine essence—not ours or anybody else's.

Motherhood is nothing like I imagined. Motherhood has brought me to my darkness more times than I would have liked. However, having said that, journeying through the darkness has enabled me to step into more of my true divine light self. The darkness is a blessing. Journeying through the darkness is Durga. However, Lakshmi partners up with Durga to nourish your heart and provide the unconditional love mothers need. Mothers love their children unconditionally. Who loves the mother unconditionally? This is Lakshmi.

My journey comes full circle with the goddess Saraswati. Saraswati is the goddess of wisdom, the arts, knowledge, education, meditation, and creativity. I have come to realize Saraswati has been my spiritual guide from the beginning of my life. Working in corporate America strengthened my left brain tremendously. However, my right brain was neglected. When I left corporate America, I was in the process of exploring what was next for me. Being a full-time mother (thank you, Lakshmi), which I had never experienced before, was one of my purposes for sure. But I knew in my heart there was more for me. I have one daughter. She was going to fly away one day, and then what? What was I supposed to do then? I knew the universe had plans for me. I had to be prepared—to be groomed—for something when that time came. But what was it?

First Durga came forth and uprooted my daughter and me from everything we knew in New York and moved us to South Jersey. Then Lakshmi came forth and blessed me with the love of my life, which provided a strong foundation for me to be a full-time mother as well as to find myself as a woman. And now, Saraswati has come forth in this part of my journey in the form of learning and exploring sacred concepts and teachings.

My first exploration was angelic teachings. I love angels. Ever since I was in college, I have had a fascination with cherubs. I would buy cherub stationery for school. When I was in college, I traveled to Italy and saw the Sistine Chapel and was in complete awe of the angels. I was mesmerized by their beauty and celestial energy.

My second exploration was being trained in playing the crystal singing bowls. Music is one of the embodiments of Saraswati. If you were to see a picture of Saraswati, she would be holding an instrument representing music and the arts. This was going to be the catalyst of the sound healing path I am currently embodying.

Saraswati's embodiment of music led me to the healing arts. My third discovery was Reiki. Reiki is an ancient Japanese healing modality. I didn't know much about Reiki, but I was curious, so I had a Reiki session. I had an experience where I saw colors and felt energy moving up and down my body. It was inexplicable but felt so true. I had to learn this modality. I couldn't fight my intuition. Upon training in Reiki, I learned that the modality was based on the chakra system and the endocrine system. This was magic to my corporate left-brain self. The chakra system is the energy system along our spine. Each chakra is associated with a color. The entire system makes up the colors of the rainbow. I loved rainbows and unicorns as a kid. I had rainbow stickers, jewelry, stationery, and apparel. Now for the endocrine system magic...my dad is an endocrinologist. What? I had to call him immediately after my training and tell him I was working with the endocrine system too but in a very different capacity. I kept thinking, "I couldn't make this up even if I tried!" I am now a Reiki master and teacher. I didn't think I had it in me to be a teacher. It's been one of Saraswati's greatest blessings to me. I love teaching Reiki.

Saraswati's energy continued in my fourth exploration—learning Vedic mantras. Saraswati is the goddess of language and speech too. Now, you need to know something about me here. Growing up I didn't resonate with the teachings of my culture. I learned to read and write Hindi, but I didn't feel comfortable speaking Hindi. It didn't feel right to me at all. I preferred English. I am American after all. Well...I was honored to meet this beautiful soul who teaches children Vedic mantras. I heard her chant one day, and a chord struck in my heart and soul that I couldn't explain. She saw my reaction and asked if I would like her to teach me. I couldn't believe I was going to say this, but I said yes. Me? Learn mantras in Sanskrit, an ancient language? I don't even enjoy speaking in Hindi. However, the sensations in my body, heart, and soul were undeniable. I have been learning Vedic mantras for four years now. I have come to learn that Sanskrit is a cosmic language. The language itself is designed for you to connect to your divine essence. No wonder why Sanskrit mantras felt extremely natural to me. They are my passion and daily practice. I am now sharing this life-altering practice through teaching these sacred mantras.

Vedic mantra opened up all possibilities. I was diving deeper into creativity. I ended up writing an original angel prayer called "One Consciousness" in the best-selling book *365 Days of Angel Prayers*. I also contributed two meditations to the book *111 Morning Meditations.*

I gave birth to Swan Goddess LLC in honor of Saraswati, who has been my guide and teacher. I also cocreated two other projects dear to my heart: Sacred Moon Fertility (Lakshmi blessings) and Blissful Warrior Empowering Program (Durga blessings).

Saraswati unleashed my creative self, which had been dormant for years. Saraswati has continued to guide me in learning healing modalities such as yin yoga, chair yoga, raindrop therapy, hypnofertility, and gong therapy. She is also igniting fiery passion in me to continue personal development through education. I am currently taking American Sign Language classes. Where this knowledge will lead me is to be determined in divine timing. All I know is to listen to my heart and soul as they do not lie. This is Saraswati.

I have started to connect the dots of my life. To see how the goddesses have been working through every person and situation in my life journey up until this point for me to step into what I am set out to be and do in this lifetime is mind-blowing. There are no words to describe this phenomenon.

The goddesses have set out a course for me greater than I could have set out for myself. I have always wanted to heal and empower women, and the three of them have found this unique way for me to express my divine essence to the world. I continue to create workshops, classes, and retreats to do just this. The energies of the goddesses work through me in service for all of you.

I encourage every one of you to trust the universe and know the universe has your back. The universe has a plan for you much greater and more fulfilling than what you have planned for yourself.

We have mostly been living within the box of societal, cultural, or religious rules. We have forgotten about intuition—our greatest gift. Tapping into the universal wisdom expressed by our intuition is life changing. It's vast, unlimited, all expansive!

In order to change the rules by which we live, we must change the foundation from where the rules were set. Doing this with love, purpose, grace, and authenticity is the way for us. This can be achieved by working with our gift of intuition and by partnering with the universe, which can help guide us every step of the way.

We are not alone!

Do not feed into fear, self-doubt, or others' opinions or thoughts. Lean on the goddesses, as they are aspects of the divine mother. Mothers protect their children, love their children unconditionally and with patience, and guide and teach their children at every step of their paths. Choose what aspect of the universe you want to partner with and go for it. They are waiting for you.

You are the warrior. You are love. You are creation.

The world needs you.

Be the change you wish to see in the world.

ABOUT SHALINI SAXENA BREAULT

Shalini Saxena Breault is the creator of Swan Goddess LLC, co-creator of Sacred Moon Fertility, and cofounder of Blissful Warrior Empowering Program. Shalini is also a coauthor in the best-selling books *365 Days of Angel Prayers* and *111 Morning Meditations*.

Additionally, Shalini is a yin yoga teacher, chair yoga teacher, Reiki master and teacher, raindrop therapy and hypnofertility practitioner, and retreat coleader.

Shalini was featured on rvntv.com in an online TV show called *Open Mind with Barb Angelo.*

She is passionate about and advocates sound healing through modalities such as crystal singing bowl meditation sessions, gong therapy sessions, drum meditation sessions, and Vedic mantra chanting classes. She also creates divinely inspired mantra *malas*, bling apparel, and workshops and classes. Please visit Shalini's Etsy store: MantraMalasbyShalini.

Shalini's desire is for women to trust—without a doubt—the intuitive gift we are blessed to have as women. We have all the answers we seek to be powerful and purposeful women, to be loving and gentle, to be inspiring and influential leaders and teachers, and to be courageous to stand for what we believe in. The change we wish for ourselves has always been inside us. It has been lying dormant for a long time. It's time for women to rise together and change the world. See and embody your journey as one of revolution to evolution.

Prior to being on the spiritual path, Shalini obtained a BBA in international business at Hofstra University in Long Island, New York, and an MBA in finance at Pace University in New York, New York.

Visit www.swangoddess.com for more information.

A TERRIBLE THING HAPPENED, BUT I AM NOT A TERRIBLE PERSON

Lauren Cavaliero

I opened my eyes early one Tuesday morning in December. The room was dark, and my husband reached for my phone to quiet the alarm. Christmas was two weeks away, but despite the pallid gray of the sky, the air was as unseasonably warm and damp as a spring day. I knew it was going to be a demanding day at work, so I planned to hurry into the office and get an early start to the day. Suddenly, my husband thrust the phone toward me. "Something's wrong. You have ten missed calls from your mom and your brother."

Nausea immediately blossomed in my stomach as I dialed both numbers, attempting to reach someone. Ten missed calls at 5:30 a.m. I put forth a futile effort to brace myself for what news might come. I didn't want to consider the possibilities as I waited, stricken, for an answer. My brother picked up the phone. My every sense was heightened to such a degree that I felt a complete sense of detachment as I heard him say that our brother John was gone. I felt my body reacting to the words before my mind could register their meaning. Shock and disbelief were immediately followed by a wave of sickness. My brother had battled addiction for so long, but recently we had had reason to hope. We had all been together for Thanksgiving two weeks earlier, and he had looked healthier than I had seen him in ten years. He had appeared healthy and strong, and I had truly believed the hard days were behind us. Why *now*? How could this be?

Over the last two years, I have found myself going back to our early years frequently, reminiscing over my own personal rendering of the good old days. They largely consisted of me and my older brothers playing flashlight tag until dark with the neighborhood kids or riding our bikes around town to the point of exhaustion. We spent summer vacations staying up late and swimming in our grandparents' pool with our cousins. We fought with the typical enthusiasm that brothers and sisters do. We were fortunate to have close relationships with our grandparents and extended family, so there were constant birthday celebrations, family dinners, and sleepovers to busy ourselves with. Toasting marshmallows at backyard barbecues, bundling up with our cousins to watch the Thanksgiving Day parade, and spending family vacations at the Jersey Shore are among my most cherished memories to revisit. I concede that I recollect my childhood through the rose-colored lenses of nostalgia. I feel a sense of wistfulness for that period of innocence that was too brief. I have spent many long nights poring over family photos of those three smiling siblings with the whole world in front of them. I try to reconcile those pictures with the present and find myself at a loss for words. Although it has been almost two years, there are still days when the reality that John is no longer with us seems like an impossibility. That he is not occupying his place in the world, getting older by the day, feels like a terrible mistake. My family is no longer whole, and that blond little boy never made it past the age of thirty-five. His future was abruptly stolen away by an epidemic that has victimized countless families like my own.

When John reached his early teen years, he took his first steps toward an addiction that he would fight for the rest of his life. Because I was four years younger, everything that ensued I experienced from the perspective of limited life experience and a lack of comprehension of the grip this addiction held over him. As the gravity of the issue became more evident, I saw in him a person I did not recognize or understand. Within our home, it felt as if we were fluctuating between periods of tentative calm followed by rapidly spiraling chaos, each episode more extreme than the last. The frustration and helplessness took their toll on our family, and the desperate attempts to smooth over the fractures to preserve a sense of normalcy were increasingly in vain. I wanted him to stop, and to my limited understanding, it should have been that easy. My exasperation changed to anger—for myself and for what had been taken from my family. The rift that developed between my brother and me seemed to grow more insurmountable, but the moments when we did connect stand out prominently, as if branded in my memory. Despite his inward struggles, my brother was outwardly confident and radiated charisma. He was a talented performer with a beautiful singing voice. I also enjoyed singing, but I struggled with the confidence that seemed to flow so effortlessly from him. When he was able to be the brother that he wanted to be, he practiced with me. When my nerves were getting the better of me, he helped me pick a song and prepare for my first high school audition. In truth, his endorsement meant more to me than almost anyone else's. He was older and popular, and in many ways he felt just out of reach. When he was at his best, he was captivating, and I remember hoping that perhaps by proximity some of that shine might rub off on me. As we grew older, the closest bond we shared was his son, who was born when I was sixteen years old. He was such a source of happiness and joy for our family when we desperately needed it, and eventually our love for him was one of the few bridges that remained between us.

The latest official statistics will tell you that ninety-one Americans die every day from an opioid overdose. The statistics are startling, but they are clinical and impersonal. They fail to tell the true-life story, to capture the gut-wrenching reality of the impact on regular families. The human toll is demonstrated by mothers and fathers, reeling, in shock, who must bury sons and daughters. It is a grieving mother who dries her tears during her commute because bills must be paid, and the world does not stop for one person's pain. It is a child who must grow up without a mother or father and then carry the burden of facing down the stigma associated with losing a parent to a drug overdose. It is to steel yourself against casual insensitivity, offhand comments about Narcan and junkies, to make it through your workday without losing composure. It is to grieve a tremendous loss and have the world react as if your loved one is some form of subhuman who deserved his or her fate. Anyone who has experienced addiction on an up-close-and-personal level knows the damage that it will inflict on anyone within its sphere of influence. There is a lack of understanding on this topic, yet misinformed opinions abound. As a result, families feel compelled to exist in a shadowy space of shame and secrecy. This makes it difficult to find support when you are living through it and to grieve when you lose someone you love so tragically. If you have not experienced this firsthand, I can only implore you to reserve judgment, practice compassion, and consider yourself incredibly fortunate not to have been touched by this. Our family struggled for many years against a force that we were ill-equipped to fight. My brother made repeated attempts to recover, seeking treatment in rehab facilities, using the gym as a healthy outlet, attending twelve-step meetings, and working with his sponsor. My father summed it up so beautifully in his eulogy; some might say the ongoing fight means he was weak, but he was the strongest person we knew. He never gave up, and he never stopped fighting.

When I learned that my brother was gone, I found myself almost paralyzed by a guilt so pervasive that it consumed my every thought. I would lie awake at night replaying my choices and cursing myself for my shortsightedness. I was the worst kind of traitor imaginable. My brother had needed me, and I hadn't saved him. The guilt was a constant presence. It loomed over me as I celebrated Christmas with my children weeks after his funeral. I forced myself to smile as I went through the motions, but deep down I felt I was undeserving of happiness. It didn't seem fair when every joyful moment was one that my brother would never experience. I woke each day with the guilt weighing heavy on my chest. At night, as I struggled to find sleep, it whispered its indictments in my ears. I felt such deep shame, and I didn't believe I had the right to grieve out loud. I hadn't been the perfect sister, so who was I to wring my hands and sob now that my brother was lost to me? I felt the judgments and heard the accusations before they could even be spoken. Real or imagined, they told a story about me that I believed to be true: I had failed him. I had not supported him. I had let him down.

When I was in middle school, I struggled to cope with the anger and helplessness that I felt in the face of the situation. What I recall most distinctly is the fear, the persistent feeling that things could take a permanent turn for the worse at any moment, that we were powerless in the face of this thing that had him in its iron grip. The resulting anxiety manifested itself in the form of migraines, hives, and panic attacks. I woke every morning with a stomach that was nervous, tumbling, full of butterflies. I felt distant from my peers, as though I were harboring a secret. The activities that I had enjoyed since I was a child seemed a trivial use of my time, and gradually I withdrew from them all. Because I was still getting good grades and I wasn't exhibiting red-flag behavioral problems, these issues were largely unnoticed. I struggled to find a healthy outlet for the stress and would have greatly benefited from learning healthy coping and stress-relief techniques, but this information wasn't readily available to me. My anxiety was triggered by routine events, such as getting on the bus to go to school or dining in a crowded restaurant, so I avoided many social engagements with family and friends. As the years progressed, I felt so victimized and defeated by the effects of the stress that his addiction had imposed on our family. I chose the path of self-preservation and made the decision to heal myself by disconnecting from my brother until he attained sobriety.

In the intervening years, I saw John at family functions and would keep updated on his whereabouts. With each life experience, I learned a bit more about myself and who I wanted to be. In time, I realized it did not sit comfortably that my brother and I were not communicating. I felt a persistent need to reach out to him, to make peace. In my younger years, anger and resentment toward the disruptive influence of his addiction had been consuming. Through no small effort, I had come through the other side of this. I had forgiven him, but I had not taken the time to tell him so. I had chosen posturing over authenticity because it felt like the safer choice. I persuaded myself it was the path with the least probability of a painful outcome and persisted with a tough-love approach, convinced that I would appear naïve if I allowed him back into my life given his history of relapse. Even at the time, I questioned my choice. Shouldn't I be able to love someone without making him or her earn my love first? What is naïve about accepting the fact that we are all inherently flawed, that we all struggle, and yet we are all deserving of compassion? I was operating in a moral gray area, excusing my own behavior based on self-protection. I was being cynical and holding my brother at a distance to guard against potential disappointment. I understand now that you cannot change the behavior of other people, no matter how desperately you may desire to. You cannot fix anyone else. What you can do, for the betterment of others and the good of your own soul, is to recognize your own limits, set reasonable boundaries, and unwaveringly extend your love and support. You don't have to understand the behavior and you don't have to condone it. Your love is not an endorsement. It is simply present, unconditional, with no strings attached. Repeatedly, a dogged thought would present itself in my conscience. Write him a letter. Tell him how you feel. Sometimes I would swat it away, distracted by more pressing concerns. Other times I would mull it over and decide, yes, I will reach out to him. But in the pace of my ever-so-busy existence, I never sat down and wrote it out. That little voice inside tried desperately to get my attention, but I ignored it. I failed to take the time, and then abruptly, the time was taken from me.

I spent the immediate days after my brother's death poring over boxes of photos for a slideshow and picture boards. It was my labor of love, my penance. It was an emotional process but also cathartic. In my mind I had allowed so much darkness to permeate his story that I had forgotten how much genuine happiness there was. The wide smile, the goofy poses with his children. It felt so important that others be left with those images as well. I continued to struggle with the fact that he had been doing so well in the last six months of his life. It seemed so cruel that our hopes had been raised, that he had seemed on the cusp of reclaiming his life only to have it end so abruptly. Our last Thanksgiving had been an added blow. Everything had felt so comfortable and effortless. It had been easy to envision our future as a family, and now our future as a family was forever altered. I was broken down, but it became the perfect point at which to rebuild a stronger foundation, a better self. In my quest for healing, I began to open myself up to new experiences and found belonging in several communities. I sought out other people who had faced similar experiences and developed very strong friendships with other women who shared a similar story. I realized that the guilt and the shame are so common, yet it is difficult to find a safe space to share those personal experiences with others. The act of speaking the words out loud and finding acceptance and solidarity can be so healing and empowering; it takes the weight of shame away to realize that you are accepted for your faults and that you are not alone. I came to the realization that I have a unique perspective to offer and that I must do all I can to facilitate creating this safe space in person, online, and through workshops for individuals and families who are attempting to navigate through similar crises on their own. I am acutely aware of the support that I needed when I was younger and want to facilitate seeing that support offered and accepted without fear of judgment. At the rate this epidemic is growing, we are all going to be touched by it in some way or another. It is time to band together and stop fighting in secret.

I also made several connections within a community focused on spirituality and mind-set, which led to multiple opportunities to completely reevaluate my thought process and my ability to move through this very difficult experience in a positive way. With the support of an entire group of similarly motivated women, I was able to push myself and stretch far out of my comfort zone. I examined my past behaviors and considered how to formulate the right mind-set and approach to make a lasting impact on the lives of others experiencing similar difficulties. Rather than living in my regrets, I found that a resounding message became clear: A terrible thing happened, but I am not a terrible person. What was I going to do *now?* The true healing began when I realized I could make this horrible circumstance mean something. I had spent too much time with regret. And as all-consuming as regret may be, it is a pointless emotion. It serves no higher purpose. The past is written, and no amount of sorrow or anger can change it. My ability to honor my brother is contained in the choices that I make today, in the lives that are influenced through my actions. I have made the choice to live with intention and allow my intuition to guide me. The most crucial aspect to this process is quieting the noise and banishing the fear-based thoughts that I allowed to echo in my subconscious. It is a daily effort and requires commitment to embracing a brand-new way of thinking. The effort is worth it. To know that my internal struggles have a larger purpose in my own story is one thing, but to have gained the understanding that my painful experiences can be a source of strength for others provided me with a renewed sense of purpose at a time when I felt truly lost. As my viewpoint shifted, I came to the realization that we were not given a false hope but rather a beautiful gift. We were granted a loving good-bye. How much more difficult would losing my brother have been if my last memory had not been of the strong, handsome man with clear blue eyes whom I said good-bye to that night? How fortunate I am to have this as my last memory of him.

To lose a sibling as an adult is to lose an intimate part of your life story. Your siblings know you in a way that others never will. They know the events that shaped you, the truth behind the carefully cultivated public persona. There is a bond forged in your shared history. You began your lives in the same nest. You are each other's first friends, first enemies, and every shade in between. Experience can be a harsh teacher, but I have learned to practice compassion, reserve judgment, and trust when my heart is telling me to act, because it is guiding me for a purpose. Shortly before he died, John texted me, and we exchanged several messages. He wanted me to know that he was sober and how well he was doing. It was a seemingly innocuous exchange, but it's something I will hold close to my heart for the rest of my life. The last words he sent were, "I'm OK." And I believe he is. I also believe I am seeing clearly for the first time in my life. I am not looking at the world from a viewpoint that is shaded by anger or resentment. Thank you, big brother, for waking me up to my purpose in life, to the person that I want to be, and to the legacy that I want to leave behind. Thank you, big brother. I'm going to be OK, too.

ABOUT LAUREN CAVALIERO

Lauren is the proud mother of two. She, her husband and her children reside happily in Southern New Jersey. They are fortunate to live in close proximity to their family and friends, and enjoy spending quality time with their loved ones whenever possible. Lauren holds a B.A. from Fairleigh Dickinson University and has over 10 years of financial management experience in the public sector. She is currently a participant in the Jack Canfield Train the Trainer Online Certification Program. The decision to be an "influencer" was significantly helped along by the valued individuals that showed her there is power and catharsis in sharing difficult experiences. Her future vision is to connect with others through speaking engagements and workshops, and to use what she has learned to have a positive influence on those faced with similar circumstances. She hopes that you will join her on this journey to erase the stigma associated with substance use disorder, and to provide support and understanding to families struggling with guilt and grief. For more information or to connect with Lauren, you can find her on Facebook, Instagram, or LinkedIn.

CHANGING THE STORY

Lana Dingwall

What the hell have you gotten yourself into, Lana? I remember asking myself just a mere thirty minutes into what would be a thirteen-hour ascent and descent of Mount Fuji, Japan's highest mountain. A solid 3,776 meters in height to be exact. I wasn't an avid hiker going on a routine climb. In fact I was a complete rookie tackling her first mountain. I grew up in the Canadian Shield, and my idea of a hike at that point was a five-kilometer walk through Algonquin Park. Better yet, I had decided that I wanted to climb the iconic mountain alone, through the night, so that I could watch the sunrise.

Just quit now, cut your losses. No one will ever know. You can just tell people some made-up story about why you didn't do it. Maybe you sprained your ankle—that is believable, right? Only you have to know the truth.

179

That voice was right! I was travelling alone through Japan, and I hadn't told anyone I was climbing at that exact moment. It would have been be easy for me to lie about how I had tried to climb, but weather or a sprained ankle had stopped me from doing it. It was dark, and I was tired; could I successfully get through the next twelve and a half hours? I stood there for a few minutes, unsure of what to do.

You're out of shape, you're cold, and you're tired. Just give up. You're never going to make it to the top. It was dumb to even think this was a feasible plan for you.

The voice in my head was really defeating and, more importantly, really convincing. This was a stupid plan. Who was I to think that I could just stroll up and climb this mountain?

I was torn. As much as I wanted to watch the sunrise from the peak, I equally didn't want to hike for another twelve and a half hours. The thought of getting a good night's sleep while tucked away in my warm hotel bed made me want to reassure myself that packing up and giving up was the right thing to do.

This wasn't the only time I'd contemplating giving up something I really wanted because the journey to get there seemed too daunting. In fact, I've done it more often than I'd like to admit.

I don't believe that it is laziness that holds us back—I believe we are held back because we let our fears, insecurities, and perceived lack of worthiness dominate our thinking. We hide behind the shield of "it'll be too much work, too much of a hassle," but everything in life worth having *is* a lot of work and often a hassle. The reality is that we're afraid that despite all our hard work, we still won't be good enough; we still won't have what it takes; we still won't get what we want. These insecurities convince us to give up before we even start, simply so that we can protect ourselves from our misguided assumptions of our inevitable failure.

It is for those reasons—my fears, insecurities, and perceived lack of worthiness—that I contemplated never coming out to my friends and family. It was those for reasons that I stalled for years on starting my own business. It is for those reasons that I almost didn't write this story.

When I was sixteen, I had my first real epiphany. I'd realized after months of thinking I was incapable of falling in love that I was simply looking for love in the wrong place. In one moment I felt overwhelming relief, only to have that relief be followed by the sickening realization that I was a lesbian.

I was a very open-minded, positive, loving teenager, but none of those qualities came into play. Instead I made up a convincing story about how everyone in my life cared about me only because they thought I was straight. If they knew the truth, they would reject me in a heartbeat. I told myself this story over and over and over. Whenever someone I knew made a gay comment or joke I instantly perceived it only as reinforcement of my story, proof that people would reject me if they knew who I really was. I told myself I could go on forever pretending to be straight because that was easier than having everyone I cared about abandon me.

About four years later, I came to a fork in the road. I realized I had a choice of which life to live. In one, I would remain so afraid of how others viewed me that I'd give up any chance at real happiness in order to "belong." In the other, I could accept myself as I was, face my fears, and have a real shot at being happy. Up until that point, I had thought the only option I had was to hide who I was. This is where I was able to change the story I was telling myself. When I believed I had only one option, I lived my life that way. The reality is, I always had the option of coming out; I was just too afraid to accept that story as true. I became so enthralled with my story's having only one ending that that story ruled me. I desperately wanted to wake up straight just so that I didn't have to face the daunting task of accepting myself, being brave, and coming out. I decided, instead of focusing on how difficult coming out and its repercussions would be, to focus on how much easier my life would be if I didn't have to hide who I was, how much happier I would be. After a few months of internalizing this new story, I was able to muster up enough courage to come out to everyone I knew. It took me four years to get there, but in less than two weeks I came out to every single person in my life.

Throughout all those years I tried to protect myself from getting hurt by hiding; I see now that I was actually holding myself back.

Sadly, with most lessons, you have to learn the lesson a few times before it really sticks. As with coming out, there was another moment in my life where I made my decisions based on fear and all the negative "what ifs" instead of focusing on all the positives that could come out of something challenging.

For years I had been talking about wanting to run my own coaching business. I had a million ideas but was taking zero action. I often told myself this story about how I didn't have enough experience; I didn't have enough time; I didn't have enough resources—the list was endless. For every opportunity I had to start my business, I would come up with two reasons not to. I was simply waiting for the "right" time to take that leap. The problem was that the timing was never going to be right. The fear of trying and failing made me make up every possible excuse so that I could put my coaching business off till some future date.

It got to the point where I was starting to understand that I had to either accept my fear and potential failure or be OK with never trying. I accepted fear and failure.

Once I stopped trying to protect myself and instead began pushing myself, my life became more fulfilling. I not only get paid to do what I'd honestly do even if I already had all the money in the world, since I love it so much, but I also get to help other women do the same. It is a gift to work with other female entrepreneurs, to help unlock their potential and help them build the businesses they've always dreamed of. Every day I acknowledge that this gift was given to me because I've accepted the constant challenge of pushing myself beyond my comforts in order to see what other wonderful things await me on the other side of my struggles.

I'm glad that I chose that same tactic while climbing Mount Fuji. Yes, it would have been easier for me to give in to my negative self-talk, pack up, and go sleep it off. My feet were aching, my legs were burning, I had a blister forming on my heel, and I was already using my walking stick for support. Instead, I consciously decided I needed to change the story playing out in my mind.

I decided to cut off my voice of "you can't do this" and instead use one of motivation and tough love. I reminded myself that people in their eighties climb this mountain every year and told myself I was overthinking the situation. I was overwhelmed, but I wasn't climbing Mount Everest here.

Lana, quitting isn't an option. Stop feeling sorry for yourself. Get up and start walking. You will get to the top of this mountain the same way every other person does. One step at a time. You've got this—go, girl, go.

With that, my new strategy was to stop overthinking. Instead of focusing on how many more hours I had to go, I broke my climb into little fifteen minute spurts. Anytime I started to feel fatigued and contemplate quitting again, I'd say aloud, "You will get to the top of this mountain the same way every other person does. One step at a time. You've got this—go, girl, go."

It was such a simple strategy and such a simple phrase, and it worked. I got to the top of the mountain by taking one step at a time.

Once on the summit, I witnessed the most breathtaking sunrise I've ever seen. I remember watching the first rays of light break free from the horizon and thinking, "Holy shit, you did it." I also thought, "I can't believe you seriously contemplated not doing this."

We like to think our biggest barriers are external. That things out there in the world are holding us back. Most of the time though, we are our biggest barriers. We all have this voice in our heads that is defeating, demeaning, and belittling. It's always the first voice to tell us the story about why we can't or shouldn't do something, the first voice to tell us we're going to fail and therefore shouldn't even try. It's the voice that often gets the most airtime in our minds. This voice's intention is to protect us, even if she is mean. She thinks the best way to protect us is to convince us to play it safe, to stay within our comfort zones and stay within the confines of our boxes.

What I learned the night of my climb, the moment I came out as a lesbian, and the day I started my business was that I had a more powerful voice deep inside me with a more powerful story to tell. I learned how to silence the voice that was trying to hold me back and replace it with one that would propel me forward. This voice doesn't want me to settle. She wants me to push every comfort zone I have; she wants me to take risks and do the hard stuff. She wants me to live my life on my terms, not the terms of others. She tells me stories in which I am brave enough, smart enough, capable enough, and deserving of the life I've dreamed of.

The best part about her is that you have that same powerful voice inside you as well. You have a voice that wants you to build the life you've always wanted; she just might not be as loud as the one trying to convince you to play it safe and settle. That negative voice inside your head is telling you that you'll never make it to the top, that people won't accept you, that you don't have what it takes. Remember: that voice is lying. Listen to and amplify the voice that believes in you. I promise you she is there just waiting to be heard.

A common story we are told is that those at the end of their lives never regret the things they did do, only the things they didn't. Don't let yourself be one of those people. Stop convincing yourself that you're happy with what you have in life if you know deep down that that isn't true. Don't settle for a life you don't fully enjoy—be brave, work hard, and go after the one you do. You still have time to change your story. I believe in you.

ABOUT LANA DINGWALL

Lana Dingwall is a business coach who is hell-bent on helping other women build and grow their businesses. She specializes in helping female entrepreneurs fill their client rosters so that they can ditch the stress and overwhelmingness associated with growing a business and instead focus more of their time and energy on using their gifts to serve others.

Lana believes that by coaching other women on how to make more money in their businesses, she can create a better world. In the development and nonprofit sector, in which she worked for six years before starting her business, there is a new wave of thinking emerging. Studies show that when support and funding are used to invest in having women start and grow businesses, the communities in which those women live are four times more likely to escape poverty than if that same funding and support had been invested in men. It isn't that men aren't doing good things with their business profits—it's that women are likely to do even more. Those findings have pushed her to focus on working with other women, knowing that in turn the communities in which these women live will benefit as well.

Lana also hosts a podcast called *Changing the Story: Kick-Ass Women in Business*. There she shares the stories and strategies of women who have created kick-ass businesses, so that other women can learn, be inspired, and do the same.

To learn more about Lana or simply to snag some free strategies on how to consistently get clients and grow your business, check her out at www.lanadingwall.com.

iTunes: *Changing the Story: Kick-Ass Women in Business—* with Lana Dingwall

Facebook: lanadingwallcoaching

Instagram: @lanadingwall

AN ARTIST "WAVE" OF LIFE

Kristy Dubinsky

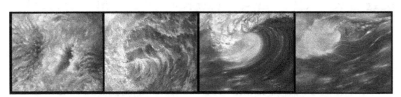

Amongst the Waves, oil on canvas, 4 x 20 ft.

I am underwater, floating amongst the waves. All my worries have floated away and are crashing upon the shore. I am alive, beautiful and independent. Thank you for this feeling.
—Anonymous

Amongst the Waves: there I stood next to my work in the largest international exhibition in the world, watching onlookers captivated by my creation. This was what I, as an artist, yearned for: to reach that emotion in someone, to have someone find a story in a picture. The art is the story, and for each person, it is experienced differently.

THE GIFT OF SEEING

I can remember viewing things differently as a child; details stood out to me in material things and in seemingly everything I looked at. All of it had beauty. I found myself capturing this beauty in photos I would take of trees and sunsets right outside my home. I collected everything from intricate glassware and trinkets to rocks, minerals, dried petals, and leaves because of how they looked and felt. I found myself enamored with making things look the same way they appeared in my mind. I loved to be creative, and I set myself apart from others with cool clothing and the unique antique jewelry and purses my mother would bring home from yard sales. My admiration for detail often set me back. My mother and father pushed me to be ready for school on time, but I had to make sure everything, from my hair to my accessories, was perfect.

I can still picture the day in elementary school when we were asked to write down our dreams. I couldn't wait to write down "to be an artist." In first grade, my teacher talked to my parents about my neatness of drawing and coloring. At some early age, I entered a drawing contest and won. That's where a lot of it started. The way I perceived things allowed me to recreate reality in my own way on paper. It was a gift that I hadn't yet taken ownership of. I recall liking to watch things unfold on paper just as I interpreted them in my mind. I didn't understand it as a child, but visuals were an important part of my communication. I learned easily by seeing something demonstrated or picking it apart in my mind as if I were creating it. My creative mind led me to draw my own interpretation of how things were made. I would create visuals to stories in my mind as the stories were told to me. Vivid dreams would come to me at night and would sometimes seem so real that I often found myself writing, drawing, and just thinking about them as though they had really happened. Seeing things differently allowed me to become the things I envisioned, and I was able to put that on paper. Somehow I could put myself into what I felt and saw, and becoming these things, in an indescribable way, helped me figure them out.

Another thing I loved was writing, making cursive letters look elegant and experimenting with a calligraphy set that I received from my aunt when I was in elementary school. In my elementary creative-writing class, my teacher always circled my cursive letters in red pen because I added too many loops, but I loved the flow in the letters and adding my own style to them. I liked watching my pen move fancifully. My teacher eventually gave up once he learned I would do it anyway. To this day I happily accept compliments daily about how beautifully I sign my name and write, especially on my finished artwork.

Because my parents noticed my abilities at a young age, they found a local art league for me to take classes at. I can remember picking challenging pictures to draw or paint, and I found it so exciting to realize I could make my own art reflect what I captured on camera or saw in front of me. I could create an interpretation of a specific vision in my mind. I became that vision and would feel it flow through me. Throughout school, my ability to easily understand techniques and my enthusiasm to experiment with new materials made my teachers challenge me. I enjoyed the challenge of discovering something new and taking things a step farther. Their comments about my "natural ability" to see and create stick with me to this day. I never really understood how I knew how to create what I did—I just did, and it felt natural; it was truly a gift.

The gift of being an artist was sometimes confusing to accept when I was younger. It was the feelings that came along with it, how details stood out and how ideas came to me. It felt overwhelming. I felt that I was different and that people would judge me and think I was weird if they knew what was going on in my head. I haven't always felt comfortable telling people that I am an artist. I have always wondered why I have been hesitant to tell people at times. I knew what I was doing was really cool, so why didn't I own it? It wasn't until I became a teacher and began expressing to students what I could do that I actually took on the title of artist. I began realizing, through the people proud of me and the number of people drawn to my work, that it was a gift that I could share. I finally felt as if I should be proud of my accomplishments. I can remember the day I made myself proudly say, "I am an artist." It was a moment of clarity and a feeling of acceptance that it was OK to see things differently and create in whatever way suited me. People loved whatever I put out there, and I appreciated what it was doing for others.

INSPIRING MINDS

They say God puts people in your life for a reason. I had put my papers and pencils away for a long thirty years, forgetting about my creativity and instead pursuing the business life. It wasn't until I met Kristy, who inspired me with her work and placed brushes and pencils back in front of me, that I kickstarted an entirely new path to my life within the arts. I have a new passion for creating that makes every one of my days feel purposeful and fulfilled. I am blessed with getting commissions on a regular basis because of Kristy. (Quote taken from a friend of mine.)

I hadn't realized how much of an impact my work as a creator could have on someone. I had no idea that I could inspire someone else's career, but that thought has since changed as a result of my own career.

When I decided to pursue art in college in 1997, my parents encouraged me to earn a degree in education as well. While in college, I became passionate about every area of art. I spent hours in the studio photo lab, hours in the painting and drawing studios and ceramic studios. I became interested in printmaking, jewelry, and sculpture. I loved it all and had a very difficult time deciding which was my favorite. I realized my passion encompassed every aspect of creating. It didn't matter what materials I used; I had visions and joy for it all. In 2002, I received my BFA in art with a concentration in ceramics; I received a teacher certification in art education in 2004.

Immediately after graduating college, I was hired full time as a high school art teacher. When I was in high school, my art teacher had inspired me and played a significant role in my development as an artist. His work amazed me, and to this day, I keep in touch with him. We discuss our art businesses, share our work with each other, and provide valuable feedback. I often think about how Mr. Weaver encouraged me to pursue art shows, and when I received awards, it helped me remember that I really was good at what I was doing.

The goal of encouraging young minds to pursue their dreams, just as I have, has impacted how I teach and share my passion. This has been one of the most rewarding ways for me to share my talents and knowledge with others. I enjoy sharing the art that I create and what I do outside the classroom to open students' minds to new art forms. I encourage students to pursue experimenting and creating from what they feel inside. Teaching them to see the world in a different way and feel something about what they are looking at can help them bring something new out in themselves. And being able to help them do that is a blessing.

THE NEW ART I "SAW" INSIDE ME

Despite this recognition of my abilities early on, my mother never let me use scissors. Ironically, my current artistic medium is chainsaw carving. Yes, I said CHAINSAW, and yes, it is a regular chainsaw. However, the difference is that the bars have more narrow tips. Other than that, gas, oil, and I run it.

I repeatedly am asked, "How did you get into chainsaw carving?" I also get comments like, "Really? I don't picture you with a chainsaw!"

Then again, I've heard a lot of these comments throughout my life. People would question that I was an artist. I think artists often fall into a stereotype, especially a woman creating art with a chainsaw.

To answer how I got into chainsaw carving, I will say that I am a firm believer that we are always learning. Even though I have accomplishments in certain areas, I still explore techniques and find new ways of working. That's what's fun about what I do. There's never an answer for how something needs to be approached. It's all within the self and what is felt. The end product may not always be to your liking, but it's the process of creating that leads to the next level of achievement. It all lies within the desire for further growth.

I also believe that people cross our paths for a reason and that it's important to embrace whatever gift or advice any of those people has to offer. In 2014, I met someone who connected me to another artist over social media. I got in touch with that artist, and that same night the person was having an artist-send-off event. I grabbed my things after work and drove to that place, which was unknown to me at the time. When I pulled into that large studio way out in the country, I remember thinking how great it was. I had chills running through my body, knowing something interesting and exciting awaited me. When I went inside, I was greeted by a group of extremely diverse and talented artists. As the night proceeded, I noticed a guy walking in with sawdust all over him. I could tell he was an artist. I laughed and asked him why he was covered in sawdust. When he told me he was a chainsaw artist, I didn't believe him, so he said to come outside. I quickly found out that Ken was a world-champion chainsaw carver. He showed me unbelievable sculptures that he had carved of the Hulk, Native Americans, and animals. I said I would love to try it. We had shared interests and backgrounds with painting, and he said that he thought I could do it with the skills and visions I already had. The rest was history. I took him up on his offer and decided to take a leap of faith and try something new. Ironically, throughout college and high school, I had wanted to pursue woodworking. My grandfather was a woodworker and always told me stories about carving little boots out of wood and making a violin on his own. His stories got me interested, and now, years later, the time had presented itself, but with a more dangerous tool.

I knew as soon as I picked up the saw that I had found yet another passion. It was a feeling that I can't explain. When I carve, time passes, and I get lost in the entire artistic process. When I paint, I am typically indoors, and sometimes the desire for perfection overwhelms me, but the chainsaw allows me to work outside and combine my love for nature with my love for art. Now I could start combining my passion for painting with my passion for carving.

A JOURNEY OF EMOTION THROUGH EXHIBITION

Josephine's Journey, oil on canvas, 4 x 9 ft.

I pursued showing my art wherever I could. I enjoyed the idea of competition, putting my work up against that of others and showing others what my abilities were. Ultimately it was about proving to myself that my work was worthy. I soon found myself actually winning awards and receiving recognitions locally, nationally, and internationally. Those experiences gave me and continue to give me the opportunity to meet many other artists and connect with people with similar interests.

In 2015, I was selected into the largest international art show in the world, located in Grand Rapids, Michigan, called Art Prize. During the first year of Art Prize, I entered the oil painting entitled *Josephine's Journey*. My goal was for the viewer to be able to understand a woman's inner self. Beauty overshadows her unspoken thoughts and feelings. Standing near my work at this show, I quickly realized that the thousands of people who would walk by wanted to know more about the journey. Sometimes I would stand back and listen to people discuss the work. At times, they would turn, see me, and say, "Are you the artist? Is that a self-portrait?" They wanted more, wanted to know the journey. I heard the different emotions and stories that people felt and discussed.

When I thought about it, I was able to connect my feelings to my creations. I often find that when I am creating a work, before I begin, I spend a lot of time feeling: feeling the colors, feeling the composition, the textures, the atmosphere, the mood, the lines and shapes. I put myself into the viewer's place and try to feel the emotions, mood, and storyline that the viewer may feel. I begin to visualize each storyline in my mind. This visualization has helped my work have life and breathe on its own, as I have been told. If my work is alive, I feel it can reach inside someone and speak to someone's soul. To me, that is so incredible. That makes it worth it.

The following year, I exhibited my work entitled *Amongst the Waves*. With my new passion for chainsaw carving, I decided to carve a bench to go with this work. What better way to look at some waves than to view them while sitting on a bench with a wave painted on it?

My intention was for viewers to become part of the piece. They could sit among the waves. The waves brought an astonishing amount of emotional response from viewers. A lot of people wanted a deep story about the waves. "Why the waves?" I would hear spoken from spectators. I did have a story about the waves, but I felt as if my story wasn't enough. I started to think about it and was able to remember my frequent dreams about crashing waves. In the dreams, the waves are beautiful, but then they crash over me, and I'm suddenly drowning, fighting for my life. I can often associate this dream with times I am particularly anxious or worried. I began relating that story of why I painted the waves. I realized that it was my intuitive emotions that had led me to paint water and waves.

Ironically, one woman looked at my paintings, and when she got to the last wave intensely crashing into itself, becoming a hole, she stated, "Oh my gosh, I can't even look at the last painting." She turned her head and said, "It reminds me of the time I almost drowned!" I couldn't believe my wave painting could bring back such a terrible memory. There were beautiful stories and frightening ones.

This past year, when I exhibited *Work Is Done*, the emotional response I received from people was far different from the response to other works I displayed. This work captured attention because of the content.

Veterans and families and friends of those in the service reacted to this work. This entire work was inspired by my grandfather, Edward Huszar, a World War II veteran. His stories of war and the vision he explained to me inspired the painting. I created a painting that portrayed his description, along with a chainsaw-carved bench. The bench includes an eagle and feathers and has a painted flag draped over it; here one may sit and reflect.

One of the most emotional responses I got to this piece was on Veterans Day. I was asked to show this work and talk about it to a group of veterans. As I was speaking about it, a World War II veteran, in a wheelchair, tears flowing from his eyes, attempted to support himself as he raised himself up from his chair the best he could, placed his hand to his forehead, and

saluted my work as I spoke. I tried holding back my own tears as I saw how much this meant to a man who had served this country. What an honor from a man of honor from the greatest generation.

DELVE INSIDE

One important thing I have realized through undertaking shows, especially the international shows, is that people want to connect. They want to connect personally and emotionally with the artist. During the months at Art Prize, standing in front of my work, I met so many people who wanted to know the story. I would stand back and hear them discuss *Josephine's Journey*. However, *Amongst the Waves* was one that really stood out in my mind. I would have crowds of people coming through to see the work and picking up a journal that I had placed on the bench.

The book I placed in front of my work for people to sign or comment in became a personal diary for people. My journal became their journal. People would write anything from short comments to two pages filled with stories of what my work made them feel and remember. People felt compelled to tell me their stories.

I have had many experiences with making work for people and pulling emotions out of people, especially with personal works for clients. I have seen tears of joy and tears of sadness. It's amazing what art can do to a person. The best part of being an artist and creator is presenting my work in front of someone and witnessing the emotional response, both verbal and physical. It's amazing what art can do for the soul. As an artist, I put my heart and soul into everything that I create.

When you purchase a piece of art, you are buying a piece of that artist's soul and taking it with you. Sometimes you meet the artist and you have a deeper connection to the piece. It becomes a great way to start conversation. Purchasing some wall art from a store doesn't have the same meaning as a piece that has had the artist's hand on it.

You don't have to be an artist, but you can reach inside, because truthfully, we are all creative—you just have to find your creativity. Make an intuitive stray mark on a paper, add some color, and throw the paper behind a little frame. Set it aside, and then go back and look at it. Think about it and how it makes you feel. Or think about what you were feeling at the time you made it. Maybe even hang it up. Talk about it when people come over. It's from your soul. It doesn't matter if people like or dislike it. If you feel a connection to it, that's all that matters. Believe in yourself. Perhaps you don't feel comfortable with picking up a tool and making marks, but at least, when you pass a work of art, really stop and look at it. Think about it and how it makes you feel. Does it remind you of anything? What do you like or dislike about it? What do you think the artist was thinking? Try to make a connection when you see a work made by someone else and appreciate it. Think about bringing a piece of art from an artist into your life if you find something you like. There is a beauty that lies within those who desire to hold a piece of art for themselves.

"I didn't expect much to happen when I sat, but as I sat, I felt waves of healing pulse through my body, sending a release of emotion."

A TIDE OF EMOTION

Just as the tides of emotions run through me and emanate through my work, I realize that it can bring out a wave of emotion in those that see my art. "I've had emotions bottled up and a certain kind of pain I've been carrying and a loss I've been hiding. I feel so connected and can feel the love that you put into this work and I am able to let my own emotions out in these waves. Pain, fear, and love get lost in the tide. I can feel every stroke of your brush, painting a new path for me made from water. I'm walking away from this with tears in my eyes knowing I was able to let go of these feelings I've kept back for so long."
-Anonymous quote taken from "Amongst The Waves" comment book at Art Prize in Grand Rapids, MI

An Artist "Wave" of Life

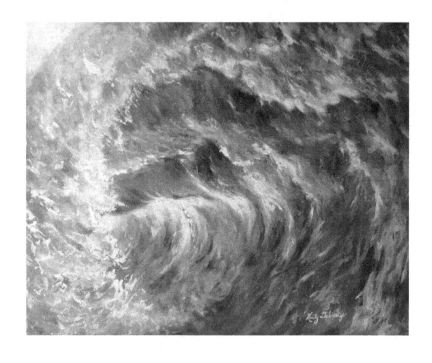

ABOUT KRISTY DUBINSKY

Kristy Dubinsky is a professional artist and art teacher at Elizabeth Forward High School in western Pennsylvania. She earned a bachelor of fine arts with a concentration in ceramics from Edinboro University of Pennsylvania in 2002 and completed her teaching degree at Carlow University in 2004. Kristy's artistic passions started at a young age, and through the years she has built a diverse portfolio, including realistic paintings, abstract works, mixed medias, drawings, ceramics, photography, murals, and chainsaw carvings.

Kristy's talents have led her to receive recognitions and awards at the local, national, and international level. She has done various commissions for clients and businesses in various mediums and subject matters ranging from public murals and chainsaw carvings to personal paintings and drawings for private collections. She has been fortunate to have had the opportunity to build a business with her work, utilizing her summers and time after work.

Kristy believes that by sharing her creative talent, inspirations, and love for the arts she can encourage others to think, feel, and portray their surroundings in a new manner as well as gain an appreciation for art. She thinks that everyone has a creative side and an innate desire for self-expression; some may need a little assistance to bring it out, but all anyone really needs to do is just reach inside. Kristy says that it's not always about an end product; it's the process and how you get there. Art is a journey of exploration, an opportunity to connect on a deeper level, to open up and allow your inner being to come alive.

To connect with Kristy, view her work, leave questions and comments, and find lessons, strategies, and articles, or for inquiries about purchasing her art or commissions, please visit www. KristyDubinskyArt.com.

Facebook business page: KristyDubinskyArt

Instagram: @KristyDubinskyArt

Twitter: @KristyDubinskyArt

Subscribe to her You Tube channel: Kristy Dubinsky Art

E-mail: DubinskyArt@gmail.com

TO THE TOP OF KILI AND BACK

Laurie Dudo

"It is in our darkest moments that we are given the opportunity
to shine our brightest."
~Laurie Dudo

THE JOURNEY

"P ole Pole" is a Swahili phrase that continues to guide
me on my journey, meaning 'slowly, slowly.' This is
said by many Kilimanjaro guides reminding us to
go slowly, and gently, to assist us in acclimatizing to the mountain's altitude.

We began our summit ascent of the magnificent Mount
Kilimanjaro (Kili), the world's highest freestanding mountain.
It was Wednesday at midnight, on the sixth day of our eight-day
trek in October 2015. My five girlfriends and I, plus our larger

team (fifteen in total), had spent months training our minds and bodies for this eventual ascent. One that would require patience, resilience and acclimation to the new environment. We began preparing for this climb at the start of the year. However, this journey for me had started back in early 2003.

In December of 2002, I had travelled to Taiwan to spend the holidays with my sister Lisa who was teaching English overseas. We had decided to spend part of our trip in beautiful Bali. One morning, as I was getting ready to lounge out by our pool, I felt something unusual in my breast as I was putting on my bikini. I could feel something palpable, the size of a bean. I vowed to myself that I would get it checked out as soon as I got back home from my three-week trip. I didn't mention anything to my sister as there was no point in worrying her. However, I knew deep down that I couldn't ignore this.

During the entire trip, I automatically checked to see if I could feel the lump, which to my dismay, was always evident. In fact, I felt that it was getting bigger. Was this possible? Or was it my imagination?

I was extremely tired but chalked it up to jet lag and the several flights to get to multiple destinations. Except this was a deep exhaustion, different than anything I had felt before. It was like I could hibernate and sleep to no end. I craved sleep, it was like a drug that I could not get enough of. I couldn't enjoy activities because I was constantly tired. Even if I slept all day and night, it seemed that it was not enough. Exploring the sites became a chore. This was not like me – I was in my twenties and I thrived on travelling and exploring. Something was wrong.

One evening after I arrived home, as I was preparing for work the next day, there was a TV special on in the background about a local news anchor who had recently been diagnosed with breast cancer. The program provided a "behind the scenes" view of her breast cancer journey, including her treatments. I heard this voice inside me say, "Pay attention, you need to hear this," but I tried to ignore it. I knew deep down that she was speaking to me and that I needed to listen, but my initial reaction was to resist it. To listen to it meant that I was admitting that a breast cancer diagnosis could be a real possibility for me. Little did I know that one day, years later, I would meet this news anchor and we would share the stage as keynote speakers for the Canadian Breast Cancer Foundation (CBCF) Run for the Cure Event.

Within a week of arriving home, I saw my family doctor to discuss the lump in my breast. She was skeptical that it was cancer. She had comprehensive knowledge of my family medical history and knew that we had no history of breast cancer. The doctor sent me for an ultrasound to be cautious, but it would be six weeks before I could get an appointment at the local hospital. I felt the lump getting bigger – this was not my imagination. She also referred me to a general surgeon for a consult. I could not bear to wait six weeks for the ultrasound appointment, and after countless calls, I was able to find a much earlier appointment at another clinic.

I was also able to get in to see the general surgeon quickly, later being told it was only due to a cancellation. I explained to the surgeon how I found the lump and that it was growing, in addition to the extreme fatigue that I was experiencing. I could see that he was skeptical about my comment regarding the growth.

I asked him if he thought it was cancer, he indicated 'no' since the lump was palpable. I assume that he thought it was a cyst. He proceeded to perform a fine needle aspiration and anticipated that there would be fluid (as is consistent with a cyst) yet, there was none. At the same time, he took a tissue sample with the needle.

At our follow-up meeting a couple of weeks later, he commented on how bruised my breast was, which was nothing compared to how it looked in the days following the aspiration. The once palpable tumor had now become hard in my breast. He indicated that the tissue sample came back inconclusive and he recommended that we have surgery to remove the lump. I was completely on board – I wanted this hard lump out of me.

However, I still did not have an official breast cancer diagnosis. He mapped out the surgery – he would perform a lumpectomy and then send the tissue to pathology immediately while we were in the OR. Pathology would be able to confirm if it was cancerous, and if this was the case, he would check the lymph nodes located under my arm, as this is normally the first place that the cancer would travel to.

I was in in limbo, but felt better now that we had a plan. I had two weeks to get myself prepared for the surgery, tell work so that I could wrap things up on my client project, and more importantly, tell my family and friends about a possible breast cancer diagnosis. This was challenging. Deep down I knew what I was dealing with. I could tell by how my body felt that something was horribly wrong. It was so difficult to concentrate at work. I tried to be optimistic and positive, but it was devastating that a potential cancer diagnosis was looming over me.

On the day of the surgery, we needed to be at the hospital for 5:30 am. I was nervous and scared. I had been in this hospital for surgery once before – when I was eight years old and had my tonsils removed. Looking back, life was so uncomplicated back then…

As the medical team was setting me up in the OR, I asked to speak to the surgeon. My fear was that he was going to open me up and find cancer everywhere in my breast and then perform a mastectomy, which was an option that we hadn't discussed. I asked him if that was the case, to just perform the lumpectomy and we would come back to do a mastectomy. I couldn't bear the thought of waking up and not having a breast - I was not prepared for this, I was still in my twenties. I hadn't even been diagnosed yet. He assured me that he would only perform the lumpectomy and remove the lymph nodes if necessary.

After a few hours of surgery, with my boyfriend Chris and our families pacing the halls of the hospital, I awoke in recovery. I knew immediately that he found cancer since I could feel the incision under my arm. The surgeon had removed the lymph nodes.

Later that day when they were able to find me a hospital bed, an oncologist came into to the room and in a matter of fact tone began to describe the situation. I was now diagnosed with breast cancer which was very aggressive and had spread to the lymph nodes. We would have to wait for the pathology report that would indicate stage and grade.

The oncologist proceeded to paint a picture of what my life would look like over the next year. I would undergo aggressive chemotherapy, I'd lose all my hair, and would need radiation.

I was told that I should not plan on working while undergoing treatment. He went on and on in detail about the side effects of the chemotherapy and treatments I would need. "Wait, stop!" I wanted to scream. It felt so unreal, like I was watching a soap opera, except that I was the main character starring in this unfairly scripted drama.

Six weeks after surgery, I began a very aggressive chemo protocol. Since I was now going to be spending countless months at home, Chris and I discussed getting a dog to keep me company. Shortly after I started chemo, we adopted a beautiful apricot toy poodle that we aptly named Fletcher. He was an amazing companion for me during my recovery, and continues to provide endless comfort, cuddles, love, acceptance, and protection.

Chemo was grueling and led me to be hospitalized for five days as it had depleted my blood counts. We then decided to switch to a different chemo cocktail that hopefully I could better tolerate. I finished radiation just before Christmas and needed over a year to recover from the treatments. I was also placed on an adjuvant hormonal therapy protocol for five long years.

I recall that since the day I was diagnosed, every morning I would wake up and there would be thirty seconds or so when things felt right in my world. And then the diagnosis would come flooding back into my mind and my world would come crashing down. Every day was like this, until it wasn't. It was probably more than two years before breast cancer was not the very first thing that I thought about. I don't think that there has ever been a day since my diagnosis that I did not think of breast cancer, but it has changed from being all consuming to more of a thread in the fabric of my life.

There has always been a fear of this dreaded disease returning. And it hit closer to home as friends whom I had met on this journey had recurrences, which became metastatic. This disease does not discriminate and has taken so many loved ones well before their time. Over the years, I was able to get my life back together. I had more energy and endurance and I started to enjoy life again. I began to travel, become more independent and trust my body again. After I came off the five years of hormonal therapy, I went back to school full time to obtain an MBA.

In the fall of 2014, a friend of mine whom I had met at the hospital going through treatment asked if I was interested in climbing Kili to raise money for the Canadian Breast Cancer Foundation (CBCF) and to climb in honour of our friend whom had recently passed away after a metastatic recurrence. I was excited, but scared – could I really do this? Then I thought, how could I not do this? I signed up for the challenge in January and started training and fundraising for the climb that was to take place in October 2015.

THE SUMMIT

It was Wednesday morning, the day of our summit and after breakfast, we completed a short hike and settled in our new camp around lunchtime. Today differed from the previous days when we had hiked all day, only stopping for a short lunch so that we could reach our new camp by late afternoon, in time for dinner. We changed camps daily and slept in tents alongside the mountain each night, preparing and acclimatizing for the upcoming summit.

The camp that we were now positioned at looked like a war zone – a sharp contrast to the camps we journeyed to previously. This camp was littered with sharp rocks everywhere, with no plant life in sight, due to the higher altitude. We ate lunch, had a group summit prep meeting and began to prepare our backpacks for the climb. We were reminded to bring only the essentials (water, snacks, layers and a headlamp) and to pack as light as possible because each pound we carried would feel much heavier as we climbed higher. We had an early dinner at 6 pm and were instructed to sleep until 11 pm. We would eat again and then leave at midnight sharp. As we were preparing to leave camp, the nervous energy of the team was tangible. Everyone was laser focused and aware of the magnitude of the task at hand.

It was cold, and dark, exceptionally dark. The only lights were our headlamps. The endless sky and the outline of the magnificent mountain were our landscape. I recall standing on the side of the mountain and looking up at the long line of climbers, with their headlamps trailing up the mountain. At one point I could not tell where the headlamps ended, and where the beautiful stars of the African sky started. It is these moments that make all the hard work, preparation, blood, sweat and tears worth the journey. These are the moments that cannot be captured on film but are etched into my memory and are there for me to retrieve any time I need inspiration.

In this long line of people, I surprisingly felt alone. It was tough and difficult, and it was up to me to get up to the top of the mountain. No one really spoke. Our energy was consumed by the very basic activity of navigating the terrain directly in front of us. One misstep could potentially lead to an injury and an abrupt end of our journey to the summit.

With each step my legs became heavier and heavier. We were moving very slowly. The guides and the porters were amazing. They encouraged each of us and sang to us as we climbed. Each time I heard the Kilimanjaro song, I welled up inside. But I needed to focus, 'pole pole,' one step at a time. I was used to this attitude (one step at a time, one day at a time), as this was my guiding mantra through my chemo treatments, radiation, recovery and years of adjuvant therapy.

As we climbed, the journey upwards became more difficult, and I was aware that I needed to choose my thoughts carefully. I started to ask my angels for help, 'Please help me get up this mountain," I pleaded. Shortly after I made this request, I felt a tap on my shoulder. One of the guides was offering to take my backpack. My initial reaction was to decline his offer, but I stopped myself. What was I doing? I had just been asking for help and here it was. I removed my backpack and thanked him for his help. How many times had I done this previously in my life? Refused help exactly when I needed it most.

Now, he didn't speak much English and I didn't speak much Swahili, however, we were able to communicate as needed as we climbed. He stayed beside me on the path all the way up. What would have happened had I been stubborn and not accepted his help?

On the way, our Leader had indicated that one of our team members had to turn back down, as she was very ill. She would not be able to summit. I felt sick to my stomach. I know how hard she had worked to get to this point. All the time, effort, energy, excitement and planning she had put into this – it wasn't fair. I was heartbroken and wanted to cry. I had to stop myself – I already had limited energy and if I expended my energy crying, I would not be able to move forward up this mountain.

My mind started to bring me new thoughts, "why don't you head down and join her? She would really appreciate some company right now. This is hard, and unless someone has done this climb, they don't realize how difficult this really is – no one is going to fault you for not climbing." These thoughts raced through my mind and I needed to take control of them or else I would not get up the mountain. It was this very type of thinking that I had to cast away during my diagnosis and treatments.

We hiked and climbed for hours. We would stop every twenty minutes to eat some of the snacks we packed. I didn't want to eat, but I forced a few bites down knowing I needed the energy to propel me. I also forced myself to drink. Being hydrated during the climb is key to summiting, and my hydration pack was frozen. Thankfully my plastic water bottle hadn't frozen in its insulated cozy. A welcomed blessing during such a challenging time.

As I climbed in the darkness I thought this was the most difficult thing I had ever done. I then corrected myself. Battling cancer was the most difficult thing that I had done. Was this climb second? No, it wasn't. Watching my aunt and my father-in-law battle cancer, and having friends fight breast and other cancers were much more difficult than this. It made me feel so helpless to watch them endure such pain and suffering because of this disease. This climb was my third most challenging experience – or so I thought.

As the sun started to rise over the horizon, it was one of the most beautiful sights I've ever seen. The emerging yellow, orange and pinkish hues of the sunrise began to contrast with the dark landscape before us. Although we were not yet at the peak, I felt on top of the world. However, fatigue was setting in and the air was getting thinner and thinner with each step.

I love taking pictures, however, the amount of energy that was required for me to place my hand in my pocket and pull out my camera phone was too much for me to expend. This is how precious energy was, the scarcity of it paralleled only by how I felt during my treatments and recovery.

Sometime after daybreak when we had been climbing for close to eight hours, we reached Stella Point, which is a milestone at 5,752 m /18,871 ft. I was exhausted at this point. Part of me thought, "maybe I'll just stop here." Would anyone really know? Perhaps not, but I would. I decided to continue the additional 143 m / 469 ft. to Uhuru Peak, the highest point on the mountain. The incremental distance isn't very far but the thinness of the air and the fatigue tested my mental and physical strength and endurance far more than the actual distance we covered.

After what seemed like a lifetime, I summited Mount Kilimanjaro with my team and it was exhilarating! The sky was clear blue with the sun shining and greeting us warmly at the African peak. We were above the clouds, and it was magical. All the hard work, tears, exhaustion, and pain became a distant memory once I reached the Roof of Africa - this magnificent moment would remain forever in my heart. Up here, problems were insignificant. Up here cancer did not exist.

Adrenaline must have kicked in as I do not recall feeling tired. I felt so proud of myself and the team. Collectively we had raised over $110,000 for the Canadian Breast Cancer Foundation (CBCF). As we started to descend, the fatigue set in. My eyes became so heavy and I just wanted to, needed to close them, if only for a few minutes.

As on the way up, my guide was by my side the entire way down. He encouraged me to keep going and sat with me during our short rest breaks. Finally, approximately thirteen plus hours from our initial summit time, I made it back to camp where I had a short twenty minute nap before lunch and then we packed up and continued down the mountain to our next camp for the night. We had one more night on this beautiful mountain, and my tired body wanted to soak in every single minute I could. It would soon be time to say goodbye to the beautiful sunrises, sunsets and everything in between, here in Africa.

This trip was life altering. I had been able to trust my body again and I felt invincible for the first time in over twelve years. Little did I know that this feeling would be challenged again a short sixteen months later.

ACCLIMATIZING TO THE NEW ALTITUDE

It was winter 2016/2017 and one night, while Chris and I were enjoying one of our favorite shows, I couldn't keep my eyes open. I had to rest before I could conjure up enough energy to climb into bed. This felt familiar. Then one morning as I was getting ready for work, Chris noticed a blemish on the same breast as my lumpectomy and I booked a doctor's appointment right away. When I saw her she didn't seem concerned, however because of my history, she requisitioned a mammogram and an ultrasound. The last one I had was the summer before, and it was clear. She did a physical exam and there were no discernable lumps in my breast.

Fortunately, I was able to get into the hospital very quickly for the tests. I did the testing with the technicians and the doctor came to see me in the ultrasound room. She informed me that the mammogram and ultrasound that I just had done were clear. What a relief! However, she proceeded to ask me what had brought me in. I showed her the blemish on the breast. She scanned the area again and saw nothing. She then said the following words which continue to stay with me and most likely saved me, "Hmmm, I'd hate for there to be something hiding behind the area. I recommend that you ask your doctor for an MRI referral." I've had many breast MRIs over the past fourteen years. I called my doctors' office and requested a requisition, and thankfully, I was able to get in quickly.

I was sitting at my desk when my phone rang. It was the hospital. They wanted me to come in for a Breast MRI guided biopsy. They could get me in the next week. I booked the appointment and hung up. I was in shock. No, this isn't happening – not again.

I called Chris and told him about the biopsy request. He tried to calm me down and reminded me that I have had several negative biopsies over the years, and that they were just being thorough. The day of the biopsy came, and the medical team was very caring and sensitive but as soon as I got into place on the machine, I started weeping. I cried during the entire biopsy procedure. I knew deep down something wasn't right.

After the procedure I felt weak and defeated. The nurse suggested that I sit in a wheelchair to be taken up for the next test, a mammogram. As she pushed me out into the waiting area, I could see Chris looking for me and the mix of surprise and concern on his face when he saw me in the wheelchair. He then pushed me up to the mammogram imaging unit and there was deafening silence between us.

It had been two weeks and my family doctor still had not received my results, and she was heading off for vacation. My breast had become increasingly sore since the exam. Over the next couple of days, I called the hospital trying to track down the report. In the meantime, I needed an antibiotic to address the breast pain and I booked an end of day appointment to see the doctor that was covering for my physician.

I went to work but the pain in my breast was so intense that I thought I was going to pass out. I took pain medication but nothing helped, and I asked Chris to drive me to the appointment. I waited in the examination room for what felt like forever before the covering doctor came in. I had never met her, and I began explaining that I needed an antibiotic as I thought I had an infection from the biopsy.

The doctor was quiet, eerily quiet, and she handed me the biopsy report indicating a positive result for cancer. I was in shock – no this can't be mine – there's a mistake! This was all behind me. The only words that I could find were, "What does this mean?" I think I repeated this phrase at least a dozen times.

I could tell she was uncomfortable. She had no answers for me. Chris had been waiting in the car and he pinged my phone, and this was a relief for her, "Is there someone here with you?" she asked desperately. I messaged Chris and asked him if he could come upstairs.

As we were waiting for him to arrive, my head was spinning. Again, I repeated, "What does this mean?" I was desperate for some answers. Thoughts raced through my mind - Am I going to die from this? If so, when? Has it spread? If so where? How am I going to tell my family? How am I going to get through this? More importantly, am I going to get through this?

The uneasiness in the room was its' own entity. Finally, Chris showed up. By this time, I had begun to weep, and I showed him the biopsy results. The doctor indicated she would set up an appointment with a surgeon at the hospital to discuss next steps. However, she did not have any other answers or info for me. Again, I reminded her that I needed an antibiotic. I think that she was reluctant to provide this to me but complied.

It was Valentine's Day, and I was just two weeks shy of my fourteen-year anniversary of my first breast cancer surgery and diagnosis. I officially despised the month of February. What is the probability of getting diagnosed twice in the shortest month of the year? Chris and I talked and agreed that we would not share the news until we had more information and a plan in place.

I was in shock and would remain in varying degrees of shock for months. Shock, denial, it all felt the same. It was extremely difficult for me to talk about this new diagnosis with others. Countless times I picked up the phone but had to hang up, as I could not find the words. It was as if my life was this beautiful ornate mirror. I had spent the past fourteen years putting the pieces of my life back together to form something that could reflect light again, and now it was shattered into a million pieces strewn across a dark floor, each piece cruelly glistening.

Would I be given the time, the ability, the health, to begin to repair this mirror again? Or would I start to collect the broken pieces only to continually get cut by their sharp edges? What had I not learned the first time? Would I be able to stop asking the questions that I would never get the answers to – why me? Why now? Why again?

It was so difficult to get any sleep that first night. Thankfully I remembered one of my favorite meditations and it lulled me into sleep. I woke up the next morning, the shock and disbelief setting in again. I somehow decided to go on with my day and not immerse myself in the countless unknowns. Fortunately, I was able to get into see an oncologist who was able to provide me with some answers. She indicated that we caught it early, and that it had a different pathology from the first cancer. She recommended chemo and one year of targeted treatments. Next step was for me to meet with a breast oncology surgeon to determine surgery options.

Throughout this journey, I have learned to be an advocate for myself, which has been extremely challenging at times. I have learned to listen to my body and heed its whispers and unassuming clues. When I reflect, I had seen the warning signs, like signposts. The indescribable fatigue, where sleep itself is so sweet and intoxicating, without the feeling of restoration upon waking. It is harder going through a second breast cancer diagnosis. I had so many decisions to make regarding surgery and treatments. Seven weeks after surgery, I started a weekly chemo protocol, which was extremely challenging.

I'm not naïve like I was the first time. I knew it would be tough, however, what I didn't anticipate was how differently I would react to the treatments. Side effects that I did not experience the first time around resulted in ending treatment early this time. There are days when I feel my body shutting down and I go into slow motion. I will be walking normally, and then it's as if someone pulls out my battery and I slow down completely. It's scary. My body is so different now, again. And I am reminded of this every day, especially when I look in the mirror for the long blond strands that no longer exist. My heart aches and I continue to grieve and mourn all that I have lost to this disease. And then somehow, I move through the moment and on with my day. But some days are much more difficult than others.

It is not lost on me how fortunate I was to find the cancer so early. It was a miracle that we were so diligent and that I had a great medical team that listened to me. Throughout this second diagnosis, my mind takes me back up to my summit night. I'm reminded how my sole focus was on my next step, and how difficult and physically exerting it was to climb in the ever-thinning air. "Pole pole." This again parallels the challenges I undergo daily with treatment and recovery. Where I was gripping my poles for support on the mountain, I am now gripping the railing as I climb my steps at home.

I have learned to acclimatize to my new altitude with this diagnosis. And how my attitude at this new altitude matters, just like it did on Kili. Putting the pieces of my life back together is a work-in-progress, and I am thankful for the support of my close friends and family. But I guess that is the point – we are all a work-in-progress creating beautiful masterpieces of art called life, supporting each other every step of the way. In the meantime, I will thankfully take in as many beautiful sunrises, sunsets and everything in between that I can.

Asante Sana

(Thank you in Swahili)

The team summited Mount Kilimanjaro on October 22, 2015.

ABOUT LAURIE DUDO

Laurie is a technology executive, author and breast cancer survivor. She is passionate about travel, education and community. As an avid traveller she has journeyed to six continents, backpacked across Europe, and climbed Machu Picchu and Mount Kilimanjaro.

Through her passion for education and development she has received two undergraduate degree's and her MBA. Laurie has also received her CPA (CMA) accounting designation.

As a breast cancer survivor, Laurie enjoys giving back and has volunteered with the Canadian Breast Cancer Foundation (CBCF), as an inspirational speaker, and with Wellspring Cancer Support Services and Rethink Breast Cancer providing Peer Navigation Support.

Laurie enjoys being active through hiking, yoga and running. She lives in Toronto, Ontario Canada with her partner Christopher and their dog Fletcher.

Laurie is passionate about sharing her story and talking to others about breast cancer and her journey. Laurie would love to hear from you and can be reached at:

Facebook: lauriedudoofficial

Website: www.tothetopofkili.com

SIDE HUSTLE SUCCESS

Gina Fresquez

Jump off the cliff and build your wings on the way down. We have all most likely heard different versions of this statement, and in my experience, many people believe that to become an entrepreneur, this is what you must do. But is it true? Is jumping off the cliff the gateway to becoming a successful entrepreneur?

From a young age, I knew I wanted to start something of my own. My father was an entrepreneur, and I constantly daydreamed about becoming one myself. Ideas would flood my brain, and my imagination would take me down paths of what I could create. Entrepreneurship was in my DNA. Therefore, it didn't surprise me when I found myself starting my first side hustle business as a life and health coach.

At the time I was also working in the corporate world, putting in well over forty hours per week, including lots of travel, yet

I was determined to make my new business a success. But over time, I was struggling to juggle it all and was beginning to feel overwhelmed and stressed out. At one point I felt as if I were running myself into the ground and became completely exhausted with adrenal fatigue. I was so busy that I didn't even have time to think. It was hard trying to balance my career, my business, my responsibilities, my family, and a social life. Many people thought I was crazy to take on so much. I felt as if where I was and where I desired to be seemed so opposing that something had to give, and it sure was not going to be me or my budding business. So I began to look for solutions.

I started paying attention to how others were handling the balance of all their endeavors. As I looked toward my peers and industry leaders, I noticed many of them were not running their businesses as side hustles. From what I could see, all those who were successful in my industry were those who were working in their businesses full time.

It was in this search that I came across a quote online about how the definition of an entrepreneur is someone who jumps off the cliff and builds her wings on the way down.

Wait, what?

While many people praised this approach to entrepreneurship, this did not sit well with me. Every time I saw someone mention it, I cringed. Why did this bother me so much?

Well, being the type A planner personality that I was, I definitely did *not* feel good about cliff jumping with no plan. It made me feel constricted and fearful. Was this the only way to become successful? "Jump!" they said. "Do it!" they said, and that is how you find success. This was all I heard in the online-coaching space, and it felt like a sort of silent peer pressure.

Now, I am not someone who skydives, bungee jumps, or cliff jumps. These activities are great for the fly-by-the-seat-of-your-pants adrenaline seekers, but me? I feel best with my feet firmly planted on the ground. When I have a well-thought-out plan with careful steps of execution that is when I really shine. Plus, I actually liked my corporate job, and I had no plans to leave as long as I was happy. So what then?

What if I didn't want to leap off the proverbial cliff? Did that make me less of an entrepreneur? I felt different from my peers and began to feel shame around having a nine-to-five corporate job in addition to my business, which did not feel good. I knew I was an entrepreneur at heart no matter what anyone said. I was just as determined, imaginative, resourceful, resilient, creative, and focused as anyone else, and I wanted to do something to make it all work in my favor. I knew cliff jumping was not the answer for me. But what *was* the answer?

At this point I decided to do things differently. My way. What would feel right to me was deciding to do both on my own terms. I decided to create a way to take the stairs instead of jumping and free falling off the cliff. What felt good to me was setting the foundation, taking it step by step, growing at a pace that felt doable and achievable without burnout, and guess what? It didn't have to be an either/or for me; it could actually be both—having the corporate job *and* running a successful business on the side, all while enjoying the work I contributed to the world without sacrificing my lifestyle, heath, or sanity on this journey. Now *that* felt liberating.

With my newfound liberation, I quickly became immersed in stress and time management. I negotiated a work schedule that felt balanced and gave me more time and freedom, and I gained traction and success in doing both. Each choice and decision I made took me to the steps I needed to gain more success in my business. I truly felt that I was taking the stairs.

Upon this success, many people were quite surprised to find out that I still had a corporate job, as it seemed as if I were in my business full time. Other coaches and entrepreneurs, who were also trying to do both, contacted me and wanted to know how I was making it all happen with such success and ease. They told me it seemed impossible to balance both; it felt so overwhelming and hard. Where was I finding the time to do it all? How did I stay focused and consistent while not burning out? I quickly discovered there were many other women like me who wanted to create and grow a business on the side but didn't want to sacrifice everything to do so. They too desired a way to take the stairs.

I began giving advice to those who reached out to me. I shared that to be successful while being time strapped, you must focus on doing one thing well. You may have many ideas you want to execute, but you must choose to master only one at a time (this goes for social media, marketing channels, niches, and so on). You can eventually do all the things, just not all the things at the same time, and now is your time to focus. I shared how you need to be a master of your time and set office hours for your side hustle to devote some consistent time to making it a success as well as developing the mindset you need to stay motivated and grow in the direction you desire.

I quickly realized that there was a need for this, and so I began a community to support this different breed of entrepreneur, the woman side hustler. This group was a safe place for women to connect, vent, and support one another in growing businesses alongside nine-to-five jobs, part-time jobs, motherhood, and any other things they were juggling. What happened next was beyond anything I could have imagined. Women showed up to collaborate with and celebrate one another, they got help in all areas of their businesses, they were honest and vulnerable, they shared struggles and successes, they found new friendships, and they gained true respect for one another. Together we were removing the shame attached to having nine-to-five jobs in addition to our businesses. We were all entrepreneurs together.

Because I was supporting women in the group by coaching them through time-saving techniques, advising them on how to find their unique gifts and maximize their zones of genius, and offering tips on stress management and maintaining their sanity by deciding where their focus should go, women within this group began to explore how to really make their side hustles successfully work for them. The discovery of how to grow a successful side hustle without feeling overwhelmed, without feeling as if they had to do everything at once, and without sacrificing their health, lifestyle, finances, and sanity was liberating to them too.

And when I really knew I had made the right decision and was exactly where I needed to be was when one client came to me needing help. A mom of two young boys, working in the corporate world, and starting a side hustle, Laurie was struggling. She was struggling with knowing what to focus on as she felt as if she had to be doing everything, and it was overwhelming. She felt that she was not very specific in her marketing but didn't know how to carve down her niche, and she was having trouble finding any more time for her business in her already demanding schedule. Laurie was burning out quickly by not taking time to nourish herself, and her family was beginning to resent her having started her business in the first place. She felt stuck and up against a wall. She was so committed to making her side hustle a success, but she needed a different way to make it happen that worked better than her current stressed-out situation.

First we approached her schedule. Together we evaluated what she was spending her time on, carved out dedicated weekly work hours for her business, and made sure her family agreed to her new schedule. Instead of making her feel that she was always trying to catch up and squeeze in working on her business here and there, these boundaries helped her open up more free time to spend with her children and husband, which made her feel joy again.

Then Laurie gained clarity on her unique gifts and specific zone of genius so that she could focus her marketing to attract more clients with less effort. As she streamlined to working only on income-generating activities and delegated the rest to maximize her efforts, her side hustle quickly grew and felt expansive again.

Over time we addressed Laurie's mindset, walking her though the process of challenging how she used to approach her career and getting past her fears of lack and scarcity. We were able to change her limiting beliefs about the success of her business, which led to massive confidence in where it was headed. With her newfound confidence, the stress melted away, and

Laurie was able not only to ease her husband's concerns about stability and security but also to craft a well-thought-out negotiation with her boss to work part time from home, which gave her the momentum she needed to finally quit her corporate job altogether within six months of our working together. Laurie had become a full-time entrepreneur in a way that felt doable and achievable without sacrificing herself, her sanity, her finances, or her lifestyle. Laurie had taken the stairs.

When I realized that what I had done behind the scenes from a foundational standpoint had accelerated the success of this client, I knew that all the things I had done up until that point had been worth it. I could make an impact on these women's lives and businesses and give them the freedom to grow and succeed in a way that felt good to them.

You *can* successfully build a business alongside working a full-time job and do it in a way that feels good, where every step of the way feels planned, purposeful, and well executed. It does not have to feel scary and hard, as if you are free falling off a cliff. Taking the stairs to success can actually feel empowering, rewarding, and liberating, and you do not have to sacrifice everything to do so. It is achievable. If you desire to have both, you can have both. And that does not make you any less of an entrepreneur.

Through my discovery and decision to do both and take the stairs, follow my intuition, and decide to do things differently, I felt total clarity and alignment in my mission. I decided to do it my way, in a way that was different from what I had been presented with, and in a way that felt good to me. Because of this clarity, I am exactly where I am supposed to be, doing exactly what I am meant to do. I was able to create a thriving coaching practice, which now provides me with the choice of whether I want to remain in the corporate world with a side hustle or take that last step into full-time entrepreneurship. But because I took the stairs, it feels not big and scary but totally doable and achievable. It is liberating to know I am in control and have the power of my success because I get to choose. It literally feels like a small step. No cliff jumping required. And that feels oh so good.

ABOUT GINA FRESQUEZ

Gina Fresquez, MS, CHC, is the founder of the Women's Side Hustle Society, where she is committed to empowering ambitious, soulful, side hustling women to bring their biggest entrepreneurial dreams to life in a way that's infused with confidence, joy, ease, and freedom—without having to sacrifice their health, sanity, or lifestyle. Gina holds a master's degree from the University of Arizona and coaching certifications from the Institute for Integrative Nutrition and HCI Transformational Coaching Method as well as being trained in stress management and mindset work.

After spending many years in corporate sales, Gina made her dream of becoming an entrepreneur come true in 2012, when she started her first side hustle. Since then she has enjoyed the journey of strategically and intuitively coaching her clients through mitigating fears and facilitating the breakthroughs, transformations, and transitions of building successful businesses in a way that feels good to them while also making a positive impact on the world. Gina accomplishes this through coaching, masterminds, and retreats. She also loves sharing stories of other inspiring, successful side hustling women on her podcast: bit.ly/WSHSPodcast.

Gina lives in Seattle with her husband, René, and three-year-old son, Ezra. Together they love traveling and exploring the outdoors, rain or shine.

To learn more about how you can gain more time to work on your side hustle, download her free e-book, *21 Tips to Time Freedom*, at bit.ly/timefreedomtips.

If you'd like help starting or growing your side hustle with more ease, joy, and freedom, or if you'd like to hire Gina to speak or facilitate a side-hustle-success workshop, reach out to her on her website.

Connect with Gina: www.ginafresquez.com

Facebook: GinaMFresquez

Instagram: womens_sidehustle_society

Join the Women's Side Hustle Society Facebook group: www.facebook.com/groups/womenssidehustlesociety

ONE NIGHT ONE VOICE FROM THE BEGINNING

Melody Garcia

What if I told you that one prayer unleashed it all? What if I shared that without leaving my own living room, I was able to move into action and help impact over 20,000 lives halfway around the world with one event that led to global connectivity and a podcast aired where sixty countries joined in to listen, an event that lead to other doors opening and finding myself inside Capitol Hill, with a following of over 200,000 readers on my column and in the circles of some of the best of the world's influencers? That one fateful evening changed the course of a lifetime that continues to unfold? And that despite the deep pain, the painful past, the labels, the limiting beliefs, the betrayals, the hurts, the brokenness...it all led up to becoming catalyst for a greater purpose? My name is Melody, and here's a glimpse of my story, my journey, called One Night One Voice...from the beginning.

You're not good enough—the labels started early.

I was born out of wedlock in a different time, in a different culture, and in a country that was strictly Catholic and did not recognize divorce. My parents fell in love in the most inconvenient way, as their lives had their own twists and turns. I was a happy child, headstrong, and creativity ran deep in my being in all directions, in reading, writing, singing, dancing, speaking, and a visionary creative outlook and out-of-the-box thinking. I was independent but grounded. The arts created a world of escape from what is quite often a cruel world. Life is fair but people aren't.

I felt discrimination at a very young age because of this relationship that existed outside traditional fairy tales. I was told I was not good enough, that I was born out of sin, by people who talked around us, even by some of the educators of a prominent private school I attended. As it most often happens, the people who you think care about you end up hurting you the most. I can think of a specific moment when a teacher asked me to produce a copy of a wedding photo, knowing full well the family situation I was born into. Both my parents demanded a meeting with the school principal that led to serious disciplinary actions later on for that teacher. They tried to protect me and my sister from the cruelty of judgment that existed. My mother, full of gracefulness, strong faith, beauty, and gentleness, always taught me that love knows no prejudice, holds no unkindness, is patient, and is unconditional. My father was a highly prominent doctor and pretty much a public figure well loved by all. His marriage was all but happy. In fact, his wife at that time was very well aware of our existence and would send her own children to my mother to watch. Yes, it was unconventional and strange, but I can be grateful for the love I did witness and the protection afforded from so many labels that could cause the strongest to have deeply seeded insecurities. I didn't realize, though, until later on that abandonment issues stemmed from the situation I was born into. Anytime my dad would "go home" to his other family, I felt sad. Needless to say, all eventually worked out. My father was able to gain the annulment needed to file the divorce, and we all lived happily ever after, but just for a moment…just for a few years.

A COUNTRY BETRAYS

Both my parents emerged from poverty. My mother didn't finish her high school degree due to lack of provisions but had the brilliance of heart language, empathy, and authentic love for others felt strongly, which paved the way to success in the field of corporate management and entrepreneurship. My father became chief of staff of two hospitals, had a private practice, and was a leader in every single professional and medical association. Both had heart, charisma, and a passion for philanthropy and were strongly grounded in the principle of giving back, since they both knew suffering. Their heart was their strength, but it also proved to be the very thing that became the kryptonite for our family.

Known to help out everyone who was facing challenges, they took in a distant relative who was struggling to support his family. During one of his odds-and-ends jobs, he came across information he wanted to share with the media that was critical to the public and was connected to some political situation. We don't know the details, just that he had to meet and air his story the next day, but he never got the chance to because he was kidnapped in front of my mom's place of business, with her to witness this, and he turned up brutally and violently murdered a few days later.

Since my mother witnessed the direct kidnapping, we were faced with very serious death threats to the point of psychological tactics used by this group in very strategical, cynical ways, and my parents had no idea we were under surveillance for some time. When direct deadly threats were made to us children and safety no longer was guaranteed, they had one recourse, to leave the country in the middle of the night. It came unexpectedly, as I was frantically woken up by our maids in the middle of the night and asked to stay quiet and get dressed as they hurriedly packed everything they could in a few suitcases. A few days later, my mother, my younger sister, and I found ourselves living with relatives in a country that we had visited as tourists and now had to call home. We had to leave everything behind, never got to say good-bye to anyone, and lived with relatives in a very small three-bedroom home. My sister and I shared the floor, while my mom took the bed in one room; my father had to stay behind for a couple of years. My mom started working at a grocery store and 7-11 for minimum wage to support us. She told me to forget the lifestyle we once had but to remember all that was good; she said life had to restart. Looking back I can only imagine the courage and the humbleness it took her as she worked those graveyard shifts focused on one thing…survival.

IT WASN'T ALWAYS ROSES

While I was living with relatives, that feeling of being made to feel I was not good enough came back at full force. For reasons I have forgiven, my sister and I were not allowed to sit on couches, just the floor. When my cleaning was not to their satisfaction, completely demeaning notes addressed to me were left on display on the bathroom mirrors, and I was forbidden to take them down. They were there for anyone to see, and my childhood best friend saw. I went to her house when I was allowed and cried some nights. I was not allowed to use the phone except for a few minutes for homework, and my mother said to take it in and forgive, as we were at the mercy of their kindness. Internally, I was angry. I couldn't understand how people could treat others that way, let alone family who went to church each weekend. Don't get me wrong—there were good memories, but there were painful memories, and as I developed into a young woman through the time we lived with them, the pain increased. I attracted young men, old men, and teenagers with the changes going on with me, not realizing that my feminine energy was strong; the sexual magnetism was getting stronger, and mixed with all the innocence of youth, it drove a lot of attention I didn't want. Some was from my aunt's own dates, but I was told by them not to say a word.

Eventually, a few years later, my mom, my sister, and my father, who eventually was able to visit us, moved to our own two-bedroom condo. Life was still a struggle, but I was happy because I felt free. I excelled in school and got into business school early—I was the youngest on campus, actually. I worked two full-time jobs, supported myself in school, and fell in love with my first love. He was my best friend, and it was the stuff dreams were made of. We were soul mates, I thought. For the next seven years of my life, he was my confidant, my biggest fan, and I leaned on him with all the trust I had. I moved to Hawaii, got a job, and soared in my career early. But fate had a different call. We started drifting apart; we had different priorities and goals. He wanted to settle down and was content with all of life's simplicity, but my soul knew I was meant for more. It was a very difficult breakup. Destiny or heart? And I cried and was deeply hurt because in that drift, I had felt someone else's presence as well, someone whom he did later marry. I was shattered and moved to Orlando, Florida, and started my life over. Then I met him, my husband, a couple of years later, and the next seventeen years of my life were anything but the happily ever after I dreamt of.

He was intelligent, charming, and caring, but I ignored signs that were evident, and we got married because "it was the right thing to do" in my book after I found out I was pregnant. The alternative presented to me by his father as an option was abortion. Every single internal cell within me screamed "No!" This was not an option. The first year was an indication of troubles that were ahead. Nevertheless, I excused it as "first-year adjustment." In seventeen years, I experienced and discovered betrayals and abandonment, became pretty much the stable breadwinner, and enabled this cyclical, toxic codependency by falling into the need to fix everything, all the crisis.

As my career continued to soar in the corporate world, his was the opposite. I felt so stifled in growth and found external ways to deal with the emptiness I felt, the sadness for all I held dearly in my heart that would never come true. I thought back to many moments of the past relationship that were beautiful. But I got so caught up in expectations of keeping a family together, religious and cultural expectations, and without realizing it until later, I also got caught up in the things that had shaped me from childhood. That feeling of abandonment from my own father's absence was deeply ingrained, and I vowed I didn't want my sons to feel what I felt, so I thought it was better to sacrifice my own happiness than theirs. But it was unhealthy, until I found the courage to face my own demons and take full accountability of having allowed this to go on for years, coming to the gut-wrenching realization that by doing so, I had enabled both my sons to feel and experience and may have created a false sense of deeply instilled beliefs that this was all OK. It was not, by any means, but I created a normalcy to protect them in the process of trapping myself.

My outlet during the sad times was to give back to the world, whether it was through volunteering, heading projects, getting involved back in the arts, traveling...the deeper the loneliness, the bigger the project. Ironically enough, I found out later that this pattern is part of an ongoing healing process, one highly recommended. In 2005, I lost both parents back to back and went through the pain of another affair, and something shifted within me after yet another blow like that. Many people have asked why I stayed, why I tolerated...it was because I've always put others before myself, and that unselfishness was both my kryptonite and my power. It was a matter of finding the balance, and although things were not clear then, all that I went through became the catalyst for the bigger things to come. To the outside world, all was well. I was in demand for various projects that exposed me to public view—television assignments, on stage, and in print, and well, suffice it to say, I was a world-class actress who could fool the world with a dazzling smile and a stage presence. I was popular in all directions, and the expectation of maintaining such positivity was always present. You see, I was almost not allowed to have my human moments, not by the world, not by those who surrounded my life then, and certainly not even at work with a position in leadership.

ONE NIGHT ONE VOICE, THE EVENT THAT BECAME THE GAME CHANGER

On November 2013, the planet's strongest typhoon made landfall and slammed the Philippines. The monstrosity obliterated everything in its path, and the death count quickly rose to the thousands. I was drawn, like the rest of the world, to follow the news, but something internally prompted me to tune in to the Internet news, to find a local channel, and at that time, the Philippines didn't censor anything. I came across one story, and it broke me completely. For in the middle of a place where it looked as if a nuclear bomb had gone off was a very frail woman holding two lifeless bodies, her only children. She looked so lost, so broken, so resigned. In her brokenness, she shared that they were so remotely cut off from help and couldn't even bury her children until help could come. So she just held them for a few days. To this day, that picture is crystallized in my memory, and I still feel her heart, her loss, her pain. It was a searing arrow that pierced me, and I could not stop crying. With heavy sobs, I felt the loss deeply. And I fell on my knees. Without much thought, I uttered a prayer to heaven, crying, " Help me, help them. Please activate everything you have given me to help me reach them." And that one prayer changed the course of my life, bringing all into focus.

THE MIRACLE JOURNEY UNFOLDS

I woke up with an epiphany: to put together a small cabaret concert and invite around twenty people who could donate to a cause to help people who were suffering in the Philippines. My first order of implementation was to gather an artist or two to sing with me. To be fair, I sent out a simple message to the Asian American community asking for people to volunteer their time and join me in singing. I woke up the next day with a flood of messages on Facebook from complete strangers. The majority were not Asian American, and I wondered if I had misdirected the message. I checked, and sure enough I had sent it to the right community. But I had more than a handful of artists from all walks wanting to be part of this, all at no cost. I thought, "Wow, that came easy."

Second, I had to find a venue. It was right on the holiday mark. Everyone wanted to charge a lot. Three friends who did not speak to each other gave me one pastor's name. I thought it was odd, but there is no such thing as a coincidence. I called him and shared my idea for a small event and wanted to see if he could donate a church hall large enough for twenty people. He said to give him time and he would see what he could do. I also partnered up with a nonprofit organization I worked with that agreed to donate 100 percent of proceeds straight to the ground.

By day three from that prayer, the pastor had called back with great news. He said a venue was being gifted at no cost, and I remember asking if it was big enough to hold twenty people plus performers. He chuckled and said, "How about a concert auditorium that holds 650 seats?" I was stunned. I had artists, a large venue, and a nonprofit all lined up in three days from that amen. *This is not normal*, was all I could think internally, and I didn't realize the guiding hand in all this. Over the next couple of weeks I took to social media and started promoting this event. And I was overcome with a feeling to call it One Night One Voice. What was the meaning behind it? I had one night to make the voices from halfway around the world count.

With dizzying, unexplainable speed, more miracles started happening in very rapid succession. A community responded expediently. Sponsorships I had never sought out started approaching me—a free graphic artist; free radio ads that were supposed to air only twice but ended up airing for a full week unexplainably; company sponsorship from Pepsi, whose representative called me at 10:30 p.m. after hearing about what I was doing; a printing press company stepping up to absorb all costs of brochures, materials, posters, and prints; two big speakers reaching out to me; and so much more…and I could no longer refute that everything that was happening was directly a heavenly response to a tearful prayer I had sent up. God did activate every talent I had…fueled by testimonial messages I started receiving from halfway around the world of people in dire need of food, finding missing relatives as the death count soared into the thousands. I barely slept for three weeks, using everything I had.

HERO OF YOUR COUNTRY, RISE UP—A FULL CIRCLE

I received a message from CNN Hero of the Year recipient Efren Penaflorida, whom I had reached out to to borrow his quote, never expecting him to respond personally. One sentence made me break down into tears: "Oh, hero of your country, rise up! Your people need you." A flood of memories came flashing back: the night we left, the threats, what we lost, what we suffered through, what we had to start with again…coming to this point. "Hero of my country"? I could not stop crying in a restaurant, surrounded by friends who didn't know what to do with me. I had never felt the rush of emotions so strongly, and everything I held inside came to the surface. I had a complete breakdown because it was a very powerful and meaningful moment for me.

The day of the concert came, and I had no idea if twenty people were going to show up or a hundred. I remember my words: "God, I don't know if there are twenty people there or two hundred, but please let them be the ones with generous hearts. You know I asked only for twenty when this started." When I stepped out to host the entire program, I barely could breathe, because three weeks from that first prayer I was met with a sea of smiling bright faces, an auditorium filled with souls who had responded to the call. "Yes, dear God, yes," I cried, because in front of me was a pure work of miracle and a sign so strong of what heaven's love can do: turn the impossible into the possible.

The funds went to start rebuilding structures and providing medical aid, and then the last recipient was the manifestation of what it was all about…the mobile soup kitchen for kids. Unlike a soup kitchen, this group had nothing but two stock pots, basic firewood, kerosene, and whatever its members could gather to cook to feed families, and by a miracle we connected by a single envelope with words scribbled by my then-seven-year-old son with his one and only dollar inside, simply stating "for the Philippines." An upload on social media became the bridge that connected it all.

A simple message led to the feeding of and providing needs to over 20,000 children in different regions of the country that was badly hit by the storm. It led to the planting of sustainability gardens across different locations and to connecting me with groups from Canada, Dubai, and other countries as we worked together to help this small group of ground volunteers to reach families and children in need. Mind you that we were at the very bottom of the barrel of funds, but it didn't matter; the story within itself became the parable of two loaves and five fishes. God multiplied what felt like nothing left at that time. The story of One Night One Voice quickly spread, and just when I thought I was done, I did my part. It was just the beginning of all things activated.

BREAKDOWN TO BREAKTHROUGH

It was not until August of 2015 that I finally decided to file for divorce, and it was rough at first. Inner voices kept screaming not to do it, but my heart and soul knew it was sixteen out of seventeen years long overdue. Though they had previously eluded me, the courage and gut-wrenching realization to come face to face with my own self during another lonely walk at the beach allowed me to reflect on the future, and I asked myself one question: "Can I continue to exist this way?" One side had all the achievements, even with all that I felt internally, and the other was emptiness. Could I go on another five years, one year? I started a countdown. Every part of me was screaming no, and then I let my heart drift to my sons, and every part of my heart broke into millions of pieces. I couldn't breathe because I had allowed the very fear that loomed over my head and that their father used—"you are going to break the family"—to become the poison that trapped all of us, and I had to turn things around fast. I went home and with clarity had a conversation with my ex, and I said I was done and was filing for a divorce. Then came the harder talk, to speak to each of my sons and take full accountability for all, for allowing this to go on and to share with them why it couldn't go on.

The next few months were beyond rough. It is in the greatest adversity that you find who your real friends are, and often you are left to your own shadow. There were plenty of talks. I fell in love fast with someone I thought was the one, and he ended up breaking my heart even more. I had ministers who walked away, friends who betrayed my trust, and finances in an uproar as I wanted complete disconnection from anything that would hold me back. I paid for the entire divorce and signed an agreement of no child support from my ex; he could visit our sons as much as he wanted, and there would be no alimony for me. It was done swiftly, but I was spiraling fast into depression, and there were thoughts in my head that entered so calmly, thoughts of ending my own life in the midst of the darkness of being completely alone. The once awesome, popular, positive woman fell from the grace of people; they found out I had my human moments of imperfections, and people were ruthless. My only anchor was to think of my two boys and who would raise them, and there was no way in hell I was going to let my ex-husband do it, knowing him well. Funny enough, it was also his imperfection that became the reason I couldn't go through with the false sense of peace that loomed. But I was angry at God: for the deafening silence, for the unanswered prayer of relentless attacks in my mind, my heart, and my soul. There were many nights of tears, of not wanting to be out and about yet having to muster strength in front of my boys. The pain of seeing them go through their own adjustments was enough to break me, but I had to hold it together, and I felt hopeless for the very first time.

A MESSAGE THAT CHANGED IT ALL

As I fell deeper and deeper into depression, disconnected from the world, and refused to answer calls, texts, and messages from others, I took time off from work and let depression take over. One night, a friend sent me a video with a thirty-second message powerful enough to jump-start a zombie existence...It said, "The attacks on your life have nothing to do with who you were but everything to do with who you will become." I played it several times, and I got angrier, but it sure got me talking to God again.

I went into my closet screaming at God... literally. I threw down the Bible, thumbed it frantically, and looked up scriptures in almost mockery. "What do you mean who I will become? Wasn't One Night One Voice enough? That's thousands of people, THOUSANDS, a lot more than what dozens of people can ever claim," I argued to a silent God, and I cried deeply because he was silent. I spent hours in that dark closet, just crying and saying, "Are you still there? You never left me since I was a child." I cried even more for all that I went through and was going through…and in between the heart-break, I said, "If you are there, please send the lifetime people, not the season or reason. I'm tired; I've been hurt over and over again, but you know this; you've seen it all. I failed, but you said you'll be there. I need you. Please send them now because I don't know how much longer I can hold on." And those people started showing up little by little as I stepped forward and infused myself back into society, going through different meetups, conventions I found I didn't even belong in, just gently invited by others, and I just attended it all. I was taking frantic notes of anything I could gain that would make sense.

I sensed they were different, for the questions they asked me were different. One mentor asked me to tell him about my deepest pain and how it had served as a catalyst to my purpose—and he asked during a networking event. I didn't sleep well that night after that question; the answers were distant. Another came a few weeks later, and his question was about my circle of influence and the principle of five. Yet another came who taught me about destiny. A college friend and confidant stepped in and sent my ass straight to my first Tony Robbins event; she knew of all my past accomplishments and potential and didn't like what she was seeing: a broken person. Strangers came as weeks went by and became links to some of these lifetime people, and my soul woke up. Peace started coming, and I knew I was changing. Although it might not have been evident externally at first, I knew something big was looming as the gentle guiding hands continued to push me forward.

As mentioned earlier, the arts also became my escape, and I found myself agreeing to write for a small start-up magazine and was grateful that its founder allowed me the flexibility to be creative with my column. In search of my own answers to life, I created Life Journey for *Manila Up Magazine*, the stories of breakdown to breakthroughs, and what started as small-scale interviews quickly grew into some of the nation's and the world's influencers being interviewed and coming face to face with me. I never had to look for them; they came my way, from the most quoted man alive to business moguls and Asian celebrities, and before I knew it, their stories became platforms that inspired readers who were growing in number.

I decided to get back into giving through philanthropy or anything to do with humanitarianism and ended up creating the fourteenth congressional advocacy team in the United States under UNICEF, and within seven months of forming a strong team, we found ourselves at a summit and advocacy day in Washington, DC, inside Capitol Hill, with me leading my team to represent the needs of children everywhere and speaking on behalf of 114 countries with children in need.

The stage opened once again, and I found myself retelling the story of One Night One Voice, of God's miracle and wisdom that poured forth. I was onstage with some of the world's best, and at times I had to wonder what in the world I was doing there with my bank account not nearly matching theirs. Then God's whisper would come: "Share your heart, because the human life is irreplaceable, and tell them of all the miracles that came about. You stand to influence nations and communities, generations, with all I have given you."

Fast-forward to now. I have earned one award after another for my contributions in writing, in speaking, in making impact, in being a thought leader, and in influence, and opportunities abound. I've been on a podcast with sixty countries tuning in simultaneously, with a few more media interviews happening. Whomever I share the story with is drawn in powerfully, and that leads to more doors opening.

My mind grew, my heart grew, and I broke free from the chains that bound me. I find myself in the company of incredible people without seeking them. I have heavenly favors showing up, and that magazine following has grown to over 200,000 readers and a launch of my own segment in a TV show that showcases what I write—to be shown all over Asia, Los Angeles, and the rest of the world—about breakdown to breakthroughs. One Night One Voice became an LLC in 2017, and several other opportunities have now shown up for the upcoming year.

I've learned from the giants like Tony Robbins, Gary Vaynerchuk, Sara Blakely, Kevin O'Leary, and many others and invested in personal development in different forums.

More importantly, my sons are happy, and the three of us continue to thrive. My relationship with my ex-husband is one of friendship and forgiveness. I'm surrounded by a circle of authentic, caring people and a lot of lessons. I speak from the heart and connect globally to inspire others in their journeys. Are there dark days? Yes, I'm not spared from life's challenges, but I don't stay in the dark too long. Do I have sad days? Yes. Have I fulfilled everything I've wanted? No, because the list keeps growing, but the theme is the same. From the ashes I rose like the phoenix rising. From the story of One Night One Voice in the beginning. From the pain becoming the platform that allows me to feel yet know how I can help impact the lives of others.

I leave you these wisdoms...

Have faith and an unwavering belief that you matter, your passion matters, and you were created to make a significant impact.

Believe in God and all he is able to do in you, with you, and all that surrounds you.

Never stop growing and learning. Invest in your personal development and be willing to be an open student of life.

Stay humble and grounded. Give openly and without conditions.

Forgive your imperfections, learn the lessons they bring, and have a higher sense of accountability.

The gurus are not perfect either. Some have perfected the art of acting—trust me on this. I've come across some the world worships, and my walk has learned to recognize the act fast, but it's not their fault; the expectation is for them to maintain the act all the time. The beauty is that I can call them on their own BS sometimes.

Speak from your heart space, not from your mind.

Love is the most powerful weapon, one that can bridge nations and generations and bring healing.

Prayer is very powerful; never ever stop believing.

ABOUT MELODY GARCIA

Melody Garcia is an award-winning writer, speaker, thought leader, and influencer. A columnist for Manila Up! International magazine with her column titled *"Life Journeys"*, with over 200,000 readers and followers, and host of her own television segment titled " *Melody in Motion*" with Manila Up! TV Entertainment. Melody also founded and leads the fourteenth congressional advocacy team in the United States for UNICEF, works for a Fortune 100 company in a frontline leadership role, and an entrepreneur and launching a Single Mom's empowerment group in Orlando Florida.

Melody's diverse creative talents have landed her onstage throughout her life, from singing, acting, and camera to over twenty years of business experience leading big-scale projects and developing coaching programs that are sought by many; she works in start-up business projects, philanthropy, marketing campaigns, and global connectivity. She has a brilliant sense for out-of-the box thinking that has helped with crisis management, highly successful project turnouts, and business launches.

From being suddenly uprooted from her home country to escape imminent death threats and violence when she was young, Melody knows what it feels like to have nothing and has felt the pains of life, the unfairness that society brings all, leading up to transforming and touching thousands and potentially millions of lives in global reach....

To book Melody for speaking engagements or television commercials, please send an email to OneNightOneVoice@ gmail.com

Social Media Handles and Contact:

Website: www.Melodygarcia.com

Instagram: Melodyliezl

Twitter: @MelodyGarciaVIP

Facebook: Melody Garcia

MODERN FEMININITY

Gabrielle Grae

Today, I feel fully alive knowing that I am being the person I was born to be, fully expressing myself while serving the world with my gifts. But it wasn't always this way…

If you had told me ten years ago, actually even four years ago, that I would be living a dream—married to an extraordinary man who fully supports me and lights me up in every way and living out my life's purpose *as a career,* on my terms—I would have told you that you had the wrong woman.

If you had told me that I would be a woman who impacts and influences the lives of thousands of women, I would have been too scared to speak up and express my doubts. If you'd said I'd be helping them live more authentically and empoweredly by connecting them to their feminine energy, I would have laughed it off, thinking, "Well, that sounds like a cute hobby, not a real job."

Well, as Steve Jobs put it so eloquently, "You can connect the dots looking backward, not forward," and looking back now, I can see my purpose was always connected to me, even though I didn't know how to connect to it.

I was always drawn to helping people. I couldn't wait to graduate from high school so I could pursue a career in psychology. The logic behind that was that if I could figure people out, then I could help them. When I was growing up, people naturally opened up to me; they let me into their lives and asked for advice. I was gifted in connection and figured if I pursued psychology in school, I would be able to help more people and make a great living.

It seemed as if no matter what job I took, I would end up counseling people, facilitating new insights, and building them up. This happened when I waitressed and bartended and especially when I was a gymnastics coach.

I coached little ones under the age of six. I found myself focusing more on building up their self-esteem and opening them up to their inner confidence than speaking about gymnastics. In my parent-and-tot classes, I would find myself counseling the parents and helping them discover new ways to relate to their children that delivered better results. It felt so rewarding to know that I was making a difference.

I felt thrilled sitting in my first psychology class at the University of British Columbia. I looked at my textbook and believed it would have all the answers. While others struggled with the notoriously tricky multiple-choice questions and long essays during the three-hour exam, I flourished. It was as if I could see the answers popping up out of the page. Everything was clear to me; it all made so much sense.

I had arrived.

Or so I thought. As I worked toward my degree, I noticed that there were some things that didn't resonate with me. We've all been there—"This is my thing! Oh, wait—what have I gotten myself into?"

It's not that I didn't believe in the field; I've seen therapists and benefited. I even recommend clients to get extra support from a therapist. I just felt that there were a few rules that would make my style less effective.

I couldn't see myself spending the next six years in school, only to graduate and be in an office all day, operating within the confines of practices that I felt wouldn't allow me to show up and serve people the best ways I knew how. The idea of maintaining objectivity (is this even possible?), keeping the clients at arm's length, and never being able to offer them the reflection of "I've been there too" felt as if it would cut off so much of how I helped people. I couldn't see how I could fully show up in my gifts as a listener, healer, and intuitive within that paradigm.

I had subscribed to the story that I had grown up with, which meant that to be successful at a career, I needed to follow the path: education, degree, at least another degree or two (if I was to survive financially), and then career directly related to the degrees.

I could not conform, so for a time I gave up. It turns out that this is one of the major reasons most people give up on their dreams.

While I always naturally had a knack for helping other people feel better and have more of what they wanted in their lives, romantic relationships were not working out for me personally.

I struggled deeply in love relationships and found myself being either a total doormat or a complete control freak (where I would choose men, turn them into projects, and focus excessive amounts of time and energy managing them into life circumstances that better suited me).

I took time off from relationships altogether to work on myself, and even though my self-esteem improved, the dating process did not. To be honest, I felt embarrassed and confused. I was so done with feeling that way. So I did what we naturally do in the twenty-first century: I googled it.

"Why do all my relationships fail?"

"Why do men cheat?"

"Am I broken?"

Amid the varied results, I kept finding myself drawn back to one website. I remember that night so well; Rori Raye's book was $19.95 and out of my price range at the time, since I was a student. But I couldn't get around it—I had to have it.

This book introduced me to the secret world of masculine and feminine energy. Men started to make sense. More importantly, it introduced me to a concept that would rock my world: the power of *femininity*. I consumed the book and started practicing this powerful, leaned-back way of being.

I practiced dating from a place of feminine power. Feminine power is the energy of attracting *and* receiving. It didn't take long before I was getting into a flow that I had never experienced before. I was feeling as if I was in the right place at the right time—opportunities (including men) came to me. After about six months of this, I was ready. I set an intention to the universe to bring me my life partner. I simply declared, "I don't know who he will be or when I will meet him, but universe, I want you to know that I am open and ready."

Six days later I met my future husband in a New York City nightclub, and we were immediately inseparable. We spent nearly every waking moment together for the next three days until I had to leave.

Without fully realizing it, I had already stepped into my feminine power. I had already tapped into my highest source of magnetism.

In my previous long-term relationship, it had taken me over a year to twist my boyfriend's arm into having dinner with my parents. With Mr. Grae, on day two I met his parents casually at brunch. We even split up while I shopped with his mom for a bit— this guy was giving me 100 percent. After the weekend romance ended, we found ourselves on FaceTime daily, and the first chance he got Iain put business on hold and flew two thousand miles internationally because he wanted to get to know me better and meet my friends and my parents! This, ladies, is the power of harnessing the divine femininity, and I had gotten really good at it.

Our relationship flowed beautifully. I was never left to question if he was really into me or not, and he continued to show up and move the relationship forward. We were married within the year.

Relationship goal accomplished, it was time to start my career. My husband, a serial entrepreneur, owned an advertising agency. It used to earn six figures a month, but he had lost interest.

With my dreams of becoming a psychologist put to rest, I had landed on advertising. I thought that this could be the opportunity I was waiting for. Using my psychology degree, I could take over in a key role immediately, earn a very healthy income, and surround myself with vibrant people who were attracted to advertising. Not only would I be able to get into an important position immediately, but with the money I would earn I'd also be able to give help to my family and even some charities.

Even though I started having what most would define as success, the illusion did not last long. After just a few months, I found myself in a hotel room in Las Vegas. I could not find a way to get motivated to go back into the trade show I was attending. Actually, I did not want to leave the room unless it was to go to the spa. I realized that everything I had wanted to do for so long was not at all what I had thought it would be. The endless sea of men trying to sell me their technology while trying to pick me up made me nauseated. I didn't need either. The ad services I was selling, while effective, were not as glamorous as I had hoped. It was super techy, all about data, conversion rates, and volume—it was a quantity game, and no one was interested in quality. It was the exact opposite of who I am at my essence. It did not matter how much financial opportunity there was to be had—I could not shake another hand. I felt soulless. So I locked myself in my room and stopped working until the point where my husband had to fire me (yeah, I was too much of a scaredy-cat to just own that I hated being there). This fear was exactly the thing that stopped me from doing everything that I needed to be doing!

This inequity in who I was being versus who I was born to be inspired me to start seeking—I did not know what for, but I knew there must be a career that could make my heart sing the way my husband and cat did at home. Fortunately, my husband was in a similar place, and we both started changing the media we consumed. Rather than watching *Zeitgeist*, Alex Jones, and other alt-media sources, though, we made a huge shift. It started with listening to GIN and self-help audiobooks in the car and then watching seminars, from TED talks to random Nikola Tesla and quantum physics documentaries. We started to find some real gold that just felt so good when we watched it—one major turning point was watching Christie Marie Sheldon speak about energetics at an event called Awesomeness Fest. Fast-forward seven months, and we were in Costa Rica at the next event, which had a theme of "belief hacking."

At first, I was incredibly intimidated. I was surrounded by three-hundred-plus people who had jobs I'd never heard of (like life coaching!) and were on the cutting edge, traveling regularly, and making bank! Not only did it seem as if they were extraordinarily happy, but everything they worked to do had a place in serving humanity. I wanted to be one of them, and looking back I can see that fear, the same freaking fear I had had before, held me back from becoming one of them right then and there.

After several events and coaching programs, learning about plant medicine, and working with energy workers, the change was incredible. I was no longer the scaredy-cat I once was. I knew that I had value to give to the world, that my voice was important. Only trouble was, I had no idea how to use my voice to best serve humanity. How could I step into my highest purpose?

I started to look at my past and reflect about where I had experienced the most growth. Where had I gained a level of mastery that so many women had not? Not surprisingly, it was the same place where I had at one time felt so much pain. Relationships.

I started to ask myself, "What is the highest and best use of my gifts?" I asked the universe. The universe responded, "You can help heal women, even the planet, by teaching women how to use energy so that they can live their fullest expressions, empowered and on fire."

The best way for me to do that was clear: through coaching and mentoring women who were ready to transform their lives. Unlike with psychology, I could coach on my own terms. I could see the world through their eyes and apply universal truths to help guide them to where they wanted to be and who they wanted to be. I could be my own boss and show up for women in a unique and effective way!

Serendipitously, three weeks later my husband asked if I wanted to have dinner with his ex-girlfriend's old roommate. Old me would have gotten all weird and jealous and shut it down. Luckily, I was in my power and open, so I said yes. It's a good thing I did, because the universe can deliver in mysterious ways!

Not only was she kind and loving, but she was a successful relationship coach!

I eagerly asked her how she got started. She said she had studied under the most amazing woman named Rori Raye and that she could get me on a call with her. My jaw dropped. Rori was the author of the book that had dramatically changed the course of my life! Tingles ran down my spine. The universe indeed had my back, and this was the career path for me.

Over the next six months, I trained intensively with Rori. The training was incredible, and I got a lot of feedback from her about how I was a natural and would end up becoming incredibly successful as a coach.

Part of me felt validated, good, and as if I knew she spoke the truth. I trusted her. The other part of me started to gather a current that turned into a tsunami of self-doubt, self-criticism, and fear. All my old stories bubbled to the surface, and they came up strong!

Choosing to take the leap of faith into starting my own career, one where I would have a big voice in the world, was the biggest and scariest leveling up I had ever confronted.

Near the end of my training, it was time to start putting what I had learned and mastered out into the world. It was time to use my voice. The assignment was to write my first six client e-mails that would eventually go out to my e-mail list. Considering how much I had studied, learned, and applied, this should have been easy. My doubts became crippling. I sat with the first draft of the first e-mail for two whole months—I even found myself lashing out at important people in my life because I was frustrated with myself! Voices in my head ran rampant. "This has all been said before and better than you could ever do it. Who do you think you are telling people how to improve their lives? Nobody will listen to you anyway. The feminists will attack you. You can't even write one e-mail—how do you think you're going to run your own business? This is all a mistake." Yes, those voices—we all have them from time to time.

Because I had invested so much time and money into the training, I could not quit. (How do I illustrate the value of paying for coaching here without getting sales-ey?) I just kept taking small steps. I just kept moving. Finally, I found the courage to take a leap. I was about to go grocery shopping one night with a forty-five-minute window before a client call when my husband stopped me. He had a vision. "How about this? How about I go grocery shopping for you, and you get on Facebook and make a bold announcement that you are going to do a Facebook Live every night at seven o'clock for the next seven days." It was 6:50 p.m., and my heart started racing. "Really? But I don't know what I'm going to say. I don't even have makeup on right now!" He reassured me, "You've got this! Ten minutes is all you need." He took my keys and grocery list and kissed me good-bye. With the pressure on, I knew the time had come.

I had to stop hiding.

I had to stop worrying about how others would receive my message.

I had to stop being in my own way.

With my heart racing and palms sweating, I did it. I showed up every night at 7:00 p.m. and did a video, adding as much value as I could.

The phone calls, text messages, and Facebook messages came flooding in. Women were so ready, so hungry for my message. The feedback I got was so positive, and it didn't match the story in my head about how I thought people would react. To this day people still talk about the videos in this series. I knew I had to keep going.

I made one simple change that allowed me to accelerate. Instead of punishing myself for having all the voices of self-doubt and judgment, I started to love them. Sometimes, we spend all this time criticizing and judging ourselves and then we add another layer of judgment about the fact that we are doing it! It can be such a vicious cycle that only leads to more pain. We can't judge the judgment enough to make it go away. We can't criticize the criticism enough to make it go away. The most effective way that I've found to move through this is to start to love the voices.

If you take and try on any one thing from me, let it be this.

When they pop up, I stop and say, "I hear you, I love you, and I know that you are loving me the best way you know how. We are safe, and I'm going to do this anyway." I'll even cap this off with hugging myself. You see, when we start to love the parts of ourselves that we would rather not have or that we want to hide or get away from, we start to love all of ourselves. This is a practice that I know has personally changed my life and the lives of many of the women who I influence. It's a way of being with yourself that will immediately start to shift you into the strongest power in the universe: the power of love. I invite you to try this with every negative voice or undesirable emotion. So instead of letting those voices make decisions and direct your life, love them into submission. It's my belief that those voices, like children acting out, just need to be loved, not punished for existing.

As a result of this, I now stand as a woman of influence. I use my voice to lead. This does not mean that I've stopped questioning myself. What's changed is my relationship to the questioning. It doesn't stop me anymore—it empowers me to grow through it.

Modern femininity is a movement in which women are reclaiming their innate feminine power. Modern femininity is the fusion of practices that, when coupled with our presence, enhance our natural magnetism. Women often seek me out because they feel undervalued, misunderstood, and shut down. After just a few months of our working together, these women begin feeling authentically aroused by themselves and their lives. They can feel and act in their incredible self-worth. Women finally can feel and experience the self-love that has eluded them—the fairy tale starts with you. Men and relationships move from mystery and drama to that romantic comedy with sprinkles of challenges to grow from. Once women understand the secret world of masculine and feminine energy, the men in their lives either become inspired to step up or move out of their way so that they can have the relationships that they've always dreamed of.

ABOUT GABRIELLE GRAE

Gabrielle Grae is the founder of Modern Femininity, where she empowers women to master their feminine power.

If you want to move quickly toward embodying your most confident, grounded, radiant, magnetic, and irresistible self, then you are in the right place.

Gabrielle supports all women, from doctors, lawyers, and high-level executives to healers and even relationship coaches, in reclaiming their feminine power and having the love lives they want.

A client who is a top CEO states, "Gabrielle's work has done more for my anxiety in four sessions than years of traditional therapy and medication."

An intimacy coach who worked with Gabrielle says, "She speaks my language and teaches what I teach, except she is teaching me lots of new practices. More nourishing than anything: I don't have to think. She has my back. She holds space for me. She is my light. I trust her, and I rely on her."

On top of being mentored and trained in the Rori Raye method, she holds a bachelor's degree in psychology and has traveled the world from Europe to South America, healing herself and learning from top business coaches, famous hypnotherapists, energy workers, and shamans.

She looks forward to working with you and seeing you have everything you want in love and life.

You can find her in her women's group, facebook.com/Groups/ModernFemininity, or by visiting her website, www.GabrielleGrae.com.

BEING A MOM

Kim Haskan

I am an author, a teacher, a friend, a sister, a daughter, and a wife, but by far my proudest accomplishment is being a mom. In the front of each of my three children's baby books, I put the poem "Before I Was a Mom," author unknown...unfortunately. It talks about the emotional changes you go through when you become a mom. This poem, read at any baby shower, will have the room in tears and the first-time expectant mother sobbing (mostly because she is so hormonal) but not fully grasping the life-changing event that is about to happen to her. The stanza of the poem that impacts me the most is this: "Before I was a Mom...I didn't know the feeling of having my heart outside my body. I didn't know how special it could feel to feed a hungry baby. I didn't know that bond between a mother and her child. I didn't know that something so small could make me feel so important."

I was diagnosed with polycystic ovarian disease when I was a teenager. The doctor who confirmed my diagnosis went through a list of the side effects: irregular periods or no periods at all; excessive hair growth usually on the face, chest, back, or buttocks; weight gain; thinning hair and loss of hair from head; oily skin or acne; and difficulty getting pregnant. The whole list sounded as if I could become an attraction at the circus. "Come one! Come all! See the bearded fat lady!" But the side effect that affected me the most was difficulty getting pregnant. I had already discovered my love of children. I taught swimming, aerobics, and dance to young learners, and I loved every minute of it. But that experience also helped to build my résumé on my road to becoming a teacher. Thoughts spiraled in my head: "Would I work with children all day and not have any of my own? Would I be satisfied because I was around children all day and that would be enough?" The diagnosis resonated in my head...until I was actually pregnant.

My firstborn, Evin, was not a walk in the park to conceive. I was married at twenty-nine (tick-tock!) to a wonderful Turkish man named Gokhan Haskan, and we did have difficulty getting pregnant. I jumped on board seeing a gynecologist early on because I already knew I had a problem. I was introduced to the drug Clomid and then Gonal. The fertility treatments increased to the point of daily shots that had to be closely monitored by the clinic with regular vaginal and abdominal ultrasounds. Vaginal ultrasounds became the norm, but I hated the full bladder ultrasound. Once I rushed in to work late screaming, "Sorry I am late; I had an ultrasound again!" and a coworker said, "You go to a vaginal or an abdominal ultrasound every day?" I responded,

"Yes, but I like the vaginal ones!" What I meant was that I liked them better because you don't need a full bladder, but the joke between my female colleagues became that they were going to request vaginal ultrasounds from their doctors because they heard from a friend that they were "really good!"

Finally, we conceived Evin! I think some people might assume that after being through my experience and struggles I would embrace pregnancy. I did not. It felt too good to be true. I worried about things that were extremely far-fetched. I told the office administrator at my school that I was worried about driving. "What if my air bag goes off and hurts the baby?" I refused to have a photo taken of myself pregnant because I worried that if something happened I would be left with this memory of something that never happened. But thankfully it did happen, and Evin William Haskan was born October 15, 2002. He was actually due on Thanksgiving Day, so I would tell people when they asked me his due date that while they were having their eight-pound Thanksgiving turkey, I would be in a delivery room pushing that thing out!

Earlier, I did mention being the mother of three, and due to our troubles with Evin, we started fertility treatments again as soon as I could. Two weeks later we found out I was pregnant with Jayda Leigh Haskan. Feeling our family was complete, we stopped the fertility treatments after she was born. Not too long afterward, we received the news of a third pregnancy and had the gift that keeps on giving, Alara Glory Haskan. I went from infertile to Fertile Myrtle as I now had a newborn, an almost-two-year-old, and a three-year-old. I had three children in diapers, and I couldn't have been happier!

Yikes! Now it was time to raise them. My husband, being Turkish, was raised Muslim. I grew up in a Catholic family with Catholic friends in a Catholic area. To say that I was ignorant of other religions would be an understatement. When I went away to university, a girl on my floor was taking Hebrew lessons on Saturdays. Later in September she said she was going home to celebrate Rosh Hashanah with her family. I said to her, "I didn't know that you are Jewish," and she replied, "You knew I was going to Hebrew lessons." Yes, I was that stupid. I didn't make the connection. So when I started dating my husband, we ran into some cultural and religious stumbling blocks with our families and some friends. The support we received when planning our wedding was minimal. I wish I looked back on the planning and preparation for my wedding as an exciting, fun experience, but the truth is it was very difficult trying to please both families. We had the wedding in a chapel on my husband's university campus, played Turkish music on the organ, had readings from the Bible and the Qur'an, and yet neither family seemed happy. I told my sister on many occasions that we were going to cancel the wedding and elope.

The big concern for everyone was, "How are you going to raise your kids?" This question was often asked by strangers and was one I had difficulty answering. I'm sure I could have scared them away with my tales of my polycystic ovaries and my revelation that my deepest fear was not having children at all (aren't you glad you asked?). However, I responded with humor and would say we were planning to raise them Jewish and have a multidenominational household. The truth was I had absolutely no idea how I would deal with the religion issue if I was blessed enough to have children. I knew I wanted a balance of both, but I did not know what that would even look like. What we discovered was that the religions are more similar than they are different. We moved to Turkey together, and I spent time celebrating religious holidays with his family. It was a wonderful learning experience of acceptance and tolerance of all beliefs. As a result, our children have participated in both religions, and in my opinion, they have become more open-minded citizens of the world. I realize now that having two religions in the house has been a gift. I wish that as a twenty-nine-year-old getting married and entering this new phase of my life I had had the insight to explain this to the unsupportive bystanders, but I did not.

Flash-forward to December 2008. I was watching Oprah interview Christina Applegate, and she was discussing her diagnosis of breast cancer. It touched me because she was the same age I was and I had watched her on *Married with Children*. She recommended that everyone get what she called a baseline mammogram so the doctors would have a point of comparison. I don't know why, but as I was watching the show, I thought, "I am going to get breast cancer." I did what she suggested and went to my doctor, who said it wasn't necessary as I was not yet forty, did not have enough family history...yadda, yadda, yadda. But I pushed, and I had my mammogram and was told, "Don't come back for five years unless you notice some changes." Fantastic! That summer, my sister called me up with some bad news about her sister-in-law (no relation to me) being diagnosed with breast cancer in her thirties. I was shocked, and that night I decided to give myself a breast exam and found a lump. It was one year after my all clear. I am very thankful that I trusted my instincts and went for that baseline mammogram. The "see you in five years" allowed me never to question if I had missed something, if I should have done more. I was absolved of the guilt that many cancer patients feel over ignoring signs, avoiding doctors, and taking their health for granted.

At the time, the children were three, five, and seven, and this was a journey I did not know how to take them through. They were so young, and my husband and I were scared. I wasn't told a lot about the cancer by doctors, only that it was aggressive and to prepare for the worst. So many negative thoughts were going through my mind. I started to think about what age my children needed to be for me to die and not have my death change the course of their lives. It was one thing for them to grieve, but to have my death negatively alter the course of their lives seemed like a huge burden. It was these negative thoughts about the impact my death would have and how horrible it would be for my children that changed my focus of the treatment. This had quickly become an altruistic journey of getting through this as a family. Our plan was to tell them slowly and share only pertinent information. We did not want to scare them with the word "cancer" at first. We worried they would hear that grandmas, grandpas, aunts, and uncles had died of cancer. The most recognizable image schoolchildren have of cancer is Terry Fox. But he lost a leg and died of cancer at the early age of twenty-two. I knew I could go through treatment, but how would their young minds comprehend it? The task of explaining that Daddy's family referred to God as "Allah" seemed so much easier compared to this.

The diagnosis for breast cancer happened on December 3, 2009. The Saturday after I was diagnosed, I wanted to lie in bed and cry. That was actually my plan for the day, but my three children came into my room, saw me in bed, and said, "You promised we were making gingerbread men today." Clearly, I had made this promise before my diagnosis. I told them I was tired and we would do it another day, but they persisted. They didn't understand that I had just had devastating news and that I wanted to lie in bed and feel sorry for myself. They wanted their mom. So I got up, put on Christmas tunes, and rolled gingerbread. I felt great at the end of that day. I don't know how my day of crying would have gone, but I am guessing not as well.

The chemo treatment I was on was called FEC-T. I had triple-negative breast cancer and was given the drugs fluorouracil, epirubicin, cyclophosphamide, and taxotere. They were all very strong drugs that had side effects I wasn't prepared for. I knew about hair loss (which was horrible enough), but I also had to deal with nails falling off, holes burned in my bladder, and huge mouth sores that left me unable to eat. I was bald, nailless, and weak and weighed eighty-five pounds. When I came home from treatment, I would lie on the cold bathroom floor to feel less nauseated. Alara would knock on the door and in her cute little three-year-old voice say, "Mommy, when you are done lying on the bathroom floor, can we go to the park?" And I would get up. Never once did I go to the park and feel worse; I always felt better. They gave me the gift of laughter, and anyone in a horrible situation knows that the ability to make the person laugh can do wonders. I must admit I was often the butt of their innocent funny comments. When I first got my wig, the neighbors were having a party. I wanted to go, but I didn't want anyone to say anything about my wig. I put it on at home and everyone said it looked great. "Liars!" I thought, but I wanted to go. So I walked into the party, and Alara said, with jazz hands flailing, "Here's Mommy...with her wig!" At first I was embarrassed, but then I realized she was just saying what everyone at the party was thinking. "Here's Kim...look at her wig." A toddler pointing out the obvious was the best thing to happen. The emperor has no clothes!

During the journey through breast cancer with the children, we discovered they had a strong interest in knowing, helping, and being a part of my recovery. They took on the jobs of cleaning my stitches, choosing my scarves, and organizing the flowers that came to the house with pride and enthusiasm. I think the teacher in me created those jobs like the many classroom jobs I created—weather expert, paper passer, line leader, communication manager (answering the phone when it rings)—to allow the students to feel that they were an integral part of the daily routines and learning experiences. I wanted my children to feel included in my journey, to feel that they were helping. What I discovered was that they *were* helping! They were exactly what I needed to get through this. They were the light at the end of my journey, the reason I was being poked and prodded over and over. Other cancer patients would ask me how I got through treatment with three young kids, and my answer was always the same: "How do you do it without three young kids?" I would have been in the fetal position a lot more often if they hadn't needed me to get up and be their mom.

Being a mom is my favorite job, but I have had the job of being a teacher for over twenty years. The answer to whether teaching would be enough if I didn't have children was no, but it has been a very fulfilling career. Teaching is the best job in the world because, like the students, you are constantly learning. Being with young children brings happiness to my days. Young children are so wonderfully unaware of the differences among them. They think, "You like Cherry Coke...I like Cherry Coke...Let's be friends!" As they get older, they begin to recognize that there are differences between them, and we don't all like Cherry Coke. As an educator I have developed individual education plans (IEPs) and made accommodations or modifications in my program to make sure all students are successful. I realize the goals set out by the curriculum can seem like mountains to some while to others they are easily attainable. My hope is that children set their own individual goals and that in doing so, they not only climb mountains but dream big enough to move them. I feel I am a better teacher because I am a mom. I can help the students do their best, but there is always a mom voice in my head that says, "What if this were Evin, Jayda, or Alara? How would I want the teacher to react to the situation if it were one of them?" I think the balance of being an author, a teacher, a friend, a sister, a daughter, a wife, a survivor, and a mom has made me a stronger, more resilient, more caring person, both inside and outside the classroom.

Of all the different hats I have worn, parts I have played, and journeys I have been through, my most cherished accomplishment is being a mom to my three wonderful children. There have been many difficult moments and sacrifices. To quote "Before I was a Mom," before I was a mom, "I made and ate hot meals. I had unstained clothing. I had quiet conversations on the phone. I slept as late as I wanted and never worried about how late I went to bed. I brushed my hair and teeth every day." As they grew, this selfless discovery continued—I discovered the complete and utter desire to trade places with them and have their pain and hurt directed at me instead of them. The failed tests, parties not invited to, hurtful comments, unsaved goals, missed shots, no one to play with, rejected tryouts. You witness these events, often with front-row seats, and your heart breaks into a million pieces. But I wouldn't change a thing because I love being a mom!

Now for the teen years!

ABOUT KIM HASKAN

Kim Haskan is from Mississauga, Ontario, Canada. She lives with her husband, her three children, and two dogs. She is a teacher, an author, and a public speaker. She has had the privilege of speaking at schools, churches, golf tournaments, and the Toronto International Book Fair and was the keynote speaker at the Evening of Hope at North Bramalea United Church in 2014.

In 2013, Kim published a children's book called *Mommy Has a Boo Boo in Her Boob*, which is a recounting of her journey through breast cancer with three young children by her side.

In 2016, she wrote and published another children's book called *What We Believe*. It reassures readers that a dual-religion household—or one where no religion is taught—does not produce children lacking in morals and beliefs.

With the knowledge she gained from her many years teaching, she wrote and published a third children's book, *Yes You Can*. Kim's hope is that the story's message will help children to recognize that everyone learns differently. Her unique writing style of combining narratives, footnotes, and comic book influences makes her books appealing to an audience much wider than the usual young picture-book readers. If you visit www.kimhaskan.com, you can learn more about the author and her books.

DAY MAKER

Danielle Loraso

I t all started in the seventh grade with the question that at that point I had been asked a million times: "What do you want to be when you grow up?" As with many kids, my answers changed through the years. I would let my imagination take over in an attempt to figure out what I could feel most excited about. Astronaut? Seemed like fun; I really loved looking at the stars. Veterinarian? I liked dogs! Model? To this day, I am not sure where this one came from. Writer? In the sixth grade I wrote a series of books inspired by the television show *Frasier*, only it was pets calling in, asking for help with their crazy owners. But this time, when the question was asked, something changed. I wrote that I wanted to be a difference maker that I wanted to make a positive impact on the world. I didn't know how, but I knew I would figure it out someday.

Fast-forward several years. I was out of college and looking for my difference-maker job. Six months after graduation, I got a job in the public service. I used all of the skills I knew about the law of attraction to obtain this job; from the time I graduated from college I had visualized myself in a position making a difference. When the opportunity for this job came around, I printed out the job announcement and read it every single day. After my interview, I imagined myself driving up and walking into the building every day. When I got the call with the job offer, I thought I had arrived at my middle school daydream. I was a difference maker for a living!

But it didn't take long for me to discover that the job didn't completely align with my vision. In 2013 I was introduced to network marketing for the first time. My network-marketing story definitely isn't one of the get-rich-quick stories. In my first company I actually didn't make any money at all when it came to my year-end totals. However, I will be forever grateful, because it introduced me to the magical world of personal development. I took a deep dive and devoured books, attended events, and met some incredible people. One such event was Jack Canfield's Breakthrough to Success. One of his principles in particular struck a chord with me. I needed to take 100 percent responsibility for my life, my journey, and my mission to make a difference in the world. I discovered that making a difference isn't about an occupation at all. It's not what you are; it's who you are. With that, I committed to being a person who brings light to the world and leaves all people I meet better than when I found them. This is what I would later call being a "day maker."

I came to find that a majority of the ways to be a day maker were simpler than I had ever thought possible and made a bigger impact than I ever could have dreamed. My day maker mission broke down to three key areas: self, personal world (family, friends, and people you meet when going about your life), and professional world.

I focus first on being a day maker for myself because it is my belief that all success rises and falls on self-love and appreciation. Self-love and appreciation can come in many forms; however, I believe that they need to start with thoughts and self-talk. I wake up in the morning and declare that it's going to be a good day, and for the most part it always comes true! Throughout the day I take time to notice the things that I appreciate, and at night I reflect on all the things that I am grateful for. Throughout the day I repeat the affirmations that help me get to my goals. To the fullest extent possible, I remove all negativity in my life. This has come in the form of no longer listening to or reading the news and instead replacing it with audiobooks and uplifting music (and dance parties when the moment is right).

I once heard that all transformation is rooted in integrity. Most often we tend to keep our word with others—a coffee date, a favor, a special deadline; however, when it comes to ourselves, we let it slide. In being an ultimate day maker for yourself, you must have the integrity to stick with the self-care practices that work best for you. Schedule them into your day and act as if each one is an important meeting with your best friend, because it is.

My top tips for becoming a day maker for yourself:

- Become as fierce with your integrity with yourself as you are with your friends. Also be as reasonable with yourself and what you can get done in a single day as you would if you were delegating all of the work to someone else. Do not overload yourself and set yourself up for failure. We want to be able to celebrate our daily wins here!

- Monitor your self-talk and flip it around when necessary. Would you put up with a friend's saying what you say to yourself? If not, change it! Once you recognize the negative self-talk and replace it with something better, you'll discover that it feels good to be nice to yourself.

- Begin the day with the positive intention that it's going to be a day filled with magic and miracles (fill in whatever intention feels best to you) and write down ten things or people you're grateful for. How you start your day is generally how the rest of it will go: start the day on a positive note!

- Create a daily practice that includes quiet time just for you. This may be meditation, journaling, stretching, yoga, or coffee or tea time—anything that feels good and is just for you! Protect this time as if your life depends on it, because it does!

- Give yourself permission to live the life of your wildest dreams. If you haven't taken the time, really think about what this looks like in every aspect of your life. Make sure what you write down is what you truly want for yourself. Don't worry about what your friends might think. This is a judgment-free zone, and you get to choose what part of your vision to share with other people!

- Reflect weekly and celebrate all of the things that you have accomplished that week.

- Find a day maker buddy to help you find things to celebrate weekly!

For many people, the world is filled with negativity. Finding the bad is as simple as flipping on the television or listening to the radio for a few minutes. When you ask someone how he or she is doing, it's much more common to hear a complaint than to hear fantastic news, especially if the person is a stranger. With our friends, many people find it easier to sit around and gossip or dwell than to brag about the amazing things happening in their lives. I have made a great effort to be a positive light in the lives of others, both those I know and those I don't. I also take this mission seriously both online and offline.

In the online world, I often hear of people wanting to take a step back because their newsfeeds are filled with negativity. For that reason, I run everything I post through a filter. Is it kind? Positive? Uplifting? Something funny to brighten the days of others? If it doesn't meet any of those criteria, I ask myself if it is necessary to share. If not, I skip it. That's not to say that my life is all rainbows and sunshine 100 percent of the time, but remember that thoughts become things, and you get to keep the story you tell over and over again!

In the offline world (a.k.a. the "real world") it is my belief that the world can use as much sunshine as humanly possible. Many people are going through tough times that we know nothing about. One of my favorite lessons in life has been to be kind whenever possible and to remember that it's always possible. There are many ways that you can be a day maker in the lives of others. Many are free, some cost a little money, and some cost more. Most often I find that you don't have to spend much money at all to make a lasting impact on the lives of others. Simple gestures and letting people know that you care can go a long way.

Here are some examples of becoming a day maker in the lives of others:

- Be your friends' biggest cheerleader: celebrate the success of the people in your life. Give a level of excitement and congratulations as if the success were yours.
- Do something just a little above and beyond a Facebook post to acknowledge their birthdays. This can be as simple as a voice message through Facebook, a phone call, or sending a card.
- Send a card in the mail to let someone special in your life know how much you appreciate him or her. I use an app on my phone that allows me to personalize the card with a picture that is special to that person. When I want to go above and beyond in making the person's day, I include brownies with the card.
- For exceptional service at a restaurant, bar, hotel, etc., consider leaving a larger-than-normal tip or a nice note of appreciation or letting employee's manager know about how the employee went above and beyond.
- Start a pay-it-forward chain in the drive-through, paying for the order behind you.
- Offer a smile to anyone who needs one. You may be the only one who makes that person feel seen throughout the day.
- Hold a door open.

Studies show that upward of 80 percent of people either hate or don't enjoy their jobs. Along these same lines, the things that keep people in their jobs more than money are appreciation, recognition and praise. At work especially I feel that it's difficult to know if you've made a positive impact unless it's pointed out directly. Some companies have a kind of award system in which employees can nominate one another. I nominated a coworker whom I worked closely with on a special project. The day he received the award, he was absolutely beaming. It meant a lot to him to know that his hard work did not go unrecognized. However, in my experience and in speaking with friends and family in other companies, this very simple action of recognition is underutilized.

I attempt to work in line with the Golden Rule, always bringing a positive energy and attitude to work. Because of that I am often a go-to person for the newer employees although that's not part of my job description. When I returned from my maternity leave, I came back to an award with the following message:

> I am pleased to recommend Ms. Danielle Loraso for a special contribution award. Ms. Loraso is being recognized for her contribution as a mentor. Ms. Loraso provided superior service in assistance to internal individuals that affects overall success of the office. Danielle was not even a mentor; yet she was always available to help, answer questions, provide training, and document manual references to all trainees (regardless of whether you were assigned to her or not). She always assisted you with a smile and was eager to help, following up to ensure you understood what to do and why. She never seemed too busy or made you feel you were imposing on her time. Each and every time you sought her assistance, she went "above and beyond the call of duty." Ms. Loraso's contribution to the office does not go unnoticed and is deserving of recognition. As a result of the

aforementioned reasons, it is my pleasure to recommend Ms. Loraso receives a special contribution award.

It's important to note that the recognition does not have to be as detailed or elaborate as the one I received. A simple "I appreciate you for making my job easier/my days better," etc., can go a long way to improve office morale and culture; after all, you spend a lot of your time with your coworkers!

Examples of being a professional day maker:

• If you're in a position to do so, suggest a culture of appreciation and recognition.

• Serve as a "good catcher" when a coworker goes above and beyond; compliment or thank your coworker directly. Alternatively, make contact with your coworker's boss to let him or her know how awesome your coworker is.

• Drop out of the "ain't it awful" club and engage in only positive conversation. Raise the vibes of the office.

I feel compelled to share my story and day-maker mission because I believe that there can be a ripple effect that makes a true difference in the world. A lot of people go through their days silently hurting, and small actions can make a big difference. I got a response from one of my cards that said, "I had a negative vibe today I just could not shake after having a panic attack last night. But when I got your card it flipped me just like a switch, and I am dreaming big, positive dreams again. Thank you for being the beautiful person that you are!"

It's important to note that not all day-making efforts will receive a response, but it's safe to assume that they have a powerful impact anyway. Can you imagine if all of our day-making actions had even a fraction of that impact? My mission as a day maker is to brighten days, one person at a time, getting one dream back on track at a time. I envision a giant ripple effect and pay-it-forward movement. If just one person a day got reset on a positive path, it could make such a powerful difference. Positive energy is so much stronger than negative energy. We can begin to change the world, just by making one day at a time. I hope you'll join me.

ABOUT DANIELLE LORASO

Danielle Loraso is the founder of the Exceptional Life Project. She is a transformational coach with a passion for helping people realize and achieve their strongest desires in life, offering both group and private one-on-one coaching as well as vision-board workshops.

Danielle has lived on the bright side of life from a very young age; it was only natural for her to become a professional day maker. She sets out daily to make the world a better place through intentional acts of kindness. Her special brand of sunshine often comes in personalized greeting cards sent to friends, capturing their favorite moments through pictures.

She is an Arizona State University alumna and has earned her certification in Jack Canfield's Success Principles Trainer Program.

She lives in Phoenix, Arizona, with her daughter Grace and fur babies Doodle, Ricky, and Zoey.

Danielle is thrilled to be leading a movement of positivity, light, and kindness.

Connect with Danielle:

Facebook: www.facebook.com/DanielleLoraso

Instagram: @theexceptionallifeproject

Website: www.theexceptionallifeproject.com

TRUSTING MYSELF

Ashley Olivine

Nearly three years of struggle took a new direction when I collapsed onto the floor of a public bathroom stall. With my cheek pressed against the cold, hard surface, my first thought was about what might be covering the floor. That's when I attempted to place my arm under my head, but nothing budged. My world was spinning. Watching the feet beneath the walls of the stall, I called out, but my voice did not follow. As the feet disappeared, I wondered how long I would lie there before someone noticed my motionless body.

As my thoughts drifted to my daughter and what would happen to her since I was unable to move, my awareness of my surroundings became foggy, and I'm not exactly sure what happened. Eventually I was rescued by the most caring paramedics I had ever met, who brought extra heated blankets to warm my uncontrollably shaking body. They didn't leave the ER until they were sure I was in good hands. When nurses took over, they went above and beyond with their kind words and care for me. As I had arrived by ambulance, they even insisted on arranging and paying for my transportation back to my car. For the first time in years, I felt hope, like things might actually get better.

Before I tell the story of the events leading up to the day I collapsed, I want to be clear that I do not blame my medical providers in any way. Except for one bad apple, they all tried to help, and they did the best they could with the training, clues, and information they were given, but modern science has its limits.

Once upon a time, life was relatively normal. My perfect husband, Max, and I were preparing for a cross-country move and couldn't have been more excited about it. He's active duty military, so we don't choose each new location, but we're always up for the adventure. Timing is never ideal, but this seemed to be the best opportunity for a baby.

Moving day rolled around shortly after that first, magical ultrasound to confirm pregnancy. Max and I sat in the front of the moving truck that held all our belongings and was pulling our car, with a hundred-pound German Shepherd on my lap and a little hairless dog squeezed in somewhere. We were ecstatic, and we drove over two thousand miles in less than three days. By "we drove," I mean Max drove the entire way, without cruise control, in an old, beat-up moving truck, while I begged him to pull over at every restroom stop.

Pregnancy was no longer happy when something didn't seem quite right. There were strange symptoms that didn't add up. When I brought them to the attention of my medical team, all my symptoms were found to be normal during pregnancy. However, my research and intuition told me it was something more. After one too many doctors told me it was just pregnancy, I fell into a state of self-doubt and focused my attention on counting down the days until I could enjoy my new baby and feel good again.

My perfect little girl, Katelyn (a.k.a. Kate, Katie, Katesie), was born as the calendar year ended, yet my condition steadily declined. Once again, I sought medical attention because I was no longer pregnant but feeling worse by the day. They ran some standard blood tests, which all came back normal. As with the previous diagnosis of pregnancy, I was told that feeling ill was normal for new mothers, especially when breastfeeding.

My career suffered. As someone who at times had to choose between using energy to get dressed or sit upright for prolonged periods of time, my only choice was to work remotely from home. OK, confession: my desk was pushed up against the couch, so sometimes I worked lying down. Prior to getting sick, I had big dreams of changing the world through meaningful and reward-ing employment. Who was going to hire and keep someone who couldn't even sit up just because she was a mom? Remember, at this point, the tests had come back normal, and the only ra-tionale was that parenting isn't easy. Once again, I took this to mean that I wasn't good enough, because so many others had careers and were making it work.

Determined not to fail, I made a promise to myself that I was going to have a worthwhile career, so I started a business with the vision of flexibility around the needs of myself and my family. Before moving across the country and having a baby, I was working as an adult sleep coach in a clinical setting. I would now offer these services remotely, so location would no longer be a limitation to accessing needed services. The idea was perfect, but I struggled to grow the business because I was stretched too thin. The previously unstoppable girl who had volunteered internationally and dreamed of using her career to give back in a big way was now the one in need of help.

My family suffered. As Katelyn transitioned to sleeping through the night, my health continued to decline, even though it was supposed to get better once I was no longer waking for feedings. She hit one developmental milestone after another, and I felt as though I was missing out on her life because I was too sick to be fully present. Max had to watch my health deteriorate, not knowing what was happening or what he could do to help. I had to stop going to watch his soccer games because I didn't know if I could walk from the car to the field, and I certainly didn't feel confident about being able to run after someone who was not yet old enough to understand that she couldn't go out on the field during the games. Since I couldn't pull my own weight, our family was stretched thin, and quality time together was sacrificed just to accomplish the essentials. My daily energy was so limited that after a full day of working, I had nothing left over for the people who deserved it most.

As someone who desperately wanted to turn a house into a home with each move, cook comfort meals, throw birthday parties for Katie, make each holiday a special celebration, and have date nights with my husband (or date days because we go to bed early), I was failing. Even as a friend I was failing, because I didn't have anything left to keep up with those relationships.

It was a strange, mystery disease that was taking control of my entire life. Some days, or some parts of some days, I felt almost normal. I was even able to run a half marathon, because on a good day, exercise helped. Other times I was so weak that I was unable to lift my arms. I can remember filling out paperwork in a medical waiting room, and I struggled to hold the pen and clipboard. My brain was foggy, and I had to reread each question multiple times before answering. Writing was nearly impossible, and circling options was confusing. I'm still not sure if any of what I filled out was accurate. By the time I got to the exam room, I struggled to sit upright. As I waited for the doctor, I stared at the floor, seriously contemplating lying down on it.

Max gave me the benefit of the doubt that something was wrong with my health, but it really did seem as if I were crazy. Even though he believed me, he didn't know what to do. When I put my hand in the blender and accidently leaned against the power button, he fixed me up and poured alcohol on the wound twice per day. What could he fix when nobody could find anything broken? Outwardly, I looked fine.

My illness was invisible and didn't show up on medical tests. I began to doubt myself and wondered if I were just weak and inadequate. This led to guilt, embarrassment, and shame. Other moms had it all together, many with multiple kids, and I couldn't even handle one well-behaved little girl. If I had plans to be in public, even if I was just going to the store for a few items, I would rest for days in preparation so my symptoms would not be noticed by anyone. There was a deceptive smile painted on my face, and if anyone asked, everything was great. Too often I opted out of leaving the house at all, partially due to fear of not being able to walk, stand, or even sit and partially because I was ashamed of what people would think if they noticed what I had become.

Asking for help was out of the question, mostly because of my own fears. As a military family, we don't stay in one place too long, and neither do the people around us. We didn't have family support nearby, and it seemed that as soon as I got close to someone, one of us left. If I had asked for help from someone I didn't know very well, especially since I didn't have a diagnosis of anything other than typical mom struggles, what would she have thought? It didn't seem like the best way to make new friends.

As time passed, I became more and more frustrated with myself and my inability to do much of anything. That meant I had to push harder to overcome, because a healthy mom of one should have been able to do more. This was the complete opposite advice I would have given to any of my clients in a similar situation, but for some comical reason, I thought it was different in my case. That's how I ended up on the floor of a public bathroom.

While lying in the hospital bed that day, I watched the clock and calculated how much time I had before I would need to pick Kate up from what we called school but was really an exceptional daycare that incorporated learning. Of course, Max was a million miles away at the time, and I had not yet learned my lesson about asking for help. There was an amazing friend I could have called, but I felt guilty because she had kids of her own and way too much on her plate for me to add one more thing without prior notice. Looking back, I know she would have dropped everything to be there, with complete support and no judgment. Instead, I removed my IV and informed a nurse that I was feeling better. She compassionately gave me "the look" and wished me the best.

That night, like many nights before and after, the mere thought of preparing food and caring for a little one was exhausting. The strategy was to get her occupied with a toy, lie down on the kitchen floor to rest, stand up to grab a food item from the fridge, lie down on the floor to rest, remove a bowl from the cupboard, lie down on the floor to rest, and repeat for each step until something was prepared enough for us to sit on the floor and eat it.

After regaining some of the energy that I had expended throughout the dinner process, I carefully collected a few toys and placed them in the portable crib. Fortunately, Katelyn had not yet learned how to climb out, so I put her in. Since she always wanted to be with me, I climbed in as well. That way, I knew she was safe and her needs were being met, but I could rest. To this day, our lying in her crib together is one of her fondest memories.

From the crib, we video chatted with Max, which was great because Katelyn always had a bad day when she hadn't been able to talk to her dad the previous night. I contemplated if I should tell him about my ER visit. He was unable to help, and I knew it would upset him, but I told him anyway. I assured him I was feeling better, but he still wished we were together so he could help. Katelyn and I missed him even more than we had before.

The next few weeks were packed with medical tests and appointments, which were squeezed in before another move. Providers that didn't have openings managed to find space, and my last appointment was the same day I gave up the keys to the house. Since I was finally starting to warm up to the idea of accepting help, a friend who was living in a different state entertained Katie on a video chat while I cleaned the oven the night before. It was a lifesaver. No, I was not all moved out in time, but I managed to reschedule the final walkthrough to later in the day. Someone else just happened to have changed her time, creating an opening.

Life started to improve as soon as our family was living under the same roof again, but my health was still a mystery. One day I was feeling a bit better, so I decided to take Katie to the park. This was something I hadn't been able to do in a while, and the guilt was building up. Kids should be able to play outside, and she wanted to go nearly every day. We walked the extremely short distance, and by the time we arrived, I had trouble standing. I sat down on the bench to regain my energy for the walk home and worried that other parents would judge me for not taking advantage of the priceless opportunity to spend quality time with my child. She wanted me to play with her and push her on the swing. My heart broke because I wanted to, but I didn't know how I would get us back safely without resting. As soon as I felt I had enough energy, we made our way home.

I had also committed to making dinner that night, but as I stumbled onto the couch, that task seemed impossible. While Max was in the kitchen making dinner, I felt more guilt because once again, he had to change his plans because of me. It wasn't that he didn't want to help. This was a man who took the red-eye just so he could chaperone Katie's first field trip and take us to dinner before flying out the next day. He had always done all he could to support us; I just didn't want him to have to constantly do my share because I was always sick.

Lying on the couch, I desperately searched every website and scholarly journal article I could find that might hold a clue to help my condition. I was beyond done living a partial life, and I was even more done watching my family suffer because of my illness. I searched and searched until the pieces started to fit together. I called to Max in the kitchen, telling him in excitement that I had figured out what was going on with my body and which test I needed. I was going to get better.

At my next medical appointment, the doctor I had just met asked me a few questions, looked me in the eye, and explained that I had multiple sclerosis. At first, I felt relieved and ecstatic that we had finally reached a discovery, there would be a treatment plan, and I was not crazy for imagining an illness that wasn't there. As he pulled out his prescription pad and started talking about different therapies, I realized why he thought I had MS and asked him about my recent brain and spinal cord MRI. He told me about the spots that were found, and I told him about my previous brain and spinal cord injuries. He turned around to review the notes again, and then he turned back to me and apologized. He no longer knew what was wrong, but he assured me that he would run more tests. I made sure he ordered the blood test I suspected would be positive.

After what seemed like an eternity of waiting, I picked up my blood test results. The anticipation was getting the best of me as I read through the results, and after thorough review, I realized the test I had requested was not listed. They told me I had all the results, and nothing else was pending. I was passed between multiple people to try to find the missing test, because I wasn't leaving without it. Finally, it was found, and it was positive, or abnormal. I called Max with the news, but he did not share my level of excitement. Apparently, he didn't want his wife to be sick (go figure), so I tried to convince him that this was good news because now I could heal.

It was real this time; I knew I had an autoimmune disease, and I was going to start getting better. Having been in the health and wellness field for years at that point, I had knowledge, experience, and friends in the industry. This was a huge advantage and helped me develop a plan of action before I could even be seen by a specialist.

Once I finally saw the specialists about the positive test, there wasn't much they could do, again, because modern medicine only goes so far. When one doctor found out I had driven two hours to the appointment, she suggested I go to the beach, as it was only a couple miles away. That was unrealistic. I didn't have the energy for the beach, and I had so much work to do. Plus, I had a business call scheduled for the drive home. When we got in the car, I begged Katelyn to nap so she would be quiet for my call, as I thought it was unprofessional to work with a child. From the back seat I heard a little mouse squeak, "Let's go to the beach!" She was right. There was scientific evidence to show benefits of spending time at the beach. So I took my call, explained what was going on, and unapologetically declared that I would be at the beach. I was still on the phone when we arrived. Katie took off all her clothes and began joyfully running in the sand. I didn't stop her. When my call was over, I played with her (but remained clothed). The beach became our appointment tradition, and it was a healing experience.

I am a strong believer in the balance between holistic and modern medicine and addressing both the body and the mind. I hold no judgment against anyone who chooses 100 percent holistic or 100 percent medicinal therapies for his or her treatment, because everyone is different, has different needs, and responds differently to treatments. There were times when I was desperate for relief and tried prescription medications. They may have helped in some areas temporarily, but overall, they made me feel worse. There were holistic therapies that may have done absolutely nothing and others that I fully believe can be credited for my recovery.

Difficulty sleeping is a common symptom of many health complications, and not getting enough quality sleep makes all health conditions substantially worse because the body and mind heal, process, and reset during sleep. As a sleep expert, I was able to keep my sleep on track. Of course, there were times where I didn't sleep as well or enough, especially when Katie was a baby, but those phases were relatively short. When I did start to struggle in that area, I got myself back on track quickly, so it never escalated into a major problem.

At some point I realized the same cognitive techniques used for sleep could be used for all my symptoms and my overall health. Once I initiated a custom program for myself, my health and my life started to improve dramatically. Additionally, retraining my neural pathways gave me the ability to follow through with challenging lifestyle changes. While I was already careful to fill my body with healthy foods and avoid harmful environmental toxins, recovering required me to take things to the next level. It may have been extreme for a while, but something worked, and I got better.

I received neuromuscular and myofascial release massage therapy, dry brushed my skin, diffused and applied essential oils, used a charcoal sponge, washed my hair with products that gave me a bad hair day every day, put my drinking water through four filters, added trace minerals, purified with supplements, followed a very strict nutrition regimen, exercised when I was physically able, tried to grow all my own food organically (that may have been a bridge too far—and Max was less than pleased with the indoor jungle), and the list goes on. All my sacrifices and efforts were completely worth it when I was finally able to function again. Life got better in every way. The needs of my family were being met, and we were all happier. Not only did my career begin to flourish, but the entire experience inspired me to branch out from sleep and develop services to support women struggling with health and life, including the typical maternal struggles. If my debilitating disease could be masked by "normal" mom struggles, every mom needs support, and I am making it more readily available. I'm determined to turn my hardship into an opportunity to help others and change the way we see our roles in our own health and happiness.

From a wellness perspective, there's a big gap when it comes to maternal and women's health and autoimmune diseases. Even after that positive blood test, I had doctors apologize and tell me they didn't know what to do to help me. There are way too many women and mothers in similar shoes but without the knowledge and resources I had available to me through my education and professional experience. Looking back at how I went from being miserable and needing others to care for me to being healthy, happy, and able to care for others, I know this world would be a better place if more of us could feel in control of our health and happiness. I have a vision that empowerment through health, both of body and of mind, will create a movement of self-fulfill-ment and contribution to society. I'm determined to reach and support as many women and mothers as possible so we can live the lives we want and enable others to do the same. Life is too short for us to be sick and miserable.

ABOUT ASHLEY OLIVINE

Ashley is a military wife and the mother of a lively little girl, and she has another baby on the way. She and her family currently live in California, where they enjoy being active outside in the perfect weather with long runs and bike rides along the ocean. They don't know where they will be next, but they are always up for a new adventure.

Ashley holds a master's degree in public health and is working on a PhD in health psychology. She also holds certifications in health coaching, cognitive behavioral therapy, and sleep science. As a cofounder of Epigen Wellness Group, she helps people fall asleep and stay asleep without medications. Her real passion lies in serving clients in her private practice and helping them overcome physical and emotional struggles so that they may gain control of their health and happiness.

You can learn more about Ashley and her mission to empower women to claim their health and happiness on her website and on social media:

Web: ashleyolivine.com

Facebook: ashleyolivineofficial

Instagram: @ashleyolivine

Twitter: @ashleyolivine

THE POWER OF CHOICE!

Laurie Ann Riker

MY STORY

When I was growing up, my parents were emotionally and sometimes physically unavailable, and I often felt frightened, confused, and alone. I did, however, have a lot of freedom and independence. I had a lot of responsibility early. I was the middle of five siblings; my older brother, sister, and I raised one another. Who knew the impact this would have on me?

I always had this nagging feeling that I had done something wrong or that there was something not quite right with me. Why else would my parents decide not to love and care for me? I did try to get my parents to love me in a cautious way. I took on the role of the "good girl." I used to think that if I cleaned the house perfectly, prepared creative meals, kept quiet, and worked to quell the chaos, maybe my parents would give me the love I was desperate for. None of these things worked, of course; I still came home to my mom passed out on the floor and my dad's ambivalence toward me or misdirected anger at the world. I learned to bury all the trauma that consistently surrounded us and ignore all the disappointments and expectations. I shut down my ability to express my feelings or to feel much of anything at all. I became numb.

I managed to survive my earlier years and make it to adulthood, even though I knew that somehow I was different. I felt that I did not quite belong anywhere. I maintained a solemn, aloof demeanor that protected me from being hurt or cracking my façade of safety. Not feeling anything kept me in a bubble, so I could look out but no one could reach in. I adopted feeling disconnected, feeling different, as a strength. My strength came to be my friend in life—a strength that kept me from participating in life.

As a young adult, I knew I was searching for something. I wanted to feel happy and excited about my life, but I still felt empty inside. I knew I needed to fill my bank with something. I needed something to fill that internal hollowness. So I want to share with you three events in my life that helped me find (create, really) a much happier and fulfilled me.

RUNNING FOR MY LIFE

I was living and working in New York. One brisk Saturday morning, I witnessed a rush of men and women of all shapes and sizes running across the finish line of the New York City

Marathon. Wow! Amazing. These people had just finished running 26.2 miles, and they were beaming—yes, some were exhausted and others outright hobbled, but they all were glowing with accomplishment. What they had was what I needed. Sign me up!

I joined a Road Runners club to start training. I had never run a race, never trained for anything physical in my life. I had no idea what I was getting myself into. The running club provided me with the basics of how to run. There were organized running groups to join (a running family!). Even better, I had a community that cheered me on and helped me focus on this one goal.

I had done a little jogging and could cover about three miles. My newfound running friends assured me that if I could run three miles, I could run six miles. I had never run that far in my life—but gullible me, I believed them, so I entered a 10K race.

When I was training with my newfound family, I found safety and a sense of belonging. I also started to mend fences with my own birth family. I learned to accept my parents for who they were and started to see that their struggles had nothing to do with me. I invited my mom and dad to watch me run.

Race day came, and I was nervous, with butterflies in my tummy and a burning need to visit the port-a-potty several times. Finally, the race started. I realized I did not want to be the last one across the finish line. My fear of this embarrassment factor served as good motivation—to my utter delight, I finished in the middle of the pack. Not bad for a first-timer. I felt my chin rise slightly higher and experienced a feeling of joy I had not felt for a long time. I did it!

I finished a few more 10K races and was thrilled when I beat my best race time. I was ready to graduate to the next level, a half marathon. This meant I had to train to run at least ten miles before the race. My training runs were longer, and I added some cross-training, such as speed drills and stairs. The Sunday before the race, I ran a ten-miler with some friends. So far, so good. Race day came, and again I was very nervous, and the same prayer came to mind: *Please don't let me be the last one across the finish line.* On you mark, get ready, bang. I was off and running. Two and a half hours later, I ran across the finish line! I was definitely wearier after 13.2 miles than after the ten miles a week before. However, I was one step closer to my goal of the full marathon.

If I could run a half marathon, I could run a whole marathon—at least that is what experienced runners told me. I learned that when you train or even finish a marathon, you enter an elite class of runners called marathoners. I wanted the title and to enter into that class. What I wanted even more was to cross the finish line after running 26.2 miles. I wanted what I had experienced in New York.

I registered for a marathon three months away in San Diego. I was working a full-time job and worked a lot of hours, and I was not sure how I was going to find the time to up my weekly mileage and work toward running twenty-two miles in less than three months. I didn't really have a runner's body. I started doubting that I could achieve this feat. Did I really want to do this? Did I really want to commit all this time toward running a race? Why was I doing this? I did know that I needed to prove something to myself, but I was not sure at the time what the impact would be. Still, it felt important enough for me to do it, even if it meant giving up other activities. I also reminded myself that if the people in New York did it, I could do it.

I knew it was going to be hard, training my body and mind to run a distance that they had never run before. Luckily, sometimes I just got lost in the run. I did experience running in the zone, which is a high in itself. It was meditative and catchy. During these training runs, I would visualize myself running across the finish line. My mantra became "one step at a time." I do have to tell you there were some days I did not want to put those shoes on, did not want to spend an hour, least of all a whole day, running. Even in the weakest moments, I focused on my goal and how it would feel to cross that finish line.

Yikes! It was race day. To my surprise, my mom, dad, younger sister, and younger brother decided to join me! My dad and sister entered the 10K race. I was really looking forward to seeing them at the finish line. Their race started before mine. I shed my extra layers at the race staging area for the start and ate the last bite of a bagel (a running staple), the gun fired, and there I was with thousands of other runners.

We ran through the rain, all through San Diego, by the ocean, downtown, and were greeted with music, food, and drinking water. Even in the rain, there were a lot of folks supporting us. I would hear an occasional, "One foot in front of the other, Laurie" (I painted that on the back of my T-shirt). I felt pretty good. Five miles, ten miles. Another shout out: "One foot in front of the other, Laurie. You can do this." I felt I really could finish that race. I had been moved to tears a couple of times already during that run. The rain was steady. I breezed by the eighteen-, nineteen-, and twenty-mile marks.

When I reached the twenty-one-mile marker, my legs almost stopped. They felt like lead. I hit the wall! Oh no! I felt panic and disappointment. I tried to start again, after walking a few feet and drinking some water. I am not sure if I heard someone say or I said, "One food in front of the other, Laurie," But I just started moving. My mind took over. I had never run this far; my body was not trained for this. One foot in front of the other, Laurie. One mile, two miles, three miles—I was so focused on my feet moving that I did not realize that I was a half a mile out. I saw Jack Murphy Stadium. I started crying, I could feel it—I was going to cross the finish line. I gathered speed and ran as fast as I could, giving it all that I had left. I ran across the finish line. I heard my name. I looked up, and there were my dad and younger sister, dripping wet! I laughed and cried as they hugged me. I was high as a kite! My parents were there; they had showed up! I did not know what was next for me, but this accomplishment filled up an empty spot in my being. I experienced joy, connectedness, and confidence! I had proven to myself that I had the capacity for hard work and the ability to retain focus and achieve a goal I had set for myself. I felt chills in that moment, and I realized that the love I so desperately wanted and needed was right there in me. I had done this for myself! I loved myself!

FINDING LIFE IN THE DEATH OF A LOVED ONE

I witnessed my sister's last breath a couple of years ago. I had heard that angels and sometimes a white light appear when a loved one passes. I waited for the angels to come and sing in my ear and the white light to appear. I didn't get any of that. She was just gone.

Susan was like a twin to me. We shared the same room until we were teenagers. We shared the same family dynamic, and we were both sensitive. We fought, shared secrets, and giggled together. I remember one time we went on vacation together. We rented wave runners. Susan and I laughed so hard that I could barely stay on the thing. I sensed she loved the freedom of riding a bit recklessly over the waves just as much as I did. I can still see her laughing like a loon. She loved being silly and attracting everyone else into her antics.

Sue definitely had her own challenges dealing with our family troubles. I was one of the people she called on. I listened to her sometimes for hours. I often held her hand.

At one point in our adult lives, something shifted between us, and instead of Sue sharing her woes with me, she asked how I was doing. I felt confused and a little uncomfortable, but I went with it. I started talking about myself. Sue was curious, wanted to know more, was excited for me. I don't know how the shift occurred. I knew she had always loved me, but now she was my cheerleader, she was excited to hear about my successes or challenges, and she believed in me. She became my friend. For a while we got in the habit of Saturday-morning coffee—we caught up over the phone with our coffees in hand. I felt loved, and I felt connected. I needed it, I think, more than she did.

I wish I had more of her. More laughter, more secrets, and way more of her big sister care.

I spent the last week of her life holding her hand, reading to her, and playing her favorite songs. She was mostly unconscious, but I believe she knew I was with her. One of my most vivid memories of her during that week was when, during a lucid moment, I took her outside the hospice center one afternoon. She was in her wheelchair. At one point, she looked up at me with her bright green eyes and made me swear a promise. The promise she had me make was that I would take my life on and live it to the fullest. What a promise. I work on it every day.

I had a sister who loved me, and I can hold on to that. I miss her and feel very blessed by her spirit. Her essence of love is with me; I can tap into it anytime I want. She encourages me whenever I ask.

A PATH TO MOTHERHOOD

I had dreamed of being a mother ever since I was a little girl. My mom had five of us. My youngest sister had three, but here I was in my early forties and I had none. After kissing a few frogs, I was blessed to fall in love with a man who shared my dreams of a family. Yeah! What I did not know at the time of our marriage vows was that I could not have children. Yes, we went through the tests and tried fertility doctors, but the results were sad and clear.

A part of me was in denial at the time; I just could not imagine not being a mother or having a baby! This was my dream and now our dream. I felt partially responsible for my body's not cooperating. My husband never said a word to me about my challenge. Adoption seemed to be the only option for us at that point. My husband was open to a conversation about the process and procedures. We found a couple of local agencies. We learned about open adoption, a common practice in America. A young woman who gives up her baby for adoption gets to choose who gets to be parents of her child, and later in life, if she changes her mind, she can reclaim her child. We were not deterred. We started down that path only to be met with sincere opposition. We were probably not going to get picked because we were older parents. Huh? Really? We were established, well-adjusted adults. We were told, "Kids who give up their babies want parents closer to their age."

I kept dreaming about cuddling my baby in my arms. I overheard a couple talk about international adoption. There I went again. My husband was indeed open to the conversation. After many months of research and discussion, we were going to adopt a baby from China. It is an arduous process. I do not have the mind-set for details; my husband does. We were interviewed and wrote life-history papers that were included in a dossier that was sent to China. We were now in the waiting period. This was a very difficult time for me. I started having doubts about my ability to be a mother. Would I love a baby that was not my own? Would I be emotionally ready? How would I understand an infant from another country? The social worker assured me that these were natural concerns. This helped ease my fears a little. We had waited almost two years, with setbacks like quotas and SARS, when we were finally matched with our baby girl, ChelseaRose.

We left six weeks later to China to bring our baby home. We were met with a plane full of adoptive parents, all going to China to bring back their babies. When the day finally arrived for us to meet ChelseaRose, I was scared and nervous. What if she didn't like me? What if I couldn't love her the way she needed me to? We were with a cohort of eight other families. We were told that our girls would be brought to us one by one. The first was brought in. The family and baby were all so happy. The next had a similar experience.

Our turn was next. Chelsea's caregivers brought her in…my heart skipped at least one beat. ChelseaRose was handed to us. The room became filled with a baby's terrified cry. Our Chelsea was petrified. I have never been so moved to love in my entire life. This was our little baby. I instantly fell in love with her. When I held ChelseaRose in my arms, I forgot all about my fears and doubts. She was ours to bring home to love and cherish. She was not too happy about us at first. However, she is now sixteen years old and the joy of my life. My sunshine. I am a mother after all. A very proud one!

Chelsea is such a gift to me and wise beyond her years. Even though I make mistakes, this lovely being has taught me to love unconditionally. My life and heart are full.

YOUR STORY, YOUR CHOICE

Thank you for letting me tell you some of my story. I had to learn that I can accomplish whatever I have set my mind to do. I want you to know that's true for you as well. We are all perfect just the way we are. And we can choose at any time in our lives to live a fuller and more joyful life. Go on now—make a choice. Run around the block and then join a running club. Find the love that's present for you, offered to you—it's there. If you have a desire to nurture, don't let circumstances keep you from the joy of parenting or the opportunity to nurture young lives. Choose it—it is your story, so make it a great one!

ABOUT LAURIE RIKER

Laurie Ann Riker is passionate about transforming dreams into reality, old stories into new stories of choice. She truly believes that you can do anything you set your mind to!

Laurie received her undergraduate degree in business administration from Long Beach State University. She has worked successfully with Fortune 50 companies in the marketing, training and development, and human resources arenas. While working on her master's degree in social work and counseling at Rutgers University, Laurie learned about the budding profession of coaching. Laurie, now a Certified Professional Ignitor Coach, recognized she was born to coach and was thrilled that she could now serve in this profession, using her gift to inspire others.

Laurie has traveled extensively, run marathons, lived abroad, and adopted a daughter from China; all have shaped her story. She enjoys playing tennis, photography, meditating in nature, and hanging with her family. Laurie is now dedicated to helping women globally visualize their dreams and create life designs that bring them into a reality.

E-mail: Lriker@qualitylifedesigns.com

Website: www.qualitylifedesigns.com

LinkedIn: www.linkedin.con/in/Laurie.Riker

BRAVING THE STORM

Kim Ruether

A few weeks ago, I was invited to travel to Arizona to meet a hockey player who had played with multiple teams, including the Boston Bruins and then the Tucson Roadrunners. His name is Craig Cunningham, and I found him to be an inspirational and delightful young man sporting an engaging smile, a great sense of humor, and lively brown eyes.

We met to pool resources with Dr. Zain Khalpey. Dr. Khalpey, a brilliant international cardiothoracic surgeon, is credited with saving Craig's life and is a wonderful individual. Our connection began after Craig, like my sixteen-year-old son, Brock, was a victim of sudden cardiac arrest. Craig lost his left lower leg and foot. Brock lost his life, and, for a time, I felt that I had lost mine.

THE GIFT OF AN ORDINARY DAY

Yesterday, standing at the bathroom sink brushing my teeth, I glanced down to see three extra toothbrushes, lined up like little bristled soldiers. They are stoically waiting to be placed in labeled bags for my sisters' kids. It is now tradition always to keep extra toothbrushes on hand. One never knows when they may be needed.

Seeing those sturdy little brushes, my memory swept back fifteen years to a time when the cubbyhole shelf in our tiny farmhouse bathroom was littered with labeled toothbrushes, separately packaged in individual Ziploc bags. To a time that was remarkable for being ordinary, when our children were young, hearty, and happy. I was entrenched in the splendor of farming, mothering, working, cooking, baking, and adoring my young family. Our kids routinely had friends over to play. And those friends would suddenly decide they wanted to spend the night to complete whatever current adventure was on tap. Invariably, they wouldn't have sleepover bags. I quickly learned to have spare toothbrushes, labeled with their names, awaiting these happy events.

I have always loved kids. I enjoy the crooked smiles, the endless enthusiasm, the twisty morning hair, the quick, hard hugs as they are tucked in after bedtime stories, and being called Momma Rue. I recall countless frenzied mornings, frantically throwing extra lunches together, looking for boots the dog ate, chasing after kids to pass off overdue library books, and watching and waving as kids piled onto the school bus. The days when too-friendly chickens had to be chased off the windowsill on our front porch, days of tripping over farm cats that would slink in as kids raced out and finally of sitting at the worn kitchen table, putting my feet up, enjoying the quiet as I wrapped the flap of my housecoat up over my knees and took that first gulp of now-cold coffee. I remember putting my head back against the old farmhouse wall, a tiny, tired smile on my face, thinking, "This is the *best* day of my life." And it was.

My mind slips back, and I am sitting on the front steps of that kind, old farmhouse, untangling tiny claws from my sweatpants as a little kitten lurches and meows its way onto my lap from the corner. Three more are snuggled into the worn foam basket on the steps, with their mom, Frosty, curled around them. I hear a noise and turn to see a cherubic face looking around the corner. Twinkling green eyes with irregular, fascinating brown dots peer at me; then Brock's tiny face splits into a beaming grin as he exclaims, "Mom! I has *ants!*" He disappears back around to the front step.

Brock and his younger brother, Ryan, had been puttering around, so very busy collecting the big black flying ants and placing them in a one-gallon ice cream pail.

His little blond head pops back into sight. "Come and wook!" he says exuberantly. I get up, putting the kitten, with its outstretched, startled little legs, back down into the basket with the momma cat.

Turning the corner, I see the two boys squatting down, peering into a black mass of wriggling ants, all trying to climb up the sides of the bucket.

I shudder, amazed at their ability to be fearless with these intimidating, scary creatures. "That is *awesome!*" I exclaim, not going any closer.

I remember feeling an overwhelming surge of love for these two inquisitive, adorable souls as I cautioned, "Make sure you let them all go when you are done admiring them—maybe take them to the barn to find their families."

Heading into the house, I find two little girls pulling the garden hose through the kitchen. I ask what they are doing. "We are filling the pools, Mom!" I see that they have finished picking and eating all the Saskatoon berries off the branch. I'd found a branch loaded with berries, broken it off the tree behind the house, and brought it into the front entrance for them to enjoy. They now have blue lips and two huge plastic tubs rolled over by the door. I laugh and am amazed that they have caught on so quickly to how I filled those tubs last week. We place the tubs on the scarred deck outside, and I unscrew the tap cap, attach the garden hose, and begin running warm water into the makeshift pools. As the girls run laughing for their swimsuits, I go and check to find out how the boys made out with their task…and think, "This is the *best* day of my life." And it was.

I had four kids in five years, two girls and then two boys: Tegan, Tera, Brock, and Ryan. We lived in a farmhouse built in the first quarter of the last century. This gentle old building had settled into its foundation with the typical arthritic weariness found in old dirt basements, tongue-in-groove wood slats, and sawdust insulation. It had a beggarly grandeur, with the beautiful hardwood ceilings, the steep, pitched roof, and the even steeper stairs that we had all fallen down at least once. It was old, and crusty, and musty, and good. It cradled our young family and provided shelter without snobbery, the old windows whistling during windstorms, the roof pattering with the sound of a hard

rainfall, the water sliding down, gently invited to fill the cor-
ners and cracks of ancient sills. I tried silicone, plastic coverings,
painting, and caulking…yet there always managed to be fresh air
sifting through the cracks into the life-filled rooms.

We moved into our new house four months before our oldest
daughter, Tegan, graduated high school. And suddenly, as well as
with high school, and sports, and cows, and farming, and work,
we were busy with college, and moving, and finding old cutlery,
and bearing witness to the beginning of an ending. As time continued to pour fuel onto the fire of change, our next daughter,
Tera, graduated and headed off to college as well. Suddenly, I had
just two wonderful boys left to fill the huge empty spaces of this
new, fancy house.

I remember sitting one evening in the basement, watching a
movie with the boys and my husband, Wayne, when I was suddenly struck with the stark realization that these days were rapidly going to be in short supply. I had a sudden tightness in my
chest, knowing that life was changing, swiftly and significantly.
I popped popcorn, brought drinks, and then was called in to
our local hospital to do an x-ray mid-movie; it was a night that
remains with me, remarkable for the simple joy of status quo.

Just a few short months later, in early May 2012, Brock stood
in the kitchen. He was standing by the little table, by the hall to
our bedroom, and he held his chest. He looked at me and said,
"Mom, my chest hurts." I rubbed his arm and told him that was
normal. We all have times that our chests hurt as we work, grow,
and play. He told me he felt as if the pain was in his heart. I assured him that people routinely have pulled rib muscles and just
odd twinges. Plus, I was busy and had no time to coddle and

soothe, to give back scratches, head rubs, or foot massages. It was seeding time, I was overwhelmed, and I had to get supper out to the field as well as pick up more fertilizer from Cargill. Brock continued to rub his chest and then hugged me tight, and I was again amazed at how huge he was now. How had my tiny, beautiful babies suddenly grown into these big, incredible, gifted beings?

The next week I was sitting on the couch, dirty and exhausted after racing around treating wheat seed, checking seed depth in the field, and throwing together meals for Wayne, Brock, and Ryan. Brock came in and flopped onto the couch with his head in my lap, and his eyes shone with good humor as he demanded, "Scratch my head, Mom!" I laughed and ran my fingers through the beautiful, wavy, thick blond strands, and he shut his eyes and smirked.

Ryan came in and said, "Come on, Brock...you said we were going on the trampoline..."

I ran my hand gently over Brock's beautiful face and then pushed his head up off my lap, laughing as I told him, "Get going! You promised!" And the two boys set the stepladder up so they might climb higher in efforts to gain big air as they jumped off and down and wrestled, and I took several minutes just to videotape the action.

The next weekend was already the May long weekend, bringing with it two wonderful girls as they traveled home from the cities they now resided in. I was ecstatic and spent hours with all four kids, enjoying this gift of togetherness. That Saturday we loaded Ryan's dirt bike to go to the track. We talked, shared, and laughed, watching Ryan do crazy jumps, and then Brock told me, "I have changed my mind, Mom. I would like to get a dirt bike too."

"You bet, honey," I told him. "Let's research it when we get home!"

In his gentle, thoughtful way, he tilted his head, watching his brother, and then said, "Well, that's kind of expensive; I will think about it. Thank you so much, Mom."

As we drove the hour-and-a-half trek home from the city, Tegan put on a country song by Chad Brownlee called "Smoke in the Rain."

Hey now, hey now,
Someday you're gonna wish that I was still here,
Hey now, hey now,
Gonna wonder how it all just disappeared...

She and Brock belted out the song together, completely amazing me with their ability to remember all the words. We sang, told jokes, talked, and laughed during the entire ride. I remember getting into bed that night, my heart brimming with love for my incredible offspring, thinking, "This was the best day of my life." And it was.

That Sunday, Tegan packed and left to head back to college. Brock helped her carry things to her car, gave her an enormous hug, and told her not to be sad. He told her she should stay another day. It seemed too short, this time together, and we were already dreading the end.

Suddenly it was Monday, and Tera was packed and ready to begin her six-hour drive back to college. As she prepared to leave, she began to cry. Brock hugged her tight, wrapping his long arms completely around her, rocking her back and forth as he told her, "Don't worry, Tera-bear! You'll be home before you know it!"

Then it was Tuesday. The Tuesday that has lived in my nightmares. In my shaky, stark memories. In the sick, hard ball of horror that forever lives in my tummy. On this Tuesday, I got home late from work, exhausted. Brock slunk up to sit at the island and stared at me. "What?" I snapped. I wondered why I felt so out of sorts and grumpy. It did not stop my scowl.

"Momma-bear, I got a bad mark on my math test," he said.

Immediately I felt angry and frustrated. "Good god, Brock! I was just telling you to put in more effort at school! Start studying! Come on already—you have time to play World of Warcraft and Risk with the buddies. How about putting some of that time and effort into your damn schoolwork?"

He then told me that it was the first practice of the season for volleyball, and instead of being my usual supportive, loving self, I was grumpy, angry, and upset. I told him to take his younger brother, Ryan, who did not want to go, and an argument ensued. Ryan slipped out, and I heard him start up his dirt bike to go off for a ride. I stomped off to run a bath and glanced back to see Brock sitting quietly, staring down at the countertop.

A few minutes later, he came and poked his head around the door, smiled, and asked, "Mom, would you like to come along to the practice with me?"

I glared over at him and snapped, "No! And you'd better enjoy this practice, Brock, because if you don't get that math mark up, it will be the last practice you ever go to."

"OK, Mom," he said quietly. He turned away, and I heard his tread as he walked to the door and out of my life. Forever. I would discover, weeks later, that he stopped at the end of the driveway in a chance meeting with Ryan, who had just returned on his dirt bike. Brock was upset and even got out of the old red minivan to hug his little brother, who tried to reassure Brock, "Don't worry about Mom—she's just tired and grumpy."

I got a call about forty-five minutes later. It was Stephanie, my friend, a teacher, mother to my kids' friends, a mom who had taken my kids along for camping trips. She said, "Kim, Brock tripped, or fell, and he isn't breathing right. We are calling the ambulance…"

I told her we would head into town and meet them at the hospital. As I changed clothes, I wondered if I should put my bra back on. I wondered if Brock had fainted, if we would have to take him to the city for a CT or other tests. Maybe this was something that had carried over from his snowboarding accident in Jasper? Maybe he tripped and knocked himself out? Multiple questions wove through my mind.

I hopped into my vehicle and drove over to the shop to get Wayne. Weirdly, as I reached to turn the doorknob, a deep, cold, shuddery sense of foreboding ran through me. I began to shake. A cavernous sense of urgency and trepidation filled my body, and suddenly, overcome with fear, I wrenched open the door. I found Wayne sitting and visiting with a neighbor. I told him that something had happened to Brock at practice; he had tripped or fallen and wasn't breathing properly. They were taking him to the hospital. I drove, and as we approached the highway, the volleyball coach called Wayne to tell him they had started CPR. I drove faster.

As we turned to drive up Main Street, I saw the fire department response pickup whip out of the fire station, approach us, turn, and race toward the school. I looked down the avenue to the school and saw the ambulance there. I started to turn in that direction. Wayne instructed me to go to the hospital—we would wait there.

It took forever. I called the doctor myself from the outpatient nursing desk. I told him they were doing CPR on Brock and begged him to "please, please hurry." The nurse working that evening was a wonderful friend. As we stood by the outpatient desk, the phone began ringing. She said it was probably the ambulance staff and answered the call. She hung up the phone, and her face looked fierce, almost angry. Her eyes lifted and locked with mine as I stood, shaking, on the other side of the desk. She got up, came around, put her hands on my shoulders, and said, "Kim, it doesn't look good."

I thought, "She does *not* know Brock." At birth, he had survived having the cord wrapped around his neck with two knots in it! Two! He had survived his snowboard accident and concussion, and he was the most vibrant, effervescent, and animated person I knew. He would be fine. Fine. Fine. *Fine, fine, fine...* It became my mantra. I repeated it over and over in my mind until they came through the emergency doors. Brock was on the gurney with a firefighter along the edge, performing CPR. The bounce of compressions rocked the stretcher.

They raced past us into the main room and quickly transferred Brock onto the ER stretcher. I was staff, so it was normal that I was there. We were a unit, a family in this tiny hospital, and no one denied us the right to be present. Compressions continued. It seemed to take forever for the physician; he finally arrived. At one point the nurse told me to go over and speak to Brock, to tell him that I loved him, to encourage him. I approached the head of the stretcher and leaned down to rest my cheek against Brock's, avoiding the breathing apparatus over his mouth. I whispered to him, "I love you so much, buddy; come on, please; I am so sorry; please, Brock, you can make it; I know you can…"

I remembered Ryan was still at home and thought that he would want to be there. I called Brenda, my coworker, explained quickly what was happening, and asked her to take call for me in x-ray and please drive to our farm to pick up Ryan.

I could hear the nurse talking in the packed waiting room to all the patients registered for the 8:00 p.m. clinic: "I am sorry, but we have a critical emergency. If your situation can wait, please come back tomorrow."

I called my daughters. They were disbelieving. I didn't know what to tell them; I didn't know what had happened. "Please come home—hurry. But drive safely," I told them. I called my sisters. I called my mom and dad. I was standing at the doctors' outpatient desk and looked back to discover the waiting room was now completely empty except for one lady and Brock's entire volleyball team, sitting silently, looking sick and scared.

I went back in to see if Brock was conscious yet. I asked permission to take pictures, knowing that Brock would find them *amazing* once we were done with this fiasco. I would show these at his graduation, at his wedding, use them as blackmail photos…

What had happened? My fingers brushed over the hair on Brock's solid, strong, young legs. I looked at the name-brand shorts he'd nabbed out of his dad's vacation stash, at the favorite blue shirt he was wearing still with chest bared. This *could not* be real. I pinched and twisted the skin on my stomach as I stood, hunched, arms folded, wondering if a good, hard pinch would wake me from this nightmare. The pinch hurt. Oh. My. God. Don't they say that if you pinch yourself and it hurts, then it is real? Could this truly be real?

Words floated past as I stood there watching the guys doing compressions over and over and over: "AED not used on scene," "dilated pupils," "anoxic," "pulseless electrical activity," "We can't transport without a heartbeat," "switch," "What exactly happened?"

Ryan arrived, and standing in the emergency room, I didn't know how to comfort him. He looked absolutely terrified. I wondered if I had done the right thing by asking Brenda to bring him there. Then, suddenly, the physician walked over to the end of the stretcher, to where Wayne and I stood, hovering over Brock's feet, stroking his legs, staying out of the way. I stared, face slack, as the physician grasped and shook Wayne's hand, telling him, "I'm sorry, we cannot save your son…" He avoided eye contact with me.

I grabbed his arm and squeaked, "*What?* What do you mean? Please, keep trying. Keep trying, I beg you, please…" He looked ill as he turned from me, instructing everyone to continue performing compressions. I went over to the head of the stretcher, again wriggled past the tubes and lines and people, crouched by Brock's ear, and whispered, "Brock, please. Please, come on, buddy…Please, I love you, I love you, I love you, I love you…"

My cheek brushed his again, and I felt where the fine stubble was growing after he had proudly shaved last week, just like his dad…

And suddenly, I stood. I gently pulled back his left eyelid and looked down into a blank, unseeing, fixed pupil. I looked up, straight into the eyes of the doctor, who quickly looked away, and I knew. After twenty-five years working in health care, I knew. I knew, and I was broken.

I begin saying, "Oh my god, oh my god, oh my god oh my god ohmygodohmygod…" Over and over. I couldn't stop. My record was stuck, and it continued as I left the room and pushed open the exit door.

I went outside and tilted my face up, repressing the scream that bubbled at my lips. I felt coolness on my closed eyelids; the day had turned rainy. I had to go back in, but I felt so shaky and sick, and my legs felt wobbly, disconnected, uncooperative. I stopped to hug the coach's wife, treasured mom of Brock's friend. Brock had spent a ton of time at their house, with their huge group of friends, playing Risk, pretending to study, playing computer games, pretending to do school projects. "How's the big guy?" she asked.

My chest felt tight, my stomach lurching, as I replied, "I don't think he's going to make it."

She cried, "No…no!" and she squeezed me tight. I let go, walked back in, and watched as they ended the code. I watched as the compressions stopped. The people left, and the room became deathly quiet. Literally.

The Royal Canadian Mounted Police member who knew Brock, who had kindly given him a ride one night after the

ski-trip meeting, who had worked so hard to perform compressions to save him, stood for a minute in uniformed, respectful silence to say his good-bye, and I stared at Brock. I looked over at Ryan; his face was white. He looked sick, scared, and horrified. I hugged him and went out to tell Brock's friends and their family members, who stood outside along the hall walls. They formed a silent group of sentries, bearing witness to the loss of one of their own. A boy whom they had stocked mustard for in their homes and provided with guidance and rides, Band-Aids and love and mittens and endless snacks.

And I tried to make everyone good; I tried to fix; I mothered. I got juice and encouraged good-byes and pasted a smile on my fragmented, shattered face.

I tried to comfort my broken husband, our devastated children, and later, I climbed up on the stretcher beside Brock, curled along his side, laid my face on his still, silent chest, and was speechless at the realness of this death. He was my baby. My sunny, funny, gregarious rapper with his quick mind, open heart, and joyous countenance. A gift of skin and bone and brightness, who knew all those words to the country song he and Tegan were singing just days before, just hours before...on our way home from the dirt bike track.

I'll be a thousand miles to the sun,
Before you even know what you've done...

And I was completely fragmented. My cells were mired and gasping, swirling in a quicksand of a horror almost too deep and profound to survive. It was a surreal, foggy nightmare, and my brain was soggy, heavy, slow. The backs of my eye sockets ached from crying, and as if from far, far away, I thought, "This is the worst day of my life." And it was.

Following Brock's death, I began to do research. I spoke with the medical examiner's office, collected medical records, requested 911 dispatch transcripts and on-scene descriptions of events, and put together timelines. I asked for posthumous genetic testing, which was denied.

A wonderful young man from the ME's office assured me that most of these young deaths are due to sudden cardiac arrest (SCA), as was Brock's. Unfortunately, SCA is listed as "sudden unexplained death" following autopsy, because the actual cause or reason that triggered the ventricular fibrillation is unknown. SCA is not a heart attack—it's the sudden onset of an abnormal and potentially fatal heart rhythm that causes the heart to beat ineffectively or not at all.

In my reading, I discovered that Brock would have had at least a 75 percent chance of survival if a defibrillator had been used quickly, which it had not. I was devastated to learn that the automated external defibrillator was at the gym doors. It was retrieved and placed on the floor, and it remained there, unused, as he died. Immediately I could see that this was not about blame; it was about doing better. As time passed, I began hearing about all these other children, teens, and young adults who were affected, who needlessly died. We must do better to save these kids.

As Parent Heart Watch states, "Sudden Cardiac Arrest is the #1 killer of student athletes and contributes to the #2 medical cause of death in youth under 25. But of the leading causes of youth death (accidents, homicide, suicide, cancer and heart conditions), sudden cardiac arrest is the only one that can be prevented through primary and secondary prevention strategies."

I researched for months, finding an abnormal chest x-ray report from when Brock was eight years old. No follow-up was ever done. This also fueled my research and my determination to create change.

Then, one day at work, I finally received a copy of the 911 dispatch transcript. As I sat at the x-ray desk, in front of the computer, I opened the e-mail and began reading the words that marked the end of Brock's life. Black, solid horror filled me. I sat shaking, unable to move or speak as I finally came face to face with the documented reality of the enormous, tragic mistakes that were made. I closed the file, shut myself in the radiologist's film-reading room, and sat and sobbed. The outpatient nurse eventually came and knocked on the door. She let me know an x-ray was waiting. I finally pulled myself together and apologized to the wonderful patient for making her wait and for my haggard appearance. She hugged me hard and long as I explained that it was a tough day. And it was.

It was several days before I was brave enough to listen to the actual recorded 911 call. I mourned deeply, listening to the frantic voices, the minute-by-minute described efforts, the desperate queries and comments, the chaotic scramble as Brock's best friends and school family were unable to comprehend what was occurring or that they should resuscitate and shock him.

Again, I was caught in the knowledge that the defibrillator had been right there. It was located less than fifty yards from Brock and was even brought to his side. Why had the dispatcher not instructed them to use the AED? She said to get the AED "in case we need it later," and it was retrieved and placed on the floor beside Brock, and then it just sat there as he died.

Brock would have had such an enormous chance of survival if that available AED were only used within the first few minutes following his collapse. The EMS documented that he was in ventricular fibrillation (V-fib), which is a shockable rhythm. I read a study in the United States that documented how if a young heart in ventricular fibrillation received a defibrillation shock within two minutes, there was a 92 percent chance of survival. By ten minutes that chance was at 0 percent.

There was no effective process currently in place to emphasize the importance of using an AED extremely quickly and the necessity of rapidly initiating CPR. As I timed actions on the transcript and worked with the bystanders to determine timelines, it became obvious that CPR had been started over five minutes following his collapse, and not one person there had known that a simple shock from an AED will restart a heart. I realized that we must provide clearer guidelines and better tools and support for those facing such an event. Additionally, it became clear that the dispatcher who had answered the call had not been trained to recognize agonal respirations (the abnormal breathing that heralds death and is common in SCA events).

I began Project Brock Society in the months succeeding Brock's death. Following the example of Project ADAM in the United States and many other foundations started by grieving parents, I was determined to create global change to save children from these needless deaths. I found countless instances from around the world of all these beautiful young lives cut short. There were too many cases of victims not having an AED available, or having one but the batteries were dead, or bystanders fearing legal ramifications who would not begin CPR, or people too afraid to use the AED, or circumstances where people did not recognize that it *was* sudden cardiac arrest, standing around as precious seconds passed.

After reviewing the 911 call, completing endless research, and making copious notes, I wrote a letter to the International Academies of Emergency Dispatch (IAED) with the help of a treasured advocate, Jill. She reviewed the call and suggested protocol changes, and a letter was drafted and submitted to Dr. Jeff Clawson. Subsequently, Brock's recorded emergency call is now used in dispatcher training worldwide.

Through this effort and with the invaluable work of the IAED and Priority Dispatch Corp., international 911-dispatch protocol has been changed. Over 29,000 dispatchers worldwide use Brock's Law to ensure rapid AED response.

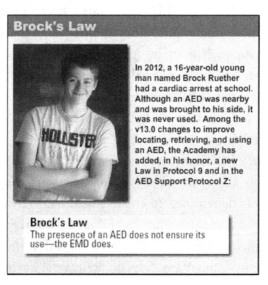

Brock's Law

In 2012, a 16-year-old young man named Brock Ruether had a cardiac arrest at school. Although an AED was nearby and was brought to his side, it was never used. Among the v13.0 changes to improve locating, retrieving, and using an AED, the Academy has added, in his honor, a new Law in Protocol 9 and in the AED Support Protocol Z:

Brock's Law
The presence of an AED does not ensure its use—the EMD does.

It is so important to determine if it is human error driving an event or a system-driven error. I believed that this was ultimately a system-driven error. According to Alberta Health Services, patient-adverse events are often described as the tip of the iceberg and are preceded by accidents, hazards, and unsafe acts or conditions. By encouraging reporting of unsafe conditions and taking action to improve these conditions, patient harm is prevented. With their support, I am taking action.

Then one day my sister Kara called. She said that during the preparations for Brock's celebration of life, she was sure she had seen an ECG (EKG) tracing in his box of treasures from a previous electrocardiogram done on his heart. I told her that I didn't think so. Kara, an RN, insisted she'd seen something that looked a lot like one. At her insistence, I searched. Sure enough, there it was. A small pink strip with the documentation of Brock's living heartbeat.

I posted a photo of this tracing on Facebook, thinking it must have been from when he had his concussion event on the ski trip. I then had a surprise visit from his friends, who outlined the next irony in this heartbreaking story.

During a drinking- and drug-awareness program, the year before Brock's death, Brock was the student selected to be hooked up to the ambulance ECG machine. As corroborated by the teacher there that day, Brock's test was vastly abnormal. The EMT or paramedic even called another health-care provider over and said, "Look at this!" Brock became upset and asked, "Is something wrong with my heart?" At that point his teacher insisted that they remove the leads, reattach them, and redo the test. This was done, and the second test was also abnormal. The staff, looking at a young, healthy, strong fifteen-year-old boy, assumed it must just be faulty equipment. They reassured Brock and his teacher that the equipment "fails sometimes" and printed off a short sample. The strip, or heart tracing, which contained a documented secret abnormality, was given to Brock. He then happily left with his treasure, which he placed in the special box without further mention.

He died a year later.

This is not about blame. It is entirely understandable that the abnormal ECG was brushed off as the result of a faulty unit. I brushed off Brock's complaints of chest pains. I probably saw the abnormal chest x-ray report and didn't think to follow up—he seemed in perfect health. If he had been forty-five or sixty years old, rapid action would have resulted, with those signs and symptoms taken much more seriously.

This must change. We must become aware that heart abnormalities from newborns to the elderly may be present. Any age, any time, any place...*anyone* may experience a cardiac arrest.

There were so many hints leading up to Brock's death that it is only appropriate to use his case as an example of what not to do as we move forward. After a quarter century working in health care, I still had *no idea* what agonal respirations were. Now, if someone called and said my teenager was on the floor and was not breathing properly, I would bellow for CPR and rapid defibrillation.

This basic learning should be available for every student, parent, teacher, and citizen. The American Heart Association reports that 9,500 youth are affected by what the National Heart, Lung, and Blood Institute calls a critical public health issue.

One student athlete dies every three days—it's the leading cause of death on school campuses. And *up to 95 percent of SCA victims die* due to a tragic delay in emergency response. Every hour, about twelve Canadian adults age twenty and over with diagnosed heart disease die. This does not capture all the toddlers, youth, and teens who fall victim to cardiac death. Due to the lack of mandatory national registries, the true prevalence of sudden cardiac death (SCD) in youth is unknown.

Parent Heart Watch provides the following information:

> The underlying cause of SCA can be a heart condition you're born with (often inherited) and/or can develop as young hearts grow. SCA can also be triggered from a viral illness, or a blow to the chest from an object or a person.
>
> **About 1 in 300 youth screened are found at risk for sudden cardiac arrest.** Because most heart conditions that can lead to SCA are not detectable with a stethoscope, a simple, noninvasive, and painless test with an electrocardiogram (EKG or ECG) and echocardiogram, a comprehensive review of personal and family heart history, and the proper assessment and follow-up of warning signs and symptoms are the best tools for primary prevention. Approximately 2 percent of youth that are heart-screened are diagnosed with a heart abnormality or concern, while 1 percent are diagnosed with a life-threatening heart condition. As children grow, their hearts change and repeat evaluations are recommended through age twenty-five.
>
> We must demand that AEDs are in our schools and youth centers and that communities are effectively trained

in the cardiac chain of survival. Ultimately, a mandatory and systematic national registry documenting the incidence of sudden cardiac arrest in the young is critical to the development of prevention protocol in youth health care.

The first symptom of SCA is often death, either because the warning signs of an underlying heart condition were not recognized, or help was not administered within minutes of the event.

Please visit the website at www.parentheartwatch.org to access excellent information and resources.

Following the review of Brock's emergency 911 call, I began working to ensure every school in our north school zone had an AED available. Through donations to Project Brock, over sixty AEDs were placed in schools across Alberta. At latest estimate, over one hundred AEDs have been placed in schools, police cars, local community halls, senior centers, public access facilities, and other buildings through our efforts and alliances. We have also worked together to train thousands of schoolchildren to use an AED and how to perform CPR, with our largest collaborative effort focused on sixteen hundred schoolchildren in two days.

I was fortunate to be invited to present at the International Liaison Committee on Resuscitation (ILCOR)/Heart and Stroke Foundation meeting in Banff in preparation for the 2015 guideline update and revisions. Being part of that extraordinary group of policy and change makers in efforts to enhance our HeartSafe guidelines was a wonderful way to create positive transformation.

The best day of my life...is yet to come. As I enjoy incredible moments with my remaining children, family, and friends whom

I so adore, I am filled with appreciation. Every day brings incredible gratitude, and a deep sense of peace washes at the edge of my awareness. I no longer feel the loss of Brock with only the familiar black horror that dims my vision and takes my breath. His enormous love and very existence are carried within my bones, as are his light, the gift that he left to this world, and the knowledge that he stands within that peace.

I believe that Brock lives on in every person saved, through every win that is provided through the learning gained from his demise. I see his face in every person revived, in every person whom I personally have performed CPR on, and I feel him in every moment that I tightly hug those who are survivors. A few times I have asked to touch the hair of those young beautiful people who have lived through an arrest event. And with their permission, I close my eyes to remember Brock lying on the couch, head in my lap, with his sparkling green eyes, saying, "I love you, Mom!" When I hug my remaining children, who are now extraordinary young adults, I have such enormous appreciation for every second that we can share together.

Every day of our lives, we are gifted with choice. I choose to promote positive change. I choose to work to save other children from preventable death events. I choose to fight for heart screening so diagnosis precedes those potentially fatal events. I choose to call for legislation so it is mandatory for schools to have a lifesaving AED immediately available. And I choose to rally for lawmaking to ensure our teachers and students are taught these life skills. There is no greater skill or gift than to be able to save a life. And I need *your* help to ensure *your* children receive skill sets and protection.

The gift of an ordinary day now arrives with a stiff bow of determination to be the change I want to see in our world and to lend myself in service.

I went to the farm yesterday to feed the dogs for Wayne. We are now separated, unable to scale this wall of grief together. The fall air was crisp; the trees, like familiar old friends, hunched around the yard, looking aged, skinny, and mostly bare of leaves. The metal wagon that traveled a zillion miles behind the little Honda trike, filled with kids, dogs, cats, toys, garden treasures, and berries, now sits empty, rusty, and dented in the crumpling old shed. I walked slowly through the yard, reminiscing, as the dogs bounded and jumped beside me. They miss me, as I do them.

As I walked into the shop, I spotted the framed photo of Brock hung above the workbench at Wayne's request. The snapshot captured Brock, arms swinging, as he bounded toward me through the waves of the Caribbean Sea. I saw his snowboard, the Christmas mailbox he created, and the dirt bike he'd ridden as he'd helped during his last spring seeding season.

I walked back to the house to collect the farm bills so I could get the business books done and fuel bills paid from harvest. Looking across the quiet, empty room, I saw the silver urn cradling Brock's ashes sitting on the desk. It sits right beside where he'd stood on that precious, ordinary day as he'd held his chest and told me his heart hurt. Oh, my treasured child, my beautiful Brock, mine hurts too. Mine hurts too.

ABOUT KIM RUETHER

Kim Ruether is an international speaker, author, educator, farmer, diagnostic-imaging technologist, certified Canfield Success Principles trainer, BLS instructor, adoring mother, and lifelong learning advocate. She is the founder of Project Brock Society, an associate of Project ADAM, a lifetime member of Parent Heart Watch, and an affiliate of ALL HEART—the Craig Cunningham Foundation. She was raised on a homestead farm in a tiny hamlet and lives in Fairview, Alberta.

Following her x-ray training, she returned to northern Alberta, where she married Wayne, and together they had two girls and then two boys. They run a small farming business, which won the Alberta Outstanding Young Farmers title in 2002.

Kim has advocated for worldwide change to 911 protocol, collaborated with organizations working to enhance child-wellness initiatives, volunteered and traveled to promote the availability and rapid use of automated external defibrillators (AEDs) in cardiac arrest events, and trained thousands of children and adults in basic life support skills.

She is now working to enhance local creative-arts programming; researching resources for those suffering PTSD, mental health concerns, isolation, and depression; collaborating on a domestic violence outreach network; and recommending legislation to ensure AEDs are available in schools. She continues her efforts to promote SCA-prevention strategies, such as youth heart-screening programs, in collaboration with other stakeholders.

Her greatest pride is her children, their family farm, her work in health care, and the pleasure found in an ordinary day. She enjoys painting, potting, carving, and building. She also can be found working, hiking, exploring, searching for fossils, picking wild berries, and finding local clay.

Please contact her at kimruether@hotmail.com.

Facebook: www.facebook.com/ProjectBrock

www.projectbrock.com

www.kimruether.com

BEAUTY FROM THE HEART

Carol Stover

Beauty is only skin deep, they say...or is it?
As a professional makeup artist, I create physical transformations on men and women of every description to make them more attractive and photogenic for television appearances, films, videos, still photography, speaking engagements, and celebratory events. For over thirty-five years, I've worked all over the country on many wonderful projects, and it is the most joyful profession I can imagine. For obvious reasons, people are intrigued by what I do, and everyone loves to see the befores and afters. But after the first few years (and few hundred faces), I began to realize that something unusual was happening when I worked on my women clients. The male subjects didn't seem to experience that much arousal of spirit, but for some reason I couldn't understand, every single woman I worked with, no matter what her age or background, displayed an emotional

awakening that seemed to move her deeply. It was more than a simple self-esteem boost. Something important was touching these women on a soul level, and I was both catalyst and witness to it. This was fascinating to me, and over the years I began to observe it more carefully with each female client. In time, it became the most meaningful part of my job. I didn't know until much later that the answer to my question would unravel a deeper understanding of my own feelings about who I was.

Artists see beauty everywhere. As long as I can remember, I've wanted to be an artist, and I drew pictures of people constantly as a child. Being entrepreneurial as well, I decided on a commercial art direction and went into the advertising field after college. But the deceptive and frantic nature of that industry, along with its near-constant sexual harassment, quickly made me disillusioned, and I searched for something I could feel more connected to. One day a photographer friend asked me to help him by doing makeup for his clients, since his regular artist had called in sick. Terrified but exhilarated, I showed up and worked all day on three models for their first portfolio sessions, using the studio's makeup kit. It felt like the best day of my life! I had never done it before, but somehow I knew exactly what to do. The highlighting and contouring I did on their features reminded me of sketching faces on charcoal paper in art school, and the colors I stroked on their cheeks and lips were just like the ones from oil painting class, only quicker and more fun. I even did their hair in all sorts of crazy styles (after all, it was the 1980s). The girls looked beautiful. And when they looked in the mirror, they each gasped and said, "I look so gorgeous!" Now, if only the photos turned out well...

And they did. In fact, the photographer was so pleased he asked me to be his new makeup artist. I had found my dream job at last.

The joy and self-confidence in the girls' faces from that day long ago have lingered in my memory through all these years. I remember watching them as they posed for their photos. Those seemingly shy twentysomethings who were new to the profession when I met them blossomed completely in front of the camera. Was it because of what I did? I hoped that it was. How wonderful would it be to make everyone I met feel this way?

Beauty by any definition is an interesting thing. We each have our own personal feelings about it, based on our upbringing as well as what we've been exposed to as young people. Beauty felt quite simple to me as I was growing up, drawing my pictures and choosing my outfits each day for school. I could never say that I was confident as a young child; rather I was shy and small for my age, content to read books beyond my grade level and play with my crayons and clay. My mother always told me I was pretty and smart (I didn't necessarily believe her on the pretty part, but I went with it). Mom was an English-literature major who loved to decorate the house with colorful, modern furnishings and listen to Beethoven records. My dad was an engineer who had studied in night school for many years to earn his degree, and he traveled a lot. Our home occasionally hosted interesting people of all kinds when my parents entertained, and it was marvelous. I loved the openness of their conversations and how different their voices and experiences sounded to me. As I became a preteen, it didn't occur to me that my unexamined ideas of what made life beautiful would shift so much. Grace Kelly changed it all.

I don't recall the name of the movie or the plot. In fact, I don't remember anything about it at all except the amazingly lovely woman starring in it. It was Grace Kelly, and it was 1968. I was twelve years old, watching black-and-white movies at home on TV, and I was mesmerized by how this woman's face seemed impossibly perfect no matter which way she turned. "She's a princess," my mom told me. "The princess of Monaco, married to Prince Rainier." Wow. That was icing on the cake, for sure. She seemed to be rocking the world without even adding in the princess part. Undaunted, I set out to recreate that flawless visage on my own undefined prepuberty face with my new pastel eye shadows and shiny lip gloss. After all, I was an artist...I labored in front of the bathroom mirror for what seemed like hours, to no avail. There had to be some mistake, some Hollywood trick I had missed. But slowly it dawned on me that no matter what I did, I would never look a thing like Grace Kelly. I just was not going to be beautiful, and that's all there was to it.

Grace, bless her soul, taught me a lot that day. Even though I was depressed over my newly discovered lack of impressive bone structure, the experience did spur me on to keep experimenting with any sort of makeup I could get my hands on. The 1960s were a time of glamour, and I had lots of role models to work with: Diana Rigg from *The Avengers*, Honey West (look her up), various versions of Catwoman, and the endless parade of Bond girls. The women of film and TV were svelte, perfectly coiffed, and *sexy*. It's funny to me now to realize how much my early ideas about sexuality were influenced by those images of ideal women. But something else stuck in my mind about them—they exuded a confidence that came from the independent spirit of the characters they played. Watching Diana Rigg take out a bad guy with nothing but martial arts and a black leather jumpsuit was a game changer for me. Confidence and strength were now suddenly beautiful. The women's movement was in its infancy at that time, and while the antics of those old TV characters seem tame to us now, they were very risqué back then. My mother used to tell me stories about how she sneaked out to feminist meetings when I was a little girl, telling my dad she was exchanging recipes with women friends in the neighborhood. "It's what you did back then," she explained with a casual shrug. Apparently, you just didn't openly attend something as radical as a women's rights discussion. Imagine!

Part of my message when I teach seminars and makeup workshops is that making yourself feel beautiful is *not* frivolous. There is an undeniable connection between feeling beautiful (in whatever way that works for you) and feeling confident and strong. And there is power in feeling your best. Body and spirit are forever entwined, and when you touch the outer self, you cannot help but touch the inner you as well. Just think back to the last time you were sick and had to pull yourself together to go somewhere. Did you drag yourself out in pajamas and dirty hair, or did you spend a little time throwing on some makeup and putting on a nice blouse to try and feel better? It worked, didn't it? For several years, I volunteered for the American Cancer Society's Look Good Feel Better program, where makeup artists and hairstylists help women cancer patients learn to apply makeup, wigs, and scarves to give themselves an emotional boost. I can tell you—from the perspective of someone who has herself had a near-miss brush with fate in the form of a large tumor—the look of triumph on the face of a woman who just learned to redraw a missing eyebrow is unforgettably humbling. Those women fully understand the complex relationship between how they look and how they feel. Many books have been written on the delicate balance between state of mind and health, and those little beauty workshops are more than just a diversion for sick people. As I share what I know and send love and humor to each of them, they in turn send it around the room to one another and return it to me as they hug me on the way out. It is a sacred experience.

What compels people to enhance themselves? Beauty has been revered as a symbol of life, health, and union with the divine since humans began forming rudimentary civilizations. These indigenous cultures painted, tattooed, and decoratively scarred themselves in their own expressions of beauty. But for women, this seems to go to an even deeper level. Women have always had ceremonies and rituals surrounding beauty, purification, and honoring the feminine as goddess incarnate in every woman. We see remnants of these revered traditions in our own religious observances today. I love the idea of honoring yourself by taking care of your body, mind, and spirit in such a purposeful way. When you understand how your inner health and your outer appearance are linked, it makes every act of cleansing and adorning a healing ritual.

A good friend who is a spiritual healer and medical intuitive tells me that having me do her makeup is "a true healing that stays with me even after I get out of your chair." This probably explains why doing makeup has always felt like a spiritual act for me. The recognition and enhancement of individual beauty in a woman can be healing on a soul level—not just for the subject but also for the one doing it. And when you consider that each of us is a totally *unique* soul with our truest beauty on the inside, the idea of prejudice based on appearance becomes insane. Race and culture discrimination through the ages has had an insidious effect on feminine power. Fortunately, our collective ideas of beauty are constantly evolving and expanding. The hottest models right now are ultra-dark-skinned girls from Sudan with iridescent skin that shines with deep tones of purple, blue, and black. Why are they considered beautiful now but were not before? The most interesting face I ever worked on belonged to an albino black woman. She was completely blind, and she had the most unusual skin tone I'd ever seen. She also had an incredible spirit, and I could see exactly who she was inside. I shared this with her and told her I was going to make her look like herself on her very best day. She closed her eyes, lifted her chin, and said with a wise smile, "I trust you." When she was done, she literally glowed with beauty. And she told me she could feel it. I think she gave me more than I gave her that day.

I am back in the makeup room again, working on a beautiful actress whom I admire for her wit and intelligence and the tenacity with which she tackles her life's challenges. She makes the usual apologies for looking tired, blotchy, not plucking this or exfoliating that...I smile and see only clear eyes filled with courage, a delicious laugh that softens a thin layer of sadness and irony, and a huge heart larger than her tiny frame, which I know will fill her life with wisdom and integrity. I paint all that onto her face, and she relaxes into her true self. How interesting that the ones considered the most beautiful among us always have the most difficulty seeing their own beauty. It strikes me with some humor that the actress I'm working on actually resembles Grace Kelly, my old movie star inspiration (what are the odds?), and I find myself wondering if Grace Kelly had the same reservations about her looks. Every woman who sits in my chair offers up the same apologies for not being something more: powerful businesswomen, dedicated housewives, dewy teenagers...it doesn't seem to matter. I love them all and give what I can to coax them into allowing their truth, their feminine fire, to emerge.

I finish my creation on the beautiful actress and step back to survey my work and wait for the moment. *There you are*, I smile to myself. She looks like a shining star out of billions of shining stars in the sky. She glances up at me, and then her eyes dart quickly to her reflection in the wall-sized mirror rimmed with penetrating lights that hide nothing. Her eyes widen slightly and take on a sparkle from within, a soft intake of breath passes her lips, and she breaks out into a dazzling smile. Electricity passes between us as she recognizes herself and decides she is whole and beautiful. She takes a deep breath and embraces it all. The room feels like the center of the universe for a timeless minute. My awkward twelve-year-old laughs and says, "Go get 'em, girl!" Grace hugs me hard and whispers, "Thank you!" before dashing away to be fabulous somewhere.

The makeup is nothing more than a vehicle, and the techniques I use are merely a conduit to reconnect a unique and beautiful soul to her powerful feminine energy. It's nothing short of magical in my mind. The geometry of a face and the colors that give us life are transparent to me, and the spirit never lies. Beauty, truth, and healing are all the same, and the opportunity to re-awaken another woman to her purpose is something we each have the power to do in our own way. This is my way, and it gives me great joy to help as many women as I can. It is my firm belief that women of all nations can step out together and conquer any problem on earth with a little love, some insight…and the right shade of lipstick.

ABOUT CAROL STOVER

Carol Stover is a professional makeup artist based in the Baltimore/ Washington area. Her approach to makeup is detailed and creative, bringing out the unique inner spirit of each subject. Her clients have included Discovery Channel, Bahamas Tourism, Marin Alsop of the BSO, Trevor Noah, and numerous political, media, and sports figures. Clean beauty, polished corporate, and red carpet are her specialties.

After Carol studied graphic design and illustration at CCBC and MICA, her entrepreneurial spirit led her to owning a photography studio and becoming a makeup instructor, a speaker and trainer for several cosmetic companies, and eventually joint owner of a video-production and marketing company.

Carol holds seminars and workshops on makeup and personal style and instructs media performers in camera-ready techniques. However, she loves teaching regular women and teens how to create their own great looks with makeup.

An avid reader with a Scots-Irish wit, Carol is interested in travel, women's issues, animal rights, and environmental causes. She and her husband live in a turn-of-the-century house with four rescued pets, where she is president of her neighborhood community association. Her dream is to start a foundation to inspire self-esteem in young girls through makeup workshops.

Carol can be contacted through her website at www.carol-stover.com.

MY OWN FORMULA

Wendi Sudhakar

Going through rape in college and sliding eight hundred feet after summiting Aconcagua, the tallest mountain in the world outside of Asia, weren't what almost took me out. It was something else altogether, though those two events certainly took their toll. But…they are stories for another day.

It was actually my health, which was at war with me for most of my adult life, that about did the job of removing me from this earth way before what I considered to be my time. Because I was a geologist, being active and traveling the world to study rocks in wild, remote places in the field and climbing big mountains were what I was about, *not* being too sick to even drag my ass out of bed. Being able to play with my son and dogs was what I was supposed to be doing, not hanging on for dear life.

Unfortunately, no matter what I did, I just kept falling completely apart. It got to the point that when I didn't think it could get any worse, it did. I became a walking (sometimes just barely or not at all), talking, toxic waste dump. Literally. I even had a stench emanating from my body that left me embarrassed and trying to cover it up by drowning myself in a chemical cocktail of perfume that ended up changing and smelling as bad, if not worse, than the stench.

Imagine living through your prime years plagued with suffering and the realization that your body is failing you. Imagine if you had no idea why this was happening. I felt helpless, hopeless, and like giving up. I was depressed, the fittest fatass I knew, and completely miserable. I hated myself, and no doubt, I was attracting exactly what I was giving off.

All of this started when I was in my early twenties. I suddenly started feeling exhausted for no reason. My entire body hurt. The constant beating of my joints and bones with a sledgehammer wore me down and out. I had horrible headaches and crazy mood swings, and I was depressed. I had a brain fog that left me feeling like a drooling idiot. I had this constant stabbing pain where my ovaries were that radiated down my sides and into my back. I had PMS that was off the charts. The worst for me, though, was the sudden weight gain that took over. Nothing I did mattered.

I was angry.

University doctors aren't exactly known for being the best in class of their profession. In fact, the ones I dealt with were asshats and cabbages. "Oh, you just have a touch of PMS or maybe a little ovarian cyst. Here, take these painkillers, and you'll be fine. You might want to lay off the sweets too, dear."

Um, f**k you.

Things got progressively worse. I finally decided I had to go see a real doctor and drove the hundred miles home to ask my father for a hundred dollars so I could go and find out what was wrong with me. I was a broke college student, paying my own way. I never asked my parents for anything. This was the one time I sucked it up and did. My father said, "No, sorry, you're on your own." I just stood there. I think I was numb.

The next thing that happened was something you can't even make up. My brother stopped by. It was unplanned, as if some invisible hand had steered him to my parents' house. I kid you not, this is what took place. My father takes out his wallet and hands my brother a Franklin right in front of me. My jaw still hurts from where it slammed into his hardwood floors. My brother was like, "What's this for?" He was bewildered. I was devastated.

So not only could I not afford to go to a doctor, but I was also handed a message loud and clear—I was totally alone.

More time went by. I really don't remember how much now. In the time that passed before I went to a doctor, I started doing research, trying to find out what the hell was wrong with me. I concluded that I probably had this "new" autoimmune disease called endometriosis. While it was scary, I also felt relieved and felt as if maybe I'd be able to get some answers and some help.

I finally went to that doctor. I brought up my self-diagnosis. We all know how much doctors love smart and educated patients. It usually goes over about as well as a fart in church. If you've never seen it, watch the *Seinfeld* episode when Elaine goes to the doctor. That was me.

This doctor did agree to do a laparoscopy just to prove me wrong. I truly believe that because she was focused on doing just that, proving me *wrong*, she was blind as a bat to being able to see what was right in front of her eyes. I was told, "There's nothing wrong with you. It's in your head. I didn't see any signs of endo." And that was that.

Fast-forward another year. I was living in New Orleans, and I was in my first job out of grad school. I was a thousand miles away from family, and I was sick, sick, sick. I would go straight home and go to bed. The exhaustion was overwhelming. The stench was out of control. I remember being in an in-house class and my friend was sitting beside me and wrinkled his nose. He said, "Oh my God, do you smell that?" Thank goodness he didn't know it was me. I just laughed it off and said I didn't notice anything. But I died inside.

Once again, I was convinced endometriosis was my problem. So I found a doctor in New Orleans who was an expert on this disease. And lo and behold, he really was. I dragged myself in there like a wadded-up, moldy gym sock, and he listened to me. When I was done sobbing and sputtering my symptoms out between shuddering breaths, he smiled and said, "You have *all* of the symptoms of advanced endo. I mean *all* of them." After a long pause, he said, "And I can help you."

I cried even harder. This time it was out of relief and also for being taken seriously. He scheduled me for surgery the next week. I even ended up becoming a case study. That was also the beginning of when my life would change drastically...

Not only did he find stage-four endometriosis—pretty much all of my internal organs were covered with it and glued together—but I also had chronic appendicitis. But that wasn't the biggie...I was twenty-seven years old, and—wait for it—I had ovarian cancer. That was the last thing a woman in her twenties expects to hear. I am really thankful for the endometriosis and for not giving up on finding a doctor who would listen. It most likely saved my life.

The next two years following my surgery, I was pumped up with all sorts of horrible drugs that forced me into a chemically induced menopause. I looked like Jabba the Hut. I was so swollen up and full of rot. All the fluid that was causing the swelling was full of toxins, and I wished I were dead. The aftermath was worse than the initial discovery. But at the time, the doctors were doing what they thought was the best thing for me. I truly don't fault them.

Things eventually did get better. I was originally told that I would never be able to have a child. It was a tough thing to learn, and it devastated me. But guess what? A true miracle happened! I got pregnant and had a son, whom I named Gabriel, because he was (and is!) my angel from God. I decided New Orleans was not the place to raise him, so we headed to Houston, where I spent the next fifteen years dealing with one autoimmune disease after another. Sometimes I'd get little reprieves, and I'd do something crazy and impossible, like going back to climbing those big mountains. I think I needed to prove something to myself, and I needed to flip my sick body the bird.

The endometriosis and ovarian cancer were at the beginning. Acute autoimmune liver failure and Graves' disease were at the other end. In between, I had a total hysterectomy at thirty-three because a uterine biopsy showed cancerous cells. I had mind-boggling allergies, Hashimoto's prior to the Graves' disease, fibromyalgia, lupus, and probably MS—basically total immune

dysfunction of epic proportions. I say probably to the MS because once again, conventional medicine failed me big time. I got
so sick and tired of being told by doctors that they *knew* something was seriously wrong with me, but they didn't know what
the root cause or the common connection was, so they would
just throw up their hands, shrug their shoulders, try and treat
the symptoms, and suggest I see a psychiatrist and get back on
antidepressants. So I probably had MS, but I stopped going to
doctors altogether and never got a formal diagnosis. But really,
did it even matter? No, it really did not matter. But I was able to
suggest a new drug to several doctors. It's called Fucitol. It works
a bit like Tylenol, but not quite the same.

As I write this, I hope I'm not sounding bitter or angry. I'm
not. In fact, I feel gratitude for going through everything I experienced. That might sound a little odd. But if I hadn't, I wouldn't
be where I am today or who I am today: a warrior helping people
and making a difference in the world. So with that being said,
as luck, or even better, the law of attraction and a lot of prayer
would have it, I did accidentally stumble into a chiropractor who
was also a functional-medicine doctor. I had never heard of functional medicine and didn't know what it even meant. I honestly
think timing is everything, and all of this was brought to me at
the right time.

This doctor, Dr. O., just happened to be one of the world's
experts on gluten. At that point, I really didn't know much about
it—gluten—but I had started wondering. So he sat me down,
spent two hours (!) with me, and explained it all. He told me that
gluten is the only scientifically proven and medically agreed-upon
cause of or contributor to all autoimmune diseases. I suddenly felt

armed and ready. I had just been handed the holy grail! Finally! Somebody knew the root cause of what had turned my body into a living, breathing toxic waste dump—severe gluten intolerance and an allergy to gluten. I intuitively knew he was correct and what he was telling me was nothing short of the truth.

I immediately made a complete diet overhaul. I cut all grains out of my life. I say all grains because gluten is so much more than the current mainstream definition. There are soooo many types of gluten or gluten-like proteins that exist, and they are found in pretty much all grains. At first, I really wasn't feeling any better. In fact, I kind of felt worse. Dr. O. told me that it could take six months or more to undo the damage and begin healing, especially since my body was unloading a lot of toxins. This seemed reasonable to me. I was OK with months after suffering for years. However, after two years into maintaining a very strict grain-free diet and continuing to work with Dr. O., I was still feeling only marginally better. Even Dr. O. didn't have an explanation. In fact, it was during this time that my liver failed, and I ended up with Graves' disease. As you might imagine, I started to lose hope again and feel despair.

It was at this same time that a massive fire was lit. They say necessity is the mother of all invention. I took my background as a geologist and put on my research cap on full throttle to find out what was going on once and for all. I was convinced that gluten and the overall toxicity in my body were the root cause. But what I didn't understand was why I still wasn't really getting better when I had removed gluten completely from my life. When I found out the truth, the relief was overwhelming. So was the shock.

What I discovered was that it wasn't just food that had exposed me to gluten. I was getting exposure through my beauty products being absorbed into my skin. There is so much misinformation out there that says gluten cannot be absorbed through the skin. Sure, if I smear a piece of whole wheat bread or an ear of corn on my arm, I think I'll be OK. But the truth is that body products are formulated to be absorbed. While this revelation was truly shocking, it planted the seeds for the next massive transformation in my life. Taking the next step, I completely removed all products that contained ingredients that were either toxic or derived from gluten. When I say I healed for *real* in a matter of weeks, that is exactly what happened! I couldn't believe it!

Of course, people around me began to notice the transformation. Sometimes they would just ask if I had changed my hair or lost weight. Others noticed my energy levels and my changed outlook on life, as if I had been reborn. I had been so low, so down, in so much pain for so long that I didn't realize what it was like to feel normal. In sharing my story with others, I realized that I wasn't the only one who had been suffering. The reality is that thousands if not millions of people are experiencing the tragic reality of a diseased life, not having any answers, and feeling totally alone, lost, helpless, and hopeless. What I have found out is that issues with gluten are actually an epidemic and one that has caused so many misdiagnoses and mistreatments, not to mention the huge lack of understanding when it comes to the root causes of all these illnesses. Most of the emphasis regarding gluten has been on celiac disease, which is only one of the many autoimmune and other diseases that can be blamed on gluten. That leaves a massive chunk of people suffering in the dark.

Fast-forwarding to now, from all of this, my own face and body care company Kudarat was born. Kudarat is a Hindi word that means "nature." I researched thousands of ingredients and gained critical knowledge about where they come from, what they do, and if they cause harm. Sadly, many ingredients commonly found in our products hurt us. I also spent a lot of time researching finished products and was really unhappy with what I found. I knew I could do better. So I developed my own brand that not only is 100 percent gluten and toxin free but also has all the skin rejuvenating advantages of the mainstream brands.

I believe that we are unknowingly sacrificing our health. I don't want anyone to ever have to go through what I went through. There is obviously a road to recovery, but it is long, and it affects everything, including relationships, careers—you name it. Once I started feeling better and healing, I didn't really appreciate how bad I'd felt. I'd gotten so used to it. It was my norm. I don't want anybody to suffer like that.

Now I know why I went through what I went through. As they say, bad things happen for a reason. There is always something good in everything. I would've never discovered all that I did. Kudarat would've never been born. Now, I get to wake up every day feeling the excitement and passion about sharing my knowledge with those who will hear. I love helping and guiding women, answering their questions, offering suggestions, and best of all, leaving them feeling empowered and armed!

ABOUT WENDI SUDHAKAR

Wendi Sudhakar is a geologist turned founder of Kudarat, a global, solutions-based, 100 percent gluten-free, vegan, and toxin-free beauty brand. After spending twenty years in the oil and gas industry, Wendi walked away from it all and started her company. This was in response to suffering for most of her adult life from everything from ovarian cancer in her twenties to several autoimmune diseases. After discovering that gluten and gluten-like proteins not just in her food but also in her beauty products were the culprit, she began a journey that involved researching thousands of ingredients, studying the many brands on the market, and developing her formulas, and after a minor kitchen fire or two, Kudarat was born!

Now Wendi is not only working on new formulas and building the company—she's also out there helping others through education and sharing her story so that no one will ever have to go through what she went through.

In between all of that, Wendi is enjoying the last bit of time with her teenage son before he goes off to college and also enjoying time with her three German Shepherd rescues, who are counting the days until they can run free with her when she leaves Texas for Colorado.

To learn more about how you can connect with Wendi and learn more about her educational blog and natural products, please visit her website at www.kudaratskincare.com.

Facebook: www.facebook.com/kudaratskincare
Instagram: @kudaratskincare
Twitter: @kudaratskincare

PUTTING THE PIECES BACK TOGETHER

Marie Svet

A t the end of 2002, my husband and I welcomed our daughter into the world. She was so sweet-tempered and calm. She didn't even cry when the nurses swaddled her on the cold, metal contraption that looked like a french-fry warmer that someone had forgotten to turn on. Fast-forward two and half years, when my daughter and I suddenly found ourselves on our own. Our happy little family of three had become a scared, tiny family of two. The reasons for the downsizing are for another story, but suffice it to say, we were completely on our own. To make matters worse, my company was closing the division I worked in, so I was about to lose my job. Being an only child myself with limited exposure to little kids growing up, I had no idea how I would raise this little girl on my own or if I was even capable. I lived far from my family, so enlisting their help was not an option. I was clueless and terrified. The future looked fairly bleak as I faced so many unknowns, but I did, in fact, know one thing. I knew that I had a gift for finding money.

By finding money, I don't mean that I had a knack for spotting loose change and twenty-dollar bills on the street, although that happens a lot, too. What I mean is that I know how to earn money, and I know how to maximize the money that I have. Plus, money always has a way of finding me whether through gifts, windfalls, or freakishly odd circumstances that are too numerous to mention. The point is, when I need it, the money unquestionably shows up. Always.

The realization that I had a gift for finding money took root during my teenage years. I was always doing extra chores and taking odd jobs to make a few extra bucks. By the time I was fourteen, I had a flourishing babysitting business. By sixteen, I was working a part-time, commission-based retail job and consistently beating my quotas. I even outsold our full-time team. I worked hard and was paid for my efforts. From that experience, I developed the trust and confidence in myself that I could and would always be able to earn money.

Then, when I was eighteen years old, I won a huge academic scholarship to Syracuse University. I almost didn't apply because the competition involved writing and submitting an essay on a topic about which I knew next to nothing. Winning felt like such a long shot, but I tried anyway, posting my submission literally at midnight on the day it was due. To say I was surprised when I learned that I had won is an understatement. That scholarship money was what enabled me to attend Syracuse.

The experience of getting into Syracuse University taught me to never give up and to go after things I wanted even when they didn't seem possible. Most importantly, it heightened my awareness of how and when money came into my possession. It seemed like every time a situation arose that required money, I would find a couple hundred dollars rummaging through old books from a garage sale or receive an arbitrary refund check in the mail. This phenomenon followed me through college and into my first job. Even though I graduated during a recession and jobs were scarce, I had an interview and was hired the day after I received my diploma. It truly felt like Christmas in May to receive that offer letter, because I had been so worried about my future.

Since I couldn't explain how I always found money, I rationalized that it was simply my gift and embraced it. As time passed and similar events occurred, my rationalization developed into an unshakeable belief that no matter what, I would always find the money I needed to survive and thrive. So, when I found myself facing an uncertain future alone with my daughter, I had confidence that I would find the money. Forcing my worry aside, I focused on finding a job that would allow me to care for my daughter. I did what was necessary to keep myself going. It was a matter of when, not if, and sure enough the money showed up.

As I expected, a consulting project fell into my lap right when I needed it. My goal was to turn that project into a full-time job, so I worked as quickly and as precisely as possible, pouring every ounce of expertise I had into it. My results were well-received, and in a few months, I was hired as a full-time executive. I worked tirelessly to build a successful team and the coffers of my company.

My success skyrocketed me toward the C-Suite of corporate America. But, my achievements felt hollow and unappreciated. I sensed that my presence in the C-Suite was tolerated as long as I consistently produced at an exceptionally high level. There was no margin for error, nor time for strategic reflection. I wasn't happy. I felt trapped. Although I loved my work and my team, my vision for the future didn't align with the actions and attitudes of senior management. My mentors and internal advocates had seemingly disappeared into thin air as well. As the months passed, it became obvious to me that the only thing keeping me there was my paycheck and a contractual obligation. I was shackled by golden handcuffs. During what would become my last year in this company, I contemplated daily about leaving. These were full-fledged visions of how I wanted my life to be, how I pictured my future, and on what terms.

I realized that I didn't want to leave this position only to find myself in a similar situation wasting my talent making another group of rich men richer. I wanted to utilize my greatest strength, my gift of always finding money, to benefit myself and other women.

Four years before I walked out the doors for the last time, I had the privilege of being accepted into the Betsy Magness Leadership Institute (BMLI) to participate in a year-long program geared toward the development of senior women leaders in the cable and telecommunications industry. The experience was emotional and transformative. My class, comprising 25 of the most intelligent, gifted and kind women I would ever meet (besides my mom), taught me that 1) I wasn't alone; 2) My corporate/career experiences were universal; and 3) By standing together, we could and would achieve anything. This group of amazing women became my tribe and my inspiration.

The Betsy Bees, as we, Class 26, affectionately named ourselves, came together as a supportive team to mentor, coach and advise one another. We each had our unique strengths and could therefore tackle the individual problems we faced in our careers, personal lives and the program itself as one efficient unit. We learned from each other's experiences and grew stronger because of them.

One incident midway through our program became a defining moment for me. While it wasn't a particularly spectacular event, it had a profound impact on me, and I'm certain, many others. The Bees and I were attending an all-women's executive conference and were really excited to learn from women who had already achieved monumental success. I was terribly disheartened to hear one of the guest speakers, a successful executive woman-turned executive recruiter, share with this power group that if you hadn't risen to the senior-executive level or C-Suite by the time you were fifty, you would never find your success. While it was a crushing pronouncement from this woman, it was a pivotal moment for me. I absolutely refused to allow this person's opinion to become my truth. I immediately set about making a new list and refining an old one of all the personal and professional things I would accomplish at or before I turned fifty years old. They included running ten marathons; completing forty-nine half marathons so that I could run my fiftieth in Hawaii, the fiftieth state, for my fiftieth birthday; competing and winning a body-building competition; and creating my own company built on my unshakable belief that I will always find money. Twelve days after my 50th birthday last year, I was running along the Maui coastline in my 50th half-marathon, with #50 as my race number! By the end of this year, I will have accomplished eight out of the ten goals on my list, and I'm just getting started.

While distance running and weight lifting provide terrific physical benefits, they also provide amazing mental and psychological boosts. The physical demands propel me into a relaxed, meditative state where I can exert concentrated focus on whatever problems or issues I'm working to solve. Such consistent, extreme focus over time has led me to develop full-blown, next-level monetization strategies that resulted in spectacular revenue results for my employers. However, as time passed, I felt I was only as good as my last success, and felt woefully under-valued. I turned to my Betsy Bees for advice only to discover that at least half of them shared similar thoughts and feelings. Our collective malaise had me back in the gym to relax, focus and think about what to do next. We were in the prime of our careers, but we needed other options, a "Plan Bee" so to speak. I thought about each of our special talents and utilized meditation to discover my professional life's purpose. At this point, I realized that the one thing I had to share was my gift for always finding money. This was my purpose: to help women like my Betsy Bee sisters find money through their own endeavors so that they too, could have options and realize their full potential, on their terms. To aid in this task, I developed a scalable, user-friendly monetization process with the intention of sharing it with others. The Profit Puzzle was born.

The Profit Puzzle is a system that synthesizes years of revenue management experience and presents it in its most essential form.

It comprises six subsystems: (1) pricing strategy, (2) negotiating skills development, (3) team-building systems, (4) sales operations and management processes, (5) metrics analyses, and (6) enterprise alignment assessments. Here are the key concepts behind these individual subsystems that lead to increased revenue and sustainable profitability:

• The price of your products and services has more impact on a company's sustainable profitability than any other lever—including how much you sell. A solid pricing strategy not only removes the guesswork, it refocuses the organization on the value of the product or service to the customer.

• Negotiation is not a debate with a winner and a loser. It's an opportunity to build a relationship while discussing specific pain points that your product or service can help resolve. That said, there are an increasing number of procurement specialists these days focused exclusively on getting the most out of their vendors at the lowest price possible. A skilled sales team will be able to move these conversations away from price and back to value.

• The key to building exceptional teams that drive revenue is alignment: routinely mapping out roles and placing the most skilled individuals into them seems obvious, but it's often overlooked. The roles and the strengths of the players should complement one another, building a cohesive, balanced unit that works together. This requires that roles be clearly defined and enforced to avoid players accidentally "playing out of position." This principle is applicable to the entire organizational structure—from top executives to the entry-level worker.

• The ability of a company to consistently deliver great revenue results quickly lies with its sales processes and *all* the ancillary processes within the organization. It breaks down into three components: streamlining and standardizing operations, documenting every step, and strict management oversight moving forward. Streamlining and standardizing enables a company to produce at cost-effective levels, repeatedly. It also means that as a company expands, it can scale its production to meet those increased demands, which leads to more revenue. Documentation enables a team to easily replicate best practices as well as protect against knowledge deficits created by the departure of a key player. Additionally, it helps facilitate issue identification in the event of a problem. Finally, having disciplined management oversight recognizes that markets are dynamic. Demand changes, and trends will be identified early and more easily analyzed for potential impact under a standardized operation, allowing the organization to respond quickly and appropriately.

• Metrics analyses are key to identifying trends, assessing return on investment (ROI), and evaluating the financial health of an organization. The critical element here is to ensure that the right data points are being analyzed and that the metrics are actually measuring what you want them to.

• Enterprise alignment assessments ask the question, "Is everyone rowing in the same direction?" A company will not successfully increase profitability if the finance and product teams are focused on cost reduction while sales and marketing are chasing increased revenue at all costs. The result will be a substandard, cheap product that sales can't sell. Similarly, adopting a reduced pricing strategy when the corporate directive is to reposition the company as a luxury brand will only create confusion in the marketplace. Such confusion typically leads to fewer sales as consumers tend to believe you get what you pay for. The vision and strategy set by senior leadership should flow through the entire organization and be the lens through which all decisions are made to ensure sustained revenue growth and increased profitability.

The Profit Puzzle System (Trademark pending):

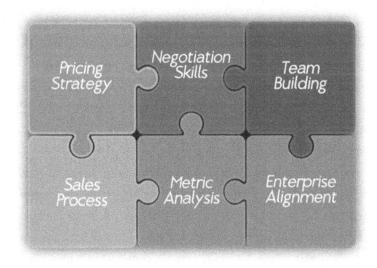

When all the individual pieces are optimized, the puzzle comes together as a business masterpiece. The secret to revenue growth and increased profitability is having each of these individual systems maximized *simultaneously*. Optimizing only one piece or two will not yield the results most companies desire. In fact, it only takes one piece to be askew, mismatched, or missing altogether to cause the business to operate at less-than-full capacity and thus fail to reach its optimal potential.

For example, a company I consulted with was a start-up firm offering a superior, personalized service. However, because they were going to compete head-to-head with large, entrenched, corporations already in the market, they thought the only way to win business would be to offer their services at below-market prices. The low-pricing piece of the puzzle didn't match with the rest of the high-value pieces. Had they followed through with the suboptimal pricing, they would never have earned enough revenue to fund the advertising necessary to generate more customers and more revenue. Their competitors would have been able to lower their prices (or not) for a short period of time, funnel money into a marketing campaign, and then simply wait until the start-up was forced to close its doors. By keeping their prices high, they would create a wider profit margin that can be reinvested in the business for continuous improvement and expansion.

Another company that I worked with had the right pricing strategy, awesome products, and a fabulous team to negotiate contracts. Unfortunately, it was a distributed, decentralized sales team without a uniform, streamlined sales process with oversight. In other words, the sales team consisted of local chapters across the country, operating independent of one another without any common goals or standard practices. That piece of the puzzle was missing. Until that piece was found and put into place, the company struggled to leverage its amazing assets, leaving millions of dollars on the table.

Lastly, one of my clients came to me in sheer frustration. The company seemed to have all the right pieces. The pieces matched and were in the right places, but still, sales were not growing. After a thorough analysis, I discovered that they were using the wrong metrics to assess the health of their business. In other words, that particular puzzle piece was the right one, but it was askew. By using the wrong metrics (or the right metrics incorrectly), they were getting an inaccurate view of their business, which led them to make poor decisions. They incorrectly thought that funding marketing activity A led to increased sales. In fact, it had almost the opposite effect. However, their data indicated that they should spend more money on marketing activity A, so they did. That decision had a compounding effect of increasing expenses and keeping sales slightly less than flat, which combined, eroded their profit margin significantly.

The Profit Puzzle is the system I used to manage revenue and yield for large companies but re-expressed as a strategic formula that I use for my own business. It's creation with the intent to fulfill my purpose is allowing me to pursue the life I fantasized about during the moments I felt trapped. As I continue on my path toward complete financial freedom, I can't help but reflect on the dream-killing prophecy made by that guest speaker several years ago. I have proven her wrong, and I am driven to help other women prove her wrong as well. The fact is, her focus was simply too narrow. Just because a woman has not reached the C-Suite by age fifty does not mean she cannot be an accomplished entrepreneur or successfully run her own company. A woman does not have to work for a male-dominated company to be an outrageously successful business person. Age is not a factor, especially in today's world where well-educated, experienced women bring incredible assets to the business world. With this in mind, it is through The Profit Puzzle *System* that I can help other women entrepreneurs gain and sustain profitability for their businesses so that they can show up and make a difference. To be clear, I am on a mission to help other women attain their personal, professional, and financial goals. So, to all women who are worried about their future, I say this: Take heart. You have not lost your value. You are just getting started!

ABOUT MARIE SVET

Marie Svet is a global, profit-focused revenue leader who streamlines resources for efficiency while building relationships. As a cross-functional strategist, she employs a holistic business approach to resolve revenue challenges. Her expertise lies in business analysis, pricing, business development, and planning across multiple lines of business.

In her most recent role as the global chief revenue officer for a major media company, Marie was recognized for her expertise in revenue management and sales strategy. Due to the effectiveness of her breakthrough strategic initiatives and leadership, the company was able to produce record-setting results for seven consecutive years.

Svet's extensive leadership experience in the advertising sales industry includes roles of progressively increasing responsibility as a leader of major digital and television initiatives at companies, such as Sonar Entertainment Inc., Nickelodeon Networks, World Wrestling Entertainment, AccuWeather, The Feedroom.com, and USA Networks. She received the 2015 Cynopsis Top Women in Digital Award, which honors "women who have helped clear a path in what is still a relatively young industry" and "those who excel in digital content, marketing, advertising, social media, and online."

Svet has an MBA from NYU's Stern School of Business and is an avid runner and certified ChiRunning coach. She is a graduate of The Betsy Magness Leadership Institute, Class 26, and the co-Founder of Women in Cable & Telecommunications NY Chapter's executive mentoring program, Prime Access. She is currently being trained by Jack Canfield in the Train the Trainer program to further enhance her team-building skills. Upon graduation, she will be a certified Canfield Trainer.

Marie works with companies on a consulting basis either as a strategic advisor or a board member. If you would like to explore the possibilities of working with Marie, you can contact her at:

www.profit-puzzle.com

marie.svet@profit-puzzle.com

GUIDING LIGHT OF MINE

Donna Wald

I f I could leave just one message to the world, it would be to listen to your inner voice! I look back at my life, and I realize that communication with God was the essence of my survival.

I was born in a one-room shack with a cookstove providing heat in the winter. I was one of six children, one being my twin brother Don, who I knew was very sick. He cried a lot, and I protected and was there for him. I remember our father bringing in two sacks of groceries, and we started grabbing at the food within. I took what I had grabbed and offered it to Don first before I took any myself.

We slept in a bed with a hole in the mattress, and I worried about Don falling through the hole. Someone took pictures of us, and we looked like refugees from a third world country, which I guess we were. My twin's stomach was protruding because he was undernourished. He spent a year in the hospital and several years of treatments by a doctor in his foster home. He recovered and became a successful engineer. I was the firstborn and obviously the stronger of the two. Yet when I was in nursing studying diseases like rickets, I felt my ribs, and the holes that the instructor was talking about for that disease, were also in my ribs.

At age two and a half, I was taken away from my parents, twin Don, siblings Dorthy, Karen and Sharon and placed in a foster home. I did not see my parents, twin or other siblings until years later. I was lonely for them, and I was what we would call depressed today. My first foster parents worried about me and gave me up because of their concern for my health. I was placed in another foster home where the twins, five years older, did not accept me and were very abusive to me. I was sent to yet another foster home, which I cannot remember as the stay was short. Finally, I ended up in the foster home where I was raised and given the family's name (but never adopted). I don't remember the fifty-mile trip to their place; by this time I felt very much alone and abandoned. I was to "replace" a daughter who was born and died days after birth. However, this foster mother was very jealous of me. If my foster father gave me some attention, she would physically abuse me when we were alone. Another tactic she used was to talk *about* me but not *to* me when I was present. I called that the silent treatment, where I felt invisible and which often lasted two weeks. Life was not easy for me in that home but guided by my inner voice, I followed the path that was told to me, most of the time.

I knew from age five I would become a nurse, and that knowledge never left me. I also knew that I was a healer. I bandaged the sick animals around the farm and said prayers over them. I instinctively sensed the anger of my foster mother and figured out ways to deflect her anger away from me part of the time. I didn't understand what was going on, but I knew something was seriously wrong with her. I tried my best to please her and make her happy, but she always found fault with whatever I had done. As I got older, I became rebellious when accused of things that I knew I had not done. I was torn between what I felt was right and what was wrong, but I did not easily back down if I knew I was right. This lead to many battles between my foster mother and me.

I'm not sure when I began to feel that the only reason they kept me was for the money they received for doing so. I remember the men climbing up the electric pole and shutting off our electricity several times and my foster parents arguing over not having enough money to pay the bills. Perhaps the fact they kept me despite these financial drains encouraged the thought that having me helped them financially. I longed to see evidence that I was *really* part of the family, but I never was hugged or told I was loved by Mom, and I wanted that so badly.

At school I was small for my age and not very athletic, so as two leaders called out names for their teams at the noon hour, I crossed my fingers behind my back that I wouldn't be the last one called, but I usually was. I tried my best to hide the tears and smile.

I always felt that I was the misfit, marching with the wrong foot. I saw many things differently than my classmates. When others teased or bullied a classmate, I could not take part. When another stole penny candy from the store and said, "They'll never know; take some." I couldn't do it. The voice inside me told me not to, and I obeyed.

In high school I felt like Jekyll and Hyde. At school I was the class clown and happy, but when I entered my home, I was the sober scholar. Sometimes I felt as if I were going crazy trying to be two different personalities at once. But it was a balancing act that got me through those emotional high school years. My older foster brother Carroll was killed in a car wreck when I was fourteen, and that was a terrible loss for me. He was the only one who verbally stuck up for me and protected me from my foster mother. How I missed him.

My folks took me to Minot, where I entered a nursing program that coordinated classes with the college. I remember thinking, " I don't care if I ever see my foster mother again," but I also knew I would miss my foster dad and other foster brother Arvin (who was a year older than I was).

When I started college, my whole world changed. I was suddenly very popular with the boys, and I realized I could be a heart breaker if I wasn't careful. What a change for me! Finally I could be myself! It was freeing and frightening at the same time. In psychology class, I gained the awareness that Mom was neurotic, bordering on psychotic at times. But the hurt was so deep that I couldn't forgive her at that time.

The first time I went home from college, I took a friend with me. I was really lonesome for my dad and brother. We caught a ride with one of my high school classmates. We walked into the house, and my mother stood in the kitchen scrubbing a pair of shoes. I said, "Hi, I'm home, and this is my friend Lois." My mother ignored us completely. I took my friend into my bedroom and with tears in my eyes told her that was my mother. She was horrified; she had thought the woman was a rude housekeeper.

I met my husband on the Fourth of July weekend of my senior year. I had broken up with a serious relationship before my two-week vacation at home. I then decided I was going to enlist in the army as a second lieutenant and see the world! I rode the train back to Minot on the third as the train was full on the fourth of July. I was due back for classes on the fifth. It's a story in itself how I met my husband, Ron, on that July 3. We hit it off immediately, and after our second date, I knew this was the man I was going to marry.

Obviously, I was hesitant to take him home to meet my family. I knew Dad and my brother Arvin and his wife Bonnie would be nice; how Mom would be was questionable. I had told Ron of my experiences with Mom, so he was somewhat prepared. However, Mom was on her best behavior.

We married on June 23, which was my dad's birthday. After a short honeymoon, we settled in a ten-by-fifty-foot trailer home on the farm. I worked at Saint Joseph's hospital until my morning sickness became a whole-day affair. Our daughter Jami was born on our first anniversary. We had a son Nathan twenty-two months later.

Ron's folks retired from the farm and built a new house in town, so we moved into the farmhouse. I cooked for hired men, took care of two children, and helped with the dairy and field work. I had a large yard to mow and a big garden, thus I canned fruits, vegetables, and meat (for quick meals). I sewed all our clothes except jeans. I was active in church activities and other community activities. Our third child, Matthew, was born the next spring. I was a very busy mom!

We left the farm and moved to a ranch in the badlands of North Dakota several years later. I loved it there, but it just wasn't big enough for Ron. He spent a lot of time helping neighbors to keep busy. So we sold the ranch and moved back to the farm. Our fourth child, Zachary, was born there.

Several years later we sold the farm and moved to a ranch in Montana, where we still reside. I have always been an active part of the ranch despite working full time. There is nothing quite like being on my horse on a beautiful day doing what I love to do. It's not work, just pure pleasure for me.

There is a saying, "You can lead a horse to water, but you can't make him drink." However, if you put salt on his hay, he will readily drink! The same is true for people; no one wants to be forced to do something. But if the situation is explained and volunteers are needed, most people will readily help. In my many different managerial positions, I have always led by example, not dictatorship.

I remember an incident that occurred when I had received my doctorate and was Director of Nursing. I made rounds in the morning, listening carefully to each patient's perception of his or her illness and hospital care. I entered a room to find that the occupant had been unable to make it to the bathroom. He was terribly embarrassed and apologetic. I assured him that this had also happened to other patients. I nonchalantly began cleaning up the mess so that someone would not slip and have an accident. I was almost done when a nurse's aide came into the room and exclaimed, "Dr. Wald, you shouldn't be doing that!" I looked at her and said, "I hope the day never comes when I am too important to assist a patient." So far that day has *not* come.

I have always felt empathy and compassion for those who are worse off than I am. However, I also believe that each of us is responsible for the state he or she is in. We can blame and accuse others, which only makes us angrier, or we can look at ourselves and realize that we have contributed in *some* way to our situation(s). I strongly feel we also have the ability to change that situation(s) for the better.

I remember well the day I was at my foster mother's deathbed, holding her hand and talking to a comatose person. I told her how abusive she had been to me and how angry that made me. I also told her that her actions had made me a stronger, better, more empathetic, and compassionate person. I also knew I had a better home with them than I would've had with my parents, and I was truly thankful for all she had done for me. I ended with, "Despite everything, I forgive and do love you Mom." She squeezed my hand and her very last words were," I love you too, Donna." Those were the very words I had wanted to hear all those years. With tears streaming down my face, I hugged and kissed her. I felt a huge weight lift from my body. She died the next day.

I received a BS in Psychology and Sociology. I worked by day as a school nurse, in the evening and for two summers I traveled 220 miles to attend university classes. I graduated magna cum laude with a Master's in Counseling. While Director of Nursing, I received my PhD in Health Services Administration. Education has always been important to me; I continue to take courses, seminars, and workshops to advance my learning. I also give educational funds to my grandchildren on their birthdays, at Christmas, and for as long as they are in school.

I have always been civic-minded and active in community affairs. I love to work with my hands—weaving rugs on an antique floor loom and making quilts that I give to the sick, terminally ill, those getting married, newborn babies, friends, my children and grandchildren. I also do wool felting, making replica dogs for those who have lost their faithful friends. I do beading and other crafts as well. These are my labors of love. Many have told me they *feel* my love in their quilts, rugs and other crafts.

I never thought about what influence I had on others until one of my daily talks with my daughter Jami, who is experiencing cancer. She is an exceptional, positive individual. I told her that day that I wished I were as positive as she. She answered, "Mom, where do you think I learned that? It was from *you!*" Wow!! That got me thinking...yes, I remember the gal who waited hours to see me because she wanted to tell me what a difference I had made in her life. The students who stood in a long line at the college on registration day because they knew I could and would help them figure out their class schedules. The people who called and asked me to help them become certified nursing assistants. Those who came to my office, abused in some way, asking for advice. The parents who came to see me wondering if it could be drugs causing their children's behavior. These were experiences I never took lightly. With my inner voice continuing to be my guiding light in life, I always do my best to help those in need of my skills and educational abilities.

As I look back, I'm so thankful for my childhood and all the events in my life that have led me to recognize and connect with my inner voice. I have learned that one doesn't have to be a victim despite the circumstances in one's life. I listened, trusted, and was guided by my inner voice and found an inner peace instead. I know that I am here to share that message with others.

Some of you have yet to discover the unique way in which your higher power speaks to you. I realize now that as a child, I attuned myself to my inner voice and readily understood its message, how fortunate for me! The difference between my thoughts and my inner voice is a recognizable sound and a tingly feeling in my body telling me I should listen more intently. Mine is a soft, yet powerful, ringing voice that speaks very few words, so it is easy to tune out. However, when I don't listen to my inner voice, I suffer some type of consequence mixed with feelings of guilt and/or shame. When I listen, I am guided down the right path and I have an inner peace.

I truly believe that I am on this earth to help others with my gifts. I am able to guide others to identify and cultivate their connection to their higher power so it becomes a valuable source of guidance and peace for them! I am willing to do speaking engagements, presentations, workshops and one-on-one sessions on this topic, as well as health, energy healing, life coaching and many other topics.

ABOUT DONNA WALD

Donna Wald lives on a ranch in Montana with her husband, Ron. They have four children, ten grandchildren, and four great-grandchildren. Family is very important to Donna. Two sons live on the ranch, raise cattle and horses, and help with other ranch activities. Ron and Donna also run a B&B at the ranch.

As a RN, Donna did private-duty nursing, was Supervisor of Surgery, taught community health, was a Red Cross volunteer teaching: First Aid, CPR, and disaster training. She has also served as a Fortunate 4 Hearing tester, school nurse, health educator, nurse consultant, chemical-dependency and family counselor, Director of Nursing, professor, Academic Dean at Little Big Horn College, Parish Nurse; additionally, she has been a 4-H leader, Cancer Crusade chairman, Secretary of her church council, and is a Lay Minister, she has been President of: Jailhouse Gallery's Board, Homemakers' Club, Sew & So, and Civic Club. The importance of education for Donna resulted in all four of her children and six of her grandchildren graduating from college.

Donna received a BS in Psychology and Sociology, Master's in Counseling, and a PhD in Health Services Administration. She is a Reiki Master, HBL Master and is studying for her Ho'oponopono certification, Life Coaching Certification, Energy Medicine Healing, NPL, and Hypnosis Certification.

She assists people in utilizing their unique gifts and potential through one-on-one coaching and group sessions. She also gives presentations on health issues, inner voice, spirituality, consciousness, hypnosis, energy healing, Foster Care Reform and other related topics.

She can be reached at her website: www.waldranch.com, LinkedIn, and Facebook.

from influence to impact

Hayley Hunter Hines

I t was the middle of the afternoon and I was sitting in the bathtub staring at the skylight with a face full of tears, and an incredibly heavy heart. I didn't know what to do and I was completely overwhelmed by the decision that I was trying to make and I needed off the roller coaster. Stay or leave. It was one of those moments I'll never forget. Have you ever cried in the tub? I think there is something about being immersed in water that somehow seems to make it more appropriate. I was trying to decide if it was time to walk away from the life I'd spent the last 7 years building and just kept having wave after wave of guilt and shame and failure.

I remember just praying for clarity and direction and now I realize that the root of the tears was not from the idea of leaving my marriage but being separated from God. I was raised to believe that divorce was one of the things that God hated and that if I made this choice that I would be 'cast out' and no longer to be in "right relationship" and so I cried. And then I finally asked for a clear sign. A sign that no matter the decision that I made that I would be okay. I would be loved and still deeply connected.

In that moment a song came on the radio that spoke so sweetly to me. "There is nothing that can separate you from the love of God" and that was the chorus of the song that just played over and over. And all of the sudden the tears stopped and I knew that I was free to make the decision that while not easy, I knew it was in the highest and best. Like this huge weight had been lifted from my chest. It was the first time I ever felt a clear message and answer to a prayer.

I'd realized over the previous months that the life I had spent all those years creating looked nothing like me and I had never been more far away than what I truly wanted and my deepest truth. I knew that I was meant for more than staying in an unhealthy, emotionally abusive marriage and so after seven years I walked away with a few pieces of furniture, thousands in debt, started over and began again. At thirty years old I had nothing to show for the past seven years other than a failed marriage and battered self esteem. That was my first experience of the blessings of being brave.

It was an opportunity to rebuild every part of my life and myself and it was both overwhelming and extraordinarily exciting at the exact same time. A clean slate. How can I create exactly what I desire? What will make me the happiest? What steps can I take to ensure this never happens again? These were all questions I dove deep into and over the next few years things began to become more and more clear. It took several years of healing and restoration, daily pep talks and inner work, like a deep renovation of my truth and who I wanted to become. I had to fall in love with myself and rediscover the true desires of my heart.

The next decade was an incredible time of growth for me both personally and professionally and I ended up as a senior level executive, traveling and consulting with large employers all over the US on how to create a healthier workplace and inspiring employees to make the changes they needed in their lives. I had paid off all the debt from my divorce and had been saving like a crazy lady because I had promised that I'd never be in a challenging financial situation ever again and I also knew that "someday" I wanted to travel the world and volunteer and make a bigger impact than what was possible from my fancy corporate office. I called it Operation Gypsy and it was born ten years earlier when I read the book Eat Pray Love by Elizabeth Gilbert.

I worked incredibly hard and had reached the peak of "success" in my corporate career, having everything I thought was important, yet feeling super overwhelmed, not healthy, and left with zero time for the things that were most important to me: freedom and resources to travel and serve in a really impactful way. My "someday" came after the tornadoes hit my hometown of Oklahoma City in 2014 and I had that moment of WHAT AM I WAITING FOR. I watched dear friends pull their children from rubble and lives destroyed in minutes. It was six months before my 40th birthday and I decided to leave. It was time.

I was ready to create something really beautiful and something that was the fullest expression of myself and my soul. Something that felt so spacious and the embodiment of my hearts desire. Deep connections with beautiful soul friends. I wanted to connect IN REAL LIFE and hug people and look them in the eye and create opportunities for them to feel seen. Known. Supported. Connected and so very loved.

When I shared this vision with a sweet friend and told her that I wanted to create magical, moving experiences for women around the world where we come together in sisterhood and support of helping make each others dreams come true she started crying because it felt so perfect. And I told her this story of one of ladies that had worked for me and I'd promoted her to a huge job and really tried to help her grow into the next iteration of herself and her leadership and how one day she steps into my office to simply say " Thank you for giving me this opportunity. You've made my soul sparkle"

And that is how Soul Sparkle was born. From a deep desire to create a safe a sacred space for women to come together and create their magic in the world. To help them step into the next iteration of themselves and the life they have been dreaming of. To know that they are not alone. Since that moment we have gathered for soirees on rooftops and hillsides, we've sparkled in the City of Lights and the city that never sleeps! We've sipped prosecco in Tuscany and Champagne in Epernay. There have been heart to heart full body hugs, sweet moments of being seen in a new and beautiful way, deep releases of things that have kept us small and afraid to speak our truth. Each experience carefully curated and designed to bring women back to the sparkle they have within. It is such an honor to witness the transformation that happens when women give themselves permission to do life differently and in a way that brings them joy. They have started beautiful soul centered businesses, non-profits, moved across the country, found their sacred soulmates and are living their version of a magical life.

At the very first sparkle experience several big dreams came true, one of which was the birth of the Soul Sparkle Spa line. All those years of pep talks, lotions and potions were so instrumental in my healing and the concepts of self love and self care were so foundational for myself and all the women I had worked with in the last decade that I wanted to create something that would help support their own self love and care. The box with the products arrived the second day of our retreat and I had a tear filled moment with the UPS delivery man! He had no idea what he had just delivered! It was so exciting to see how beautiful everything was.

This same weekend, I'd asked my dear friend to craft something lovely we could give as a gift during a special ceremony for the ladies. She created a piece that was so perfect and so lovely that the ladies asked for additional pieces that may go along with the bracelet, like earrings and a necklace. So she created those and then more and from there we launched an entire collection of jewelry, which along with the spa line became the Soul Sparkle Collection.

The most beautiful thing happened along the way, loves. Remember when I asked for a sign and received the blessing of the song? Well I kept asking and these signs of magic and guidance began showing up in the form of feathers, most of them white. They came in the most interesting and beautiful ways and unexpected places. Sticking out of telephone poles and hotel room walls, in places and spaces completely closed off and so unlikely, yet so perfect. Sweet signs from my angels that I was on the right path. Whenever I felt uncertain or needing con-firmation it was always then that they showed up. They have become part of the collections to remind us we are never alone and each time we sparkle together each woman receives a special piece of jewelry to remind her of the experience, the connection, the transformation but most of all the magic. We also wanted to share it with the world.

I wanted to share this blessing of the collections by donat-ing a portion of all the profits to a group of women in need and we really wanted to find a group of ladies that would be inter-ested in handcrafting the pieces for us. I sent dozens of emails to artisan collectives around the world and got zero response. I thought it was such a good idea but not a single email back, it seemed so crazy to me! The story that unfolded was so perfect and so magical that I realize now it couldn't have happened any other way.

I knew that another part of the Soul Sparkle vision was to offer service trips, where we take a group of women on an ex-perience where they could really get their hands dirty and con-nect with the local people. I've also always felt like I shouldn't be leading or teaching something I haven't done myself, so in July of 2016 I went on my first service trip to Nicaragua. It was com-pletely last minute but it just felt so right.

We built 24 homes in two days in a small village and then drove a few hours away to the beach town of Jiquillo. As we walked around visiting some of the projects I mentioned to our host that we were looking for a women's collective that we could work with on our jewelry collection in hopes it would help them create an income. He stops me right there on the dirt road and says that there is a collective of women that he felt certain would be interested in working with us. I met the women that afternoon and shared our dream with them and by the end of our conversation we were all hugging and crying and knowing this was the perfect next step! The next few hours unfolded so beautifully and magically and by the end of the conversation they were signed up and thrilled to work with us. It was a gorgeous moment I'll never forget. I asked the leader of the group what the dream of the ladies was and she says they would love to all live together on a farm, in safe and secure homes. The homes they were currently in were at risk of being washed away and were patched together pieces of metal and wood.

I left that conversation knowing that we would be funding a farm and 10 homes for these women and children that had been abandoned by their husbands/fathers, which is so common in the culture. We started the process of how we would raise the funds and within 10 days of getting home I got news that the ladies had been *gifted* a 25 acre farm and within another month they had been given permission to build the new "forever homes"! It was such a gorgeous miracle to witness such a precious gift!

We began fundraising right away for the homes and have had so many beautiful souls reach out in support. It was amazing to watch as people stepped forward to support this vision and dream. I was able to be there when the first house was completed and I just stood there in a pile of happy tears as we painted, completely covered in tears and paint and love. It's amazing what happens when we dare to dream bigger than we ever have before, isn't it? It was so lovely to see all of the other ladies show up to help, such a beautiful example of sisterhood. As of this writing the third home has just been completed and we are so excited to be part of something so sweet.

Since that initial meeting, we've taken a gorgeous group of ladies back with us on what I call a "service-meets-sparkle" trip under our Soul Sparkle Seva initiative. I wanted to redefine the paradigm of what it means to serve and that service doesn't mean have to mean suffering. I want to inspire women to come again and again so this was a beautiful example of what it could be. We went back another time to work with the ladies again to craft additional pieces of jewelry and are so excited to watch the expansion of the line unfold with hundreds of pieces being sold. Our hope is that this will provide a long term and sustainable way for the women to care for themselves and their children.

Of all the things I've ever done in my life, finding this way to feel like my life and my work are truly making an impact is the most rewarding thing I've ever done. To know these women personally, to connect with them deeply, to know that every dollar we are raising is going toward helping them create a better life. It's such an honor to serve in this way, both these ladies in Padre Ramos but also them women that feel called to sparkle with me, wherever I am in the world. It is my greatest joy to have them come again and again and to watch them re discover the sparkle they have within, just like I had to over 14 years ago.

And the best part? Remember how I told you about Operation Gypsy and my dream of traveling the world, speaking, teaching and serving? I'm doing it, loves. After all those years I finally put my things in storage in October of 2016 and have been doing it every day since. Teaching women around the world how to step into their next level of soul centered leadership and spiritual activism and how to live life on a magic carpet ride. I am living the fullest expression of my most magical life and loving each and every sweet moment. We are continuing to raise funds for the homes in Nicaragua and are now curating the global expansion of the sparkle collection which will include items I love crafted from women's collectives all over the world with a portion of proceeds going to the home project. We are creating sacred sparkle sanctuaries all over the world where you can come to rest and restore and experience gorgeous transformational retreats. I'm writing this from Morocco and I've just met a women's collective here and we will be adding their gorgeous items to our collection and creating our next Soul Sparkle Seva experience here to work with them in 2019.

What are dreaming of, love? What do you want to create in the world? What do you want your legacy to be? Can you craft a life that gives you the time and space to do what you were born to do? You were created for something beautiful, you know. It's time for you to light up the world with your magic. Now more than ever we need more light bringers and hope givers. If you have a big dream and a deep desire of your heart to create a life that lights you up from the inside out, keep going. The life you have been dreaming of is waiting for you to step into who you need to be to have it. We need the next evolution of your love, life, and service. Your soul can sparkle and your light can shine, love. Trust and believe that it is all possible, and it's all happening! Keep following your highest excitement and asking yourself what else is possible. My vision is that together, we will inspire the women of the world to serve the women of the world and as we step into our greatness, we will discover the next evolution of our work in the world. We will embody our deepest truths, our highest calling and give others permission to do the same. By allowing ourselves to do life differently we inspire others as well. It's a gorgeous thing when women come together in solidarity and sisterhood. Welcome to the new paradigm of leadership, loves. We've been waiting for you.

ABOUT HAYLEY HUNTER HINES

Hayley is the CEO of Soul Sparkle, Inc. global experiences and the creator of the Soul Sparkle Collection. She is a mentor to executive women called to create a Soul Centered business and life, a spiritual teacher and author of the forthcoming book Becoming a Soul Centered CEO. She is the host of Soul Sparkle Radio and The Soul Centered CEO Podcast and creator of Soul Sparkle SEVA, global service trips and experiences and is an expert in transformational travel. Hayley is one part fun fairy, one part wise sage, with a burning desire to bottle up and light on fire all things magical that bring women back to their own soul and the sparkle within.

Hayley spent over 20 years in the corporate wellness industry consulting over 200 employer clients and as a senior level executive leading strategy/innovation and new product development for a national health management organization. She has always felt called to help other women craft a business that gives back and makes a global impact. She has created the Soul Centered CEO mentorship and mastermind for women executives around the world.

Her vision is big - a million women serving a million women. In October 2016, she left her corporate path and since making the leap she has literally sprinkled her magic across multiple continents, fully living her Soul Sparkle life of wandering the world, giving back, and successfully running a highly impactful business.

www.soulsparkleliving.com

THE INSPIRED IMPACT BOOK
SERIES AND MOVEMENT

The philosophies are to love more, give more, and care more than necessary…always. Not because the things you give will come back to you (although they will) but because it's what we believe is right.

The coauthors of this book are here to serve others, sprinkle glitter, spread magic, and make a massive positive impact on the world.

We will meet you where you are, without judgment or confinement. We want to walk with you on this journey because together we rise up to our brilliance and greatness.

If you feel called in any way to become a part of this book series or movement, we encourage you to reach out.

We want to hear your story. We want to celebrate your truth. We want your story to impact the world right along with us!

We promise you your time is now.

Come visit www.katebutlercoaching.com/books.

Together we share inspired impact that will change the world.

With love and gratitude,

With a Grateful Heart
– Kate ♡

ABOUT KATE BUTLER

Kate Butler is a #1 Best Selling Author, Certified Professional Success Coach and International Speaker. Kate has been featured on HBO, in the Huffington Post and many other televisions, news, and radio platforms.

Kate's children's books, *More Than Mud* and *More Than Magic*, have received the prestigious Mom's Choice Award for Excellence®, the Readers Favorite International Book Award® and have also been endorsed by popular children's brands, Kidorable® and the Garden State Discovery Museum™.

Kate received her degree in Mass Communication and Interpersonal Communication Studies from Towson University, MD. After 10 years in the corporate industry, Kate decided it was time fulfill her true passion.

Kate now follows her soulful mission to guide people to activate their core brilliance so they can impact people's lives and ignite their own. In pursuit of this mission, Kate has impacted thousands of lives through her books, keynote speeches, live events, and coaching programs in her business as a Certified Professional Success Coach.

WAYS TO WORK WITH KATE:

Coaching- You're invited to experience more miracles in your life through the Pathway to Miracles coaching program. In this program, Kate coaches you through the 37 most common ways we block miracles in our personal, professional, and daily lives and how you can stop blocking them so you can unlock the pathway to miracles and live your greatest life. Kate takes a practical approach on how you can create real miracles in your everyday life and in this program, miracles are guaranteed.

Visit: www.katebutlercoaching.com/miracles

Publish a book- If you have always dreamed of sharing your story or publishing a book, then let's connect and discuss how we can make this happen for you!

Visit: www.katebutlercoaching.com/books

Speaking- Whether you are hosting an intimate women's circle or a massive seminar, Kate would love to support your work by speaking at your next event. Kate is not just an inspirational speaker, but also an *experiential* speaker, bringing the audience through exercises that will create energy shifts and mindset expansion right there on the spot. The audience will leave feeling inspired, empowered, uplifted and with a renewed sense of clarity. Kate's main mission is to inspire women to align with their soul's path and she would love to partner with you in order to impact more people!

To connect for collaboration: www.katebutlercoaching.com/speaking

Author Visits- Inspiring children is where it all begins, and Kate does this through her school visits. Kate travels across the country to share her books with schools, often times with her daughter, Bella, who co-wrote *More Than Magic*. Through reading their books and sharing the writing and publishing process, they encourage children to believe in themselves and their dreams.

To book Kate for your child's school, visit: katebutlercoaching.com/speaking

Are you a woman who ignites?
Are you a woman who inspires?
Are you a woman who influences?
Are you a woman who impacts?
Then we want to connect with *you*!

The Inspired Impact Movement is looking to connect with women who desire to share their stories and serve the world. If you have dreamed of publishing a book, then this is for you. If you have dreamed of bringing your message to a larger audience, then this is for you. If you have dreamed of exposing your business through a new platform, then this is for you. If you have dreamed of inspiring women all over the globe, then this is for you.

We want to hear your story!

Visit www.katebutlercoaching.com/impact

May your soul be so inspired that you are moved to inspire others,

the women who influence

PERMISSIONS

Tammy Anczok. Reprinted with permission.
Darlene Whitehurst. Reprinted with permission.
Adrienne Dorison. Reprinted with permission.
Susan Faith. Reprinted with permission.
Tonya Harris. Reprinted with permission.
Lindsay Smith. Reprinted with permission.
Violeta Potter. Reprinted with permission.
Brenda Walton. Reprinted with permission.
Desiree Peterkin Bell. Reprinted with permission.
Deanne Deaville. Reprinted with permission.
Alyssa Gavinski. Reprinted with permission.
Tamara Benson. Reprinted with permission.
Alexa Bigwarfe. Reprinted with permission.
Shalini Saxena Breault. Reprinted with permission.
Lauren Cavaliero. Reprinted with permission.
Lana Dingwall. Reprinted with permission.
Kristy Dubinsky. Reprinted with permission.
Laurie Dudo. Reprinted with permission.
Gina Fresquez. Reprinted with permission.
Melody Garcia. Reprinted with permission.
Gabrielle Grae. Reprinted with permission.
Kim Haskan. Reprinted with permission.
Danielle Loraso. Reprinted with permission.
Ashley Olivine. Reprinted with permission.
Laurie Ann Riker. Reprinted with permission.

Kim Ruether. Reprinted with permission.
Carol Stover. Reprinted with permission.
Wendi Sudhakar. Reprinted with permission.
Marie Svet. Reprinted with permission.
Donna Wald. Reprinted with permission.
Hayley Hunter Hines. Reprinted with permission.